"Philip K. Howard's book rings true. Teachers have such a hard time being themselves, dragging around the millstone of bureaucracy. Will all our well-intentioned efforts to regulate and manage our way to social welfare backfire, creating a society where people aren't free to exercise their own judgment and good will?"

—WENDY KOPP
Founder & President, Teach for America,
and author of *One Day, All Children* . . .

"Howard is on to something. . . . [He] makes his case through anecdotes, and he packs some powerful ones."

—*The Washington Post*

"This book provides unique insight into important aspects of modern life. Philip Howard has a gift of clear vision into these vital issues, and is sure to provoke fresh debate on how our society is organized."

—FORMER SENATOR HOWARD BAKER, JR.

"[A] rich seam of anecdote . . . Howard writes well, punctuating his text with skillfully told tales and choice quotations from the good and wise."

—*The Economist*

"Philip K. Howard has identified . . . the price we pay for our distrust of authority. By pointing to . . . the intricate array of rights and legal safeguards, he makes a provocative case which should provoke spirited debate."

—DEREK BOK
President Emeritus, Harvard University

"I have been a huge fan of Philip K. Howard since I first read *The Death of Common Sense*. This book is even better and explains so well much of what is wrong with modern America. This book will surprise you at every turn. It is like a gale of fresh air."

—SENATOR ZELL MILLER

"A powerful . . . look at our litigious society."

—*Publishers Weekly*

ALSO BY PHILIP K. HOWARD

The Death of Common Sense:
How Law Is Suffocating America

THE COLLAPSE OF THE COMMON GOOD

THE COLLAPSE OF THE COMMON GOOD

HOW AMERICA'S LAWSUIT
CULTURE UNDERMINES OUR
FREEDOM

PHILIP K. HOWARD

(Originally titled *The Lost Art of Drawing the Line:
How Fairness Went Too Far*)

BALLANTINE BOOKS / NEW YORK

A Ballantine Book
Published by The Ballantine Publishing Group

Copyright © 2001 by Philip K. Howard

www.ballantinebooks.com

Library of Congress Catalog Card Number: 2001119478

ISBN 0-345-43871-X

Manufactured in the United States of America

First Ballantine Books Edition: February 2002

10 9 8 7 6 5 4 3 2

To my father, Rev. John R. Howard,

and to the memory of my mother,

Charlotte Stewart Howard (1920–1999),

who taught everyone she met

the power of the human spirit

CONTENTS

In *The Death of Common Sense,* published in 1995, I observed that Americans' frustration with government regulation was caused not mainly by what is regulated—everyone wants a safe workplace and clean air—but by how regulation works. Government regulates us like central planning, using ironclad legal dictates that effectively banish human judgment and good sense.

Following publication, I was gratified when observers from both the right and the left seemed to agree. I was surprised, however, when people kept asking me for a solution. The solution, I thought, could not have been clearer: Unchain people from detailed rules and bureaucratic process and let them take responsibility, to succeed or to fail. Judge how people do; don't tell them how to do it.

What I did not appreciate was that America has lost the idea that people with responsibility, like judges and school principals, should have the authority to make decisions just because it seems right. Authority has become a suspect concept, the enemy of individual rights. Letting someone decide about someone else isn't fair. Who are they to judge?

The triumph of individual rights over authority has implications far beyond the functioning of regulation. Because almost any decision affects someone, ordinary choices are often paralyzed. Fear and suspicion now infect daily dealings in the workplace. Schools are falling apart, literally and figuratively. The common good is pervaded with a sense of apathy and powerlessness. This book explores the relationship between individual rights and authority in a free society.

THE COLLAPSE OF THE COMMON GOOD

THE LOST ART OF
DRAWING THE LINE

⚜

The double slide in Oologah, Oklahoma, donated to the town park by the Kiwanis Club, was a local landmark. For fifty years this slide, looking like two legs of a spider, had provided fun for the children of Oologah. In 1995, however, a child suffered minor injuries while playing unattended on the slide, and the parents made a claim against the town. "I knew it was going then," said Judy Ashwood, fifty-three, who herself had played on the slide as a child. "It's hard for me to think that people who live here would actually sue the city if their child fell off the slide." But the town board decided it had no choice, notwithstanding a citizen petition asking that the slide remain in the park. It auctioned off the slide to a resident of a nearby town, getting $326.50, and the Oologah park slide was carted away.

All across America, playgrounds are being closed or stripped of standard equipment. In 1997, Bristol, Connecticut, removed all of the seesaws and merry-go-rounds from its playgrounds. When told of the decision, the face of thirteen-year-old Jennifer Bartucca fell with disappointment. "Every time I come here, I ask a friend to go on the seesaws. It is one of my favorite things to do at the park," said Jennifer: "I love merry-go-rounds. My father would push me on them when I was a little kid." Nicole LaPierre, sixteen, was equally disappointed. "If you play right, you're not going to get hurt."

Being safe has come a long way since Ralph Nader pointed out the absence of safety guidelines for cars and other consumer products. Avoiding risk is now practically a religion. But it's not clear that the results are necessarily what most people want. Some towns, for example, have the resources to replace the playground equipment with new, safer alternatives, including transparent tubes to crawl through and a one-person seesaw that works on a spring. Can you wait? The new equipment is so boring, according to Lauri Macmillan Johnson, a professor of landscape architecture at the University of Arizona, that children make up dangerous games, like crashing into the equipment with their bicycles.

The headlong pursuit of safety is killing off the simple pleasures of life. Why take a risk on an activity that's not absolutely necessary? The town of Park City, Utah, had a proposal to make bicycles available for free to tourists and others, both to alleviate the traffic and to make the town more attractive. Most people old enough to ride a bicycle are aware of the hazards. But accidents happen, and after concerns were raised about the possibility of a horrible accident, the plan was stopped. Better safe than sorry. Larck Lake, in West Virginia, had been open to fishermen and picnickers since 1993. But the owners got scared because teenagers coming up to a party there often decided to go swimming. "We felt that, sooner or later, there would be an accident," said Fred Stottlemyer, an official with the company that owns the lake, "so we decided to close the lake to recreational use." Bob Petryszak, who bought a house nearby because of the lake, was disappointed. "This is a great place to fish. The recreation it provides is a great asset to the area. There should be a way to keep it open."

Fun is optional, of course. The prophets of safety certainly practice a gloomy earnestness. But some activities that we've cut out are pretty important. Psychologists tell us, for example, that children need affection. Even before there were psychologists, most people, and animals as well, showed affection to their young. But in America, hugging or, indeed, even a pat on the back is now considered so dangerous that teachers can't do it. "Our policy is basically don't hug children," said Lynn Maher, speaking for the New Jersey chapter of the National Education Association (NEA). The guidelines of Pennsylvania's NEA chapter urge teachers to do no more than "briefly touch" a child's arm or shoulder. Michigan passed a law that forbade teachers to touch students for any reason. We're well on our way to a society where, as Ann Welch, a special-education teacher in Virginia, put it, "we tell children that karate is okay and hugs aren't."

Being safe, maybe extra-safe, is what we say is happening. But nobody really believes that. What's going on has little to do with risk to other people. It's mainly about avoiding legal risk for the person conducting the activity. "Ultimately, we came to the conclusion we were exposing ourselves to too much liability" by allowing people to keep using Larck Lake, said Mr. Stottlemyer. Charles Montgomery, who bought the double slide from the town of Oologah and set it up for his children in the backyard, put his finger on the problem. "It's a shame," Mr. Montgomery said. "I just see a kind of dying part of most people's childhood. It's going away because of society and lawyers."

People talk about the "litigation explosion" whenever a headline announces a huge verdict on some ordinary accident, like the $2.9 million verdict against McDonald's (later reduced to $640,000) when an elderly lady spilled the hot coffee while pulling away from the drive-thru window. Exorbitant verdicts are the exception, however, and don't directly touch the lives of most Americans. But law has changed our culture. Instead of looking where we want to go, Americans are constantly looking over our shoulders.

The effects are sometimes tragic. Christopher Sercye, fifteen, was shot while playing basketball on a playground close to the Ravenswood Hospital in Chicago. With the help of two friends, the boy made it to within thirty feet of the hospital entrance. When Christopher collapsed, almost at the hospital door, his friends ran in to get help, but the emergency-room staff refused to come out. Hospital policy was that they should not leave the hospital because, as the explanation later indicated, of fear of possible legal liability for neglecting patients already in the hospital. But going thirty feet outside the hospital is not much different for staff than going thirty feet inside. As Christopher lay bleeding on the sidewalk, a policeman begged the staff to come out. But the hospital staff refused to budge and instead placed a call to 911. Christopher lay on the sidewalk for twenty-five minutes before a police sergeant arrived and commandeered a wheelchair to bring him in. The boy died shortly afterward.

Life-and-death decisions used to be more important than anything, certainly more important than legal niceties about duties to sick people thirty feet in one direction versus thirty feet in another. But Americans today act as if we're wearing legal blinders that block any sensible perspective. When a possible legal risk pops up before our narrow range of vision, however remote or ridiculous, we react like rats to an electric shock. Why take the legal risk?

A new medical school graduate, one week away from getting her license to practice, was recently driving in suburban New York when she came upon a motorcycle accident with the rider sprawled on the side of the road, obviously badly injured. After a brief discussion with her mother, she decided not to stop because she might be liable for practicing without a license. At first blink, her logic seems perfectly reasonable. But this only shows how warped we've become. How about helping out because you're a human being who happens to have the skills to save a life?

Some suggest that Americans are just being irrational, pumped up by scare tactics of corporations and greedy co-conspirators wanting to undermine the American legal system. Put yourself in the position of the doctor whose patient has a bad headache. Is it aspirin, or a CAT scan? Pretend you're in charge of making decisions on the school playground equipment. Are you a little uneasy?

The air in America is so thick with legal risk that you can practically cut it and put it on a scale. A volunteer teacher in East Harlem was working with a group of nine-year-olds when one kept shoving the others, ignoring the teacher's repeated requests and commands that he stop. Finally, she put her hands on his shoulders to tell him that he would be sent home if he didn't stop. The response of this youthful aggressor? "You can't touch me, that's against the law."

The accepted wisdom is that America is a diverse country, and the values of Americans have changed. But do contemporary Americans really suffer from differing views of what's too risky and what's not? Do most Americans really disagree on whether the bleeding boy should be attended to? Is society really so fractured over, say, the risk of letting the public enjoy a mountain lake? If everyone generally knows what's right or sensible, why doesn't he or she just make that decision? Not many years ago, we felt comfortable with these decisions. Today it's unthinkable.

We accept this perpetual legal anxiety as we would an incurable disease. What do you do? After all, people have their legal rights. The relevant issue is whether you can prove your position. We barely even question the system because, well, that's how law works.

More powerful than any invading army, than any constitution, is an accepted frame of reference. Today, Americans believe that fairness to individuals is the goal of justice. Of course it is, you're probably thinking. This is America. But what does it mean to be fair? What's fair, as most adults know, depends on your point of view. The reason we know American justice is fair, unassailable in its fairness, is that it avoids anyone's point of view. American justice is neutral. Fairness in modern America comes not from asserting beliefs but from avoiding them.

Judges see their responsibility, as Professor Michael Sandel observed, to make a "morally neutral judgment."

Who, even a judge, has the right to decide what's fair or not? Justice, we've been taught, is a matter merely of determining entitlement. Written law sets forth the standards, and the person will either prove the claim or not.

This neutral ideal of fairness has become a creed of our enlightened culture. Our children are trained from an early age to avoid making what are pejoratively referred to as "value judgments." "Everyone's views," Wake Forest University president Thomas Hearn recently noted, are now "as legitimate as anyone else's." Alan Wolfe, in *One Nation, After All,* a study of contemporary American values, suggests that there is now "an eleventh commandment: Thou shalt not judge."

Neutral justice appeals to almost everyone. It has a pure quality, as if untouched by human hands. It is available to anybody, at any time, fitting neatly in the American tradition of self-help.

Most important, neutral justice neutralizes authority. Americans of every political persuasion cringe at the idea of people imposing their beliefs of right and wrong. Liberals see justice that is neutral of personal values as protection against bigoted southern sheriffs. Conservatives see it as protection against power-hungry bureaucrats. Even critics of American litigation never question the premise that every individual should have the right to his day in a court proceeding untainted by personal beliefs. We lean back and close our eyes, reassured that there's a perfectly neutral forum to hear our point of view if someone tries to do something to us. That's what makes American justice fair, fairer than any in the history of civilization.

But fair to whom? How teachers got to be so nervous is

easy to see. Just a charge of sexual harassment or abuse can ruin a career. An elementary school girl claimed sexual assault when a music teacher helped her position her fingers on a musical instrument. The teacher was cleared, "but the investigation and public embarrassment ended his life as he knew it." Some schools now require a second teacher or video surveillance in music and art class. The effect, according to an education official, is that "everyone's nervous" all the time, a kind of pedophilic version of the Red Scare.

Everyone was warmed up and ready to play in the Little League baseball game in Slingerlands, New York, but because of a scheduling glitch, the umpire didn't show. The coaches talked; several parents volunteered; everyone wanted to play, but the longer the discussion went on, the more nervous everyone got. "And what would happen if someone got hurt?" There might be legal liability, the coaches suggested, without the official umpire. The game was cancelled. Several teams of disappointed children went home.

Justice stands sentinel on the horizon of our daily choices and certainly looks fair with its perfectly neutral processes. First you argue, then I argue, and then the neutral decision. We like the fact that it's self-executing. It honors the right of each individual to make his case. But something is missing.

Law, we believe, is a system of individual rights. We almost can't imagine any other conception of fairness. But what about fairness to society as a whole? Stated differently, how about fairness to individuals as participants in society, like the players in Little League? Law serves a social function as well as an individual one. That used to be considered its main function. The rule of law was the main concern of our founders, but not, as one reformer put it, because they were expecting America to sue its way to greatness. Law is essential to a free society because it sets the rules we all abide by. As Justice Benjamin Cardozo put it, law must stand for "standard[s] of right conduct" that find expression in "the *mores* of the time."

When working properly, a law professor once said, justice is like the liver. You never notice it. People go through their lives comfortable with their instincts of right and wrong. We're not defensive. "Most of us live our lives in conscious submission to the rules of law," Cardozo noted, "without necessity to resort to courts to ascertain our rights and duties." Law is an instrument of freedom, not mainly as a forum to resolve disputes but because it allows us to act freely, confident that law will defend reasonable conduct. America's commercial law, generally well known and reliable, is the bedrock of our thriving economy. By letting everyone know where they stand, law liberates people to make free choices.

Social relations in America, far from steadied by law's sure hand, are a tangle of frayed legal nerves. Any dealings in public—whether in hospitals, schools, offices, or in the ebb and flow of daily life—are fraught with legal anxiety. An undertow pulls at us constantly, drawing us away from choices that we believe are reasonable. Legal fear has become a defining feature of our culture.

Americans today seem to abide by a kind of law by journalism, reacting to whatever risks newspapers write about. Several New York private schools instituted peanut-free cafeterias after publicity about horrible reactions that can occur in people born with the peanut allergy. Nationally, only a few people every year die from allergic reactions to food of all kinds (estimates range from 5 to 120). Moreover, those with the peanut allergy know it, and most carry an antidote syringe at all times. But peanut butter is undoubtedly a terrible risk to a tiny fraction of the population, and after the newspapers spread the word, who will protect you from liability if the unlikely but terrible allergic reaction occurs? Try getting peanuts on most airlines now. In one fit of fear, the miracles of George Washington Carver are swept away.

Doing something wrong is not what scares most Americans. What we're afraid of is someone claiming we did. Who and for what? We don't know. It almost seems it could be anyone, in almost any situation. A sick person who gets sicker. A child who misrepresents a touch, or just wants to make a claim and see what will happen.

Litigation reforms are suggested all the time, and some are enacted, but without doing much to soothe raw nerves. The one suggestion no reformer has made, to my knowledge, is that America has too little law. Law, as everyone says, is all around us. We're tied up in legal knots. What's the effect, we constantly ask ourselves, on so-and-so's rights? But we don't pause to ask ourselves why the answer is almost never clear. Do we have too much law, or too little law that anyone can rely upon? While we talk about rights all the time, what kind of legal right is it that no one can identify with any clarity?

We can't get the notion out of our heads that justice is about being as fair as we can to every individual who shows up at the courthouse. The allegorical figure of Justice is carved above the courthouse door. There she calmly sits, her eyes blindfolded to symbolize impartiality. Just the image gives us comfort. Justice has integrity. Nothing is rigged. Courts have always had to be impartial, of course, but our aspiration for neutrality goes much further than making sure judges have no personal stake in the controversy. Modern justice is almost monastic in its self-denial. Appear before an American court and you will be given every chance, every benefit.

But is that what it means to live under the rule of law? Justice Oliver Wendell Holmes, Jr., once defined law as "the prophesies of what courts will do." Maybe Justice Holmes has put his finger on our problem. Today in America, justice may be neutral, but nobody has any idea what a court will do. Our quest to achieve individual fairness through neutrality has had an unintended side effect: America, so proud of its rule of law, has lost the law needed for people to have a sense of what they can and can't do.

Archaeologists a thousand years from now will dig up our remains and give us a name: Instead of the Age of Reason, we'll be the Age Without Reason. Our amused descendants may not figure out that the seesaws disappeared in a fit of legal frenzy. What they'll see, in plain language, are the warning labels on every product. Then we'll be found out: We were the society that lost the guidance of law, and, with its demise, lost the ability to distinguish between what's reasonable and what's not. In the ruins at Yale Law School, they'll find plastic bags warning against throwing the "mortarboard" graduation caps up in the air.

Weren't Yale law students smart enough to deal with the hazard? All preconceived notions of our eating habits will be thrown for a loop when they find a federal form cautioning against eating the toner of the photocopier. They'll really wonder about the coffee. What did we mean by warnings on practically every cup about its being extremely "hot"? Was coffee some kind of aphrodisiac?

The test of justice, Justice Cardozo once observed, is how people feel about it. If our system of justice is fairer than it used to be, people sure are reacting in an odd way. Americans are scared, but they're not scared of vigilantes roaming free in a land without justice. Americans are scared of justice itself, because it no longer is based on law.

RIGHTS WITHOUT LAW

In the spring of 1996, in the sandbox at Charles River Park in Boston, Jonathan Inge, then three years old, kicked another three-year-old, Stacey Pevnev. Stacey's mother told Jonathan to stop in no uncertain terms. The mothers proceeded to have words. Jonathan's social graces left something to be desired, and there was a pushing incident. At this point, Stacey and her mother could have left the playground or gone to another area, but Stacey's mother had her own problems in the social interaction area, and she decided instead to call the police. The police punted. The Pevnevs then decided to go to court. Within days, they were arguing away in Suffolk County Court. Did the judge toss the case out with a laugh? In the new America, the judge actually adjudicated the dispute, granting a preliminary injunction requiring the parents "to keep each child supervised and separated from each other while in the playground" and prohibiting the mothers from talking to each other.

Just think of the possibilities. Have you had an argument with anyone lately? Why deal with it face-to-face when you can go to court? Traditionally, courts were not official versions of *The Jerry Springer Show*. A Boston lawyer, Roderick MacLeish, observed dryly that "we need to take a serious look at what's going on in this country."

What people claim as their rights, at least from a distance, is pretty entertaining. A bank robber in New Jersey sued the teller for slander: He only demanded money at gunpoint and did not, as she testified, threaten also to shoot. How dare she draw that inference? Typical bank-teller prejudice. Boston judge Hiller Zobel has been asked to decide a custody fight over a dog, a claim over a missing prize in a Cracker Jack box, and a lawsuit over ownership of birth control pills between a fifteen-year-old and a thirteen-year-old. These claims usually don't succeed, but they are symptoms of a society-wide preoccupation with rights.

You can't do much that's significant, or even funny, without thinking about your or someone else's rights. Rights cruise back and forth through our consciousness like a police car on patrol. If the Gallup polls could register the thoughts that most often cross American minds, number one would be easy to predict. But rights would be right up there.

Any dispute immediately reverts to the language of rights. We can't think of the law except as a matter of individual rights. Law is rights, rights are law. My suggestion that American society needs more law to let people know where they stand seems like a bad joke. We know where we stand: on a legal battlefield. Rights are everywhere.

But what is a right? For all we've thought about it, a right could be a quark. We can describe well enough individual rights that we learned about in civics class—basically constitutional rights against government abuse. There's the right of free speech, and no prosecutor can put us in jail on a whim. Our founders made sure Americans had rights to prevent government from using state power to interfere with our freedom. But these hallowed rights against government coercion—what philosopher Isaiah Berlin referred to as "negative liberties"—aren't the kinds of rights, happily, that most Americans worry about day to day.

Rights in our daily thoughts concern suing and being sued by other people. We can't readily describe what gives someone the right to sue someone else, but we know how this "right" operates: like a legal jack-in-the-box, ready to pop up whenever there's a misunderstanding, or an accident, or any bad event.

Because the theory of rights is one of legal entitlement, no one questions the ability to sue. A court will determine that a person either has the right or he doesn't. Rights are like a piece of property. That's why they're called rights. "A person's rights are what belong to him as his due, what he is entitled to," Professor Peter Weston stated, "hence what he can rightly demand of others."

Law as a whole, we've been taught, is like an interlocking puzzle of everyone's rights. This is a conception that philosophers like John Rawls advocated in the 1960s and 1970s. A just society doesn't impose its own views of right or wrong in a particular dispute; it only provides "a framework of rights, neutral among ends." As Professor Mark Tushnet put it, we envision "a world of autonomous individuals each guided by his or her . . . goals, none of which can be adjudged more or less legitimate than those held by others."

Something obviously slipped between Rawls's theory, however, and the actual practice of his system of rights allocated around society. Most so-called rights that people assert look a lot more like selfishness dressed up in legal clothes.

A young couple in our neighborhood, a doctor and an actress, visited his parents on New Year's Eve. The sidewalk was icy, and just as they were getting to the front door, she slipped and broke her ankle. Her response came out of the new American playbook: She sued his parents. The goal was not to recover medical costs (apparently she was insured), and certainly not to hit up her in-laws. The idea was to go after a windfall from the parents' insurance company. The broken ankle would certainly affect her dancing abilities. She got a huge settlement from suing his parents. Now that's certainly ingenious. But isn't insurance supposed to be for real lawsuits? Doesn't that attitude just raise the costs of everyone else's insurance? Never mind. Accidents are assumed to be an occasion to make money. You almost feel like a chump if you don't at least threaten to sue.

Three employees of the Seattle Police Department got disability a few years ago for falling out of their swivel chairs. There's a new one. Actually not: A few years earlier the city of Miami had a rash of disability claims from employees for falling out of chairs, suffering paper cuts, and similar tragedies. But what do you do? The doctor's letter says it is an injury, and the injury happened in the line of duty. The legal logic is open and shut. Instead of telling the cops to get another job, Seattle dutifully replaced the suspect equipment with straight chairs. Now the employees can't swivel around to talk with their buddies, and they're complaining about cricks in their necks. Life has so many pitfalls. Maybe they should all collect disability or, better yet, call 911: "My chair did it."

The question in each case, we're told, is one of legal entitlement. But latching onto a legal principle doesn't seem that difficult. A depressive professor fired for abusing women sues under the Americans with Disabilities Act (ADA) to try to get his job back. When it passed the ADA, Congress had in mind accommodating the disabled who couldn't make it into the job market, not keeping abusive people on the job. But legal arguments soon spin a web that protects abusers against the abused.

Each dispute must be viewed on its own terms, evaluated against a neutral standard, and decided by a jury or other neutral decision maker. Individual rights, as Rawls suggested, are "not subject . . . to the calculus of social interests." There's no one with authority to, say, distinguish between a broken leg and a scrape, or between a self-indulgent creep and someone with multiple sclerosis. People are regarded "as isolated islands of individuality," as Professor Tushnet puts it, whose dealings with one another and society "can metaphorically be characterized as foreign affairs."

Rights have an almost theological power. Like primitive

people before a holy man, when someone asserts their rights are violated, we immediately shrink back, cowed by the possible forces that might be unleashed against us.

Even judges find themselves frozen by the power of someone's asserted rights. The judge knows that the sandbox case involving the three-year-olds is ridiculous, but if he furrows his brow and looks at the sandbox case as a matter of individual rights, the claim is perfectly logical, almost open-and-shut. How dare Jonathan Inge monopolize the sandbox with his bullying tactics. The sandbox is a public facility. The Pevnevs have just as much right to be there as he does. A dispute over three-year-olds sharing the sandbox is absurd, but what can he do? People have their rights.

Fairness is guaranteed whatever the result, we believe, because each party to the dispute had an equal right to make his arguments. But that view assumes that justice is only about fairness to the particular parties.

In 1995, confronting evidence that air bags could kill short adults or children, the federal government authorized a program that, by written permit, allowed air bags to be switched off. More than thirty thousand official federal permits were issued. But, after a year, barely one thousand cars had been modified. Dealers refused to make the modification because of fears of liability. Donna Nye, barely five feet tall, couldn't find anyone to turn off her air bags. "It's driving me berserk. What good is getting permission if no one will do it?" Janet Saker of Arlington, Massachusetts, four feet eleven inches tall, had the same problem: "I'm driving around with my heart in my mouth, and I'm afraid of the air bag blowing up and killing me."

Car dealers weren't trying to torture short people. They just perceived, correctly, that justice in America focuses on the predicament of the individual victim in the particular case, not on whether the dealers acted responsibly. After all, you never know when there'll be an accident or who'll be driving the car in the future. In the words of one Ford dealer in Rhode Island: "We're afraid, like everybody else. It's all fine and dandy until some attorney gets a hold of it."

In 1995, Harvard admitted an applicant on the basis of her excellent academic record and glowing recommendations from her high school. On an anonymous tip, Harvard learned that the student had killed her mother several years earlier by bludgeoning her with a lead crystal candlestick, and Harvard withdrew the acceptance. This fact, probably the most important event in the student's life, was omitted not only from her application but also from all of her recommendation letters. How could teachers and guidance counselors not have revealed this?

Guidance counselors are "afraid of telling the full truth" for fear of interfering with a student's rights, said Joyce Smith, executive director of the National Association for College Admission Counseling. "They'll write that Johnny took these courses and was a great student, but they won't tell you that Johnny burned down the gym. Whose job is it to tell admissions officers about that?"

Rights imply an interlocking puzzle where all entitlements fit, if not neatly, at least roughly, together. Consistency is, indeed, the indispensable feature of every system of law worthy of the appellation. The "basic moral principle, acknowledged by every legal system we know anything about," Professor Eugene Rostow once observed, "is that similar cases should be decided alike."

Justice based on individual rights, instead of striving for consistency, is closer to the opposite: single combat with an infinite line of potential claimants. In 1993, General Motors was found liable for $105.2 million when a GMC pickup exploded after being hit on the side. The explosion would not have occurred, the victim's lawyer pointed out, if the side-mounted gas tanks had been located somewhere else. Six years later, in 1999, General Motors was found liable for $4.9 billion (a dollar doesn't go as far nowadays) when a Chevrolet, stopped at a light, exploded when rear-ended by a car traveling at high speed. The argument was that the explosion might not have occurred if the gas tank were moved away from the rear. Practically everyone would be happy if vehicles used no gasoline, obviating the need for gas tanks altogether. But car design involves thousands of trade-offs of risks and costs. Where is a manufacturer supposed to put the tank?

There seem to be multiple rights at stake in each of these situations: the rights of the current car owner, and the rights of the future accident victim; the rights of the angry student, and rights of everyone else to an honest recommendation system. Whose right is more important?

Big companies just treat inconsistent claims as a cost of doing business, raising everyone's prices. But real people don't have that luxury. For most people, the possibility that a decision can be claimed to breach someone's rights is a good reason not to do it. Risk aversion is a powerful feature of human nature. Why take the chance?

For decades, reformers have given plaintive sermons about how people should act less like plaintiffs. Polls show that Americans bemoan selfish values, but every person, we believe, has the right to bring legal claims when they feel aggrieved. At least we know American justice is pure.

The more society frays, the tighter we cling to our ideal of neutral justice. A legal system that honors every individual's rights, we tell ourselves, will also protect us. Justice almost reeks of neutrality. Practically no claim is too extreme or disingenuous. Whenever there's a dispute, we reflexively drop to our knees before the altar of neutral process. Please, please, let justice be done.

Like ancient Mayans accepting human sacrifice or Catholics in the Middle Ages buying indulgences, Americans today accept that being sued is the price of freedom, and that diving for cover is the natural response to reasonable daily choices. Our faith in individual rights keeps us from pausing even to question this conception of justice. But should individual rights include the right to go to court over a sandbox disagreement involving three-year-olds, or to milk the system whenever there's a freak accident, or to scare towns and school systems out of seesaws and peanut butter? The idea of individual rights derives its moral force from the rhetoric of liberty. But is this what our founders had in mind when they organized a society around the freedom of each individual?

Actually, no. Our founding fathers would be shocked. There is no "right" to bring claims for whatever you want against someone else.

Suing is a use of state power. A lawsuit seeks to use government's compulsory powers to coerce someone else to do something. Asserting individual rights sounds benign, like praying in the church or synagogue of your choice. Sticking a legal gun in someone's ribs, however, is not a feature of what our founders intended as individual rights. The point of freedom is almost exactly the opposite: We can live our lives without being cowed by use of legal power. The individual rights our founders gave us were defensive, to protect our liberty. Liberty, we somehow forgot, does not include taking away someone else's liberty.

We assume justice is neutral. But it doesn't feel neutral. How well would you sleep at night if you were sued for, say, $100,000 when a child falls off your swing and breaks his leg? Suing is not a neutral event any more than being indicted for a crime is a neutral event. Both involve the risk, coming down to that fateful verdict by a jury picked at random, that the power of the state will compel a person to do something. Putting someone at risk, even if the claim is weak or ridiculous, involves the exercise of state power over him.

Courts are not supposed to be commercial establishments where, for the price of a lawyer, anyone can buy a chance at a raffle. Courts supposedly represent the wisdom of law, overseeing when those powers can be used against others in a free society. There's no right to sue except as the state permits.

I can practically feel your confusion. How else can we organize justice? People obviously have the ability to go to court. But by what rules and standards? Our modern consciousness is so focused on individual rights that we can't conceive of another way to ensure fairness. But if lawsuits are recognized as an exercise of state power, perhaps the state should make conscious judgments of who can sue for what. That's what legal rules and interpretations are for.

It's hard to remember, but until a few decades ago, people didn't go through the day worrying about suing or being sued. Students didn't threaten legal claims against teachers. Lawsuits were something only lawyers and judges worried about. Society wasn't perfect, but people felt free to make daily judgments based on what they believed was right.

People didn't used to talk about their rights to sue other people because law was considered a hurdle to surmount, not a free pass to a lottery. In a free society, you have no rights over another free citizen except when he affirmatively owes you a legal duty. Only when a court finds a legal duty is there a legal right to present a claim to a jury. You have a "right" to sue for breach of contract only because the contract imposes a duty. You have a right to sue a careless driver for a car accident because the law imposes a duty to drive like a reasonable person.

Looking at the sandbox dispute between the three-year-olds as a matter not of individual rights but of legal duty leads to a different result. In ordinary social interaction there is no legal duty to others. People are allowed to be rude, children are expected to be unreasonable. Citizens of a free society have to learn to deal with it. The case of three-year-old Jonathan Inge, and every case like it, must be dismissed unless there is a legal duty. Otherwise, we infect ordinary encounters with legal fear.

Medicine has been transformed. It's as if someone smashed the vial containing professional judgment. Legal fear has a "corrosive effect" on the doctor-patient relationship, according to Professor Robert Kagan, as "physicians, in a corner of their minds, regard patients as potential medical malpractice claimants." "We know we don't need [X rays]," one doctor admitted, "but you have to prove it in court." Medical students learn defensive practices, according to Professor Marshall Kapp, sometimes even "to falsify records": " 'A skillful lawyer could come back. . . . So you pad it a little.' "

Another common reaction, according to Dr. Christine Cassel, former president of the American College of Physicians, is that in critical situations doctors "turn over critical decisions to the family, which then makes the family feel like it's their fault when the patient dies." A doctor, Dr. Cassel says, should be "brave enough to put her arm around someone's shoulder and say medical science cannot keep your mother alive much longer, but she will not suffer and we will take good care of her." One study found that thousands of unconscious elderly people are kept alive by feeding tubes, not because people believe that's the right thing to do, but because doctors and relatives are legally afraid to make humane choices. One doctor described a patient who for six years "has not moved, spoken, or given any indication of consciousness," while "being supported by a tube in her windpipe attached to a respirator, by a tube in her stomach to continuously feed her, and by around-the-clock nursing care."

Legal fear has also poisoned professional relations, causing what Professor Kapp describes as "moral paralysis." In Phoenix a few years ago, three doctors resigned from a case because they believed another doctor was putting the patient's life in jeopardy with too high a medicine dosage.

But, fearing a lawsuit, they did not tell the patient or his family of their judgment. The patient went into shock and lapsed into a coma. As one of the doctors put it: "It is very difficult to intervene . . . because doctors are afraid the other doctors will sue them. And the supervising physicians and hospital administrators are also afraid to intervene because they might be sued later for letting the doctor have privileges in the first place."

Defenders of the current legal regime claim that, with the overhang of possible legal liability, doctors have an incentive to give the very best treatment. But if we consider patients in the waiting room and beyond, it's closer to a formula for medical meltdown. Every unnecessary half hour with one patient is time not spent with another, every CAT scan for someone who really doesn't need it is a CAT scan not available to someone who really does. Multiply the incidents by 700,000 doctors, making millions of choices every day, and the misdirection of medical resources is huge. Billions are squandered in unnecessary tests and treatments ordered by nervous doctors, and then partially recovered by managed care plans that resist treatment to all but the most insistent. The biggest losers are those who can least afford it, the weak and the elderly. Perhaps the ultimate irony is that, when called to account, bad doctors invoke the sanctity of their individual rights to keep practicing on unsuspecting patients.

Viewing justice through the lens of individual rights turns out to be an incomplete idea. The "rights" asserted by the parents of the child injured on the Oologah slide aren't the only rights that can be asserted. How about the "rights" of the parents who want to keep the slide for their children and grandchildren? They're not in the courtroom. Who's looking out for their interests?

A system of individual rights is almost irresistibly seductive. It empowers any individual to reach to the law. Everyone can do legal battle with, well, almost everyone. Anyone tries anything on us, and we can reach for its sword. It sounds so fair. It is so reassuring. But what if someone reaches for its sword to do something to us? What happens to us then? Organizing social relationships in a crowded society by individual rights is like handing out weapons to use whenever someone gets in the way, and then assuming everything will work out.

Individual rights don't exist in a vacuum. They're just "conclusions," as Professor Cass Sunstein observes, "masquerading as reasons." Allowing anyone to claim individual rights in a process that is value-neutral is not the rule of law. It's closer to a system of anti-law: a rhetorical society dedicated to individual self-interest.

NATURE ABHORS A VACUUM

American justice, I can hear the chorus, requires proof. You can't just drive straight to the bank. Making every litigant prove his claim is the foundation of modern American justice. That's why, we believe, a neutral system of justice is fair. Americans like the idea of proof. Making people prove their case sounds, well, like truth itself. Why is it, then, that modern justice generates such anxiety in our daily choices?

Several years ago, a homemaker brought the groceries home, put a large soda bottle next to a hot stove, and came back some time later to open it. Instead of grabbing hold of the cap and twisting it off, as the top is designed, this particular consumer took a knife and began carving at the plastic perforations around the bottle top. Now super-pressured by the heat of the stove, the soda popped. Shooting off like a rocket, the bottle top as a projectile caused her to lose an eye. Just look at her. Imagine the force. Did you know carbonated beverages could cause such damage? Why wasn't there a warning? How much would that have cost? Not even a penny. Don't these rich companies care?

Every day millions of people, including young children, successfully negotiate the opening of soda. Is carbonated soda an unreasonable risk of life? But the victim of a freak accident got rich. Take a closer look the next time you buy soda in a large plastic bottle. Joining all the other warning signs that litter the landscape, some bottlers now dutifully place warnings about the risks of soda popping.

Our ideal of neutral justice is guarded by layers of pre-conceptions. Pull away one, like the belief that law is an interlocking puzzle of individual rights, and you will en-counter another, like our belief in proof. There were unde-niably no warnings against the dangers of carbonation or against putting the bottle near heat. So what exactly needs to be proved? What it means to prove a claim has received about as little thought as the scope of individual rights.

Let's take a simple case. How do we prove whether the slide in Oologah is unreasonably dangerous? It's probably not a frivolous claim. After all, the slide is high, and chil-dren aren't always careful. We have the evidence of a child who was hurt. Does that mean that the slide is unreason-ably dangerous?

Seesaws are even more of a red flag. I could argue that seesaws are *likely* to be misused by some children. I recall standing at the middle of the seesaw using it as a balancing bar. I don't remember any bad falls on seesaws, but I do remember at age six trying to walk the banister of a friend's front porch as a kind of tightrope, falling headfirst into the water spigot, and being driven to the emergency room with blood flowing down my face. Does that mean my friend's mother should be sued for letting us play unattended on the front porch? How about letting us climb trees? The mimosa tree in our front yard in Tifton, Georgia, was particularly user-friendly, with smooth bark and long, low-hanging branches that were almost like a ladder up to higher branches. All the risks from these activities are easily foreseeable, but does that mean that slides and seesaws (and trees?) are unreasonably dangerous?

Let's go to hot coffee. The poster case arose when Stella Liebeck got third-degree burns when the McDonald's coffee spilled as her daughter drove her away from the drive-thru window. How do we prove whether hot coffee is unreasonable? Hotter coffee brews better and stays warmer longer. It can also scald. Hundreds of people had complained about McDonald's coffee over the years. But billions of cups—over one billion cups per year—kept being sold, indicating some measure of market acceptance. Why should a drive-thru window sell such hot coffee? Why not, aren't drivers grown up? Where do you draw the line? You can argue it either way.

No objective facts, no dispositive logic, can get you to a correct answer to these questions. So how do we decide? We can't, at least not on any provable basis. None of these cases hinges on proof. What's required is a value judgment. Value judgments, however, aren't provable. They're made of the one thing justice is trying so hard to avoid: what someone believes. Almost every claim involving a standard of safety, or care, or fairness requires a value judgment. Do we think carbonated soda is an ordinary risk of life or not?

But someone has to decide who wins. What's wrong with a jury just making the value judgment? Juries, studies show, generally get to sensible results. But any claim that turns on a value judgment usually not only affects the immediate litigants but, as in medicine, has consequences that ripple out into society: Do we want doctors to feel they should give CAT scans for every bad headache or not? Making these societal decisions, however, has nothing to do with a jury's responsibilities. The jury's job in a civil case is to resolve disputed facts between the immediate parties. Juries don't even have the power to make rules for society. Consistency is impossible. Win or lose, nothing prevents someone else from bringing a similar, or contradictory, claim tomorrow. The jury usually brings community values, and perspective, and good sense. Nine out of ten juries might conclude that the playground equipment is reasonable, or that the car dealer is not liable for shutting off the airbags. But, who knows—maybe the next accident victim will get Johnnie Cochran on the case.

Let's look a little closer at why Americans are so scared. Being at risk of someone's self-interested value judgment feels far different from being at risk on a disputed fact. There's no way to disprove the claim. Each case boils down to a version of a playground spat: yes it is; no it isn't. Back and forth the lawyers go: the coffee is too hot; no, it's not.

Doctors should order X rays for bad coughs; no, only if the cough persists. Where's the proof? It doesn't exist. You can't disprove a value judgment. It's just argument.

Does it seem to you that anyone can bring a claim for practically anything? They can. When justice turns on a value judgment, all anyone has to do is make up a theory. Nothing could be easier. Someone always could have done something differently. A canoe rental company on the Delaware River was found liable on the theory that it should have stationed lifeguards for miles along the river-banks. Literally any harmful event can be a lawsuit, even being struck by lightning, as the city of Denver recently learned when sued by a golfer.

We call it "proving" a claim, but letting any private person make claims based on their own value judgments is basically allowing anybody to make up their own proposed rule, and then present it to a jury. It's like law à la carte. America is no longer a nation of laws, but an ad hoc plebiscite, applied retrospectively on whatever theory anyone cares to invent. The air is thick with law, but it's not law that judges and legislators decided makes sense. Like the weather, this new law is changeable from jury to jury. Even if you win, what about next time? Juries are amazingly effective at keeping their fingers in the dike. But does it make the doctor breathe easier that the chances of losing a baseless claim are only, say, one in twenty? Those are the odds of a test pilot, not a caregiver.

For years, litigation anxiety has been casting a darker cloud over ordinary choices. Even if you're not sued, what could someone dream up? Every few weeks we read about lawsuits over some previously accepted part of life, like soda pop or peanut butter. If America is based on a rule of law, how is it that new legal rights seem to be discovered at the pace of modern technology?

Most Americans probably believe that litigation has merely shifted to a new level that we tolerate in the name of individual rights. Without standards of what's reasonable and what's not, however, justice loses its footing. Claims become self-referential. Everyone else has a warning, why didn't you? Our fear becomes a substitute for law. Other schools don't allow touching children, why did your school? We wanted a system of justice based on proof, not anyone's personal beliefs. But our own anxiety is now supplying the proof. A gnat-sized theory makes otherwise sensible people turn tail. As soon as a few people start running, it's almost inevitable everyone else will. Billions of cautionary coffee cups, because of one jury verdict.

Nothing is sacred. In response to publicity about an unsuccessful litigation against a church after a parishioner committed suicide, churches have begun implementing policies discouraging counseling by ministers. Instead, parishioners are referred to psychologists and other therapists. The legal exposure to risk is too great, according to Reverend Charles Darwin, a minister at Park City's Baptist Church, an 8,500-member congregation in Dallas. "What I'm saying," said Reverend Glen Evans of Calvary United Methodist Church in Arlington, Virginia, "is that 'I'd like to see you, but I'm afraid you might sue me.' " When Michael and Theresa Dunne of San Diego sought counseling for marital problems, their church referred them to a therapist who advocated "leaving that God stuff outside the door." Reverend Darwin doesn't like it—"I don't really know what they're getting"—but feels safer diverting his parishioners to Freud than even thinking about possible legal liability.

Americans know opportunity when they see it. "An act is illegal," Professor Donald Black observed, "if it is *vulnerable* to legal action." Empowered by their own imagination, individuals with a certain predisposition grab hold of the magic cape of individual rights and fly over society, looking for someone who might be called to account for some accident or perceived grievance, or for whatever purpose suits them.

New industries are springing up to meet the demand. Vidal Herrera in Los Angeles pioneered 1-800-Autopsy. "Business is great," said Mr. Herrera, who has so much business that he tells prospective clients that autopsies are not generally necessary. "But so many people want to sue," he observed, "that they don't listen." One recent caller said that her ninety-two-year-old mother had been working in her garden two days before she died in a local hospital. On questioning, the daughter admitted that her mother was a smoker with diabetes, high blood pressure, and a variety of other ailments. But the daughter was insistent: "I think they killed her."

Approaching each disagreement as a matter of individual rights doesn't seem to bring out the best in anyone. The effect is more like stoking a bonfire. Believing in "an unattainable order of things," Vaclav Havel notes, people start trying to "confirm [their] identity by sounding off at others and demanding [their] rights." Whoever is asserting a right comes to believe it, and the sense of legal entitlement leads to bitter conflict.

Talk to principals. Parents, particularly in more affluent schools, often act like maniacs. Their anger is startling. One tried to run over a principal in a parking lot. The situation in Orange County, California, got so bad that the Capistrano Unified School District adopted a civility code, which can result in misdemeanor charges against parents who scream at school staff or use obscenities. This attitude of sometimes violent entitlement is apparently a reason the principals are quitting and retiring in record numbers. "We're no longer educators," said one. "We're legal targets."

Right and wrong, as practically everyone has noticed, are increasingly defined in legal terms, not moral ones. Reputation seems almost like a quaint concept, replaced by an analysis of individual legal rights, as if, Professor Mary Ann Glendon notes, we "roam at large in a land of strangers." But this new legalistic morality, once legal claims are understood as self-created, can be reduced to a more straightforward understanding: It's no morality at all.

A schizophrenic strain has crept into the society, with people edging around the baseboards, looking this way and that before doing anything in the common realm, but then, when they can, aggressively using law to gain a personal advantage. There's a "litigation neurosis," Chief Justice Warren Burger noted almost twenty years ago, developing "in otherwise normal, well-adjusted people." The wife of a doctor who is probably paranoid about legal liability doesn't hesitate to milk the system by suing his parents. Like savages, rather than citizens of a great civilization, we pounce when there's an opening and cower in our caves the rest of the time.

Americans are constantly told that justice purged of personal values is an essential condition of a diverse society, just part of a social structure that must accommodate different interests and values. We trudge along like self-flagellants repeating the mantra, "Who am I to judge?" But most Americans probably share basic values of social interaction, like not making unreasonable demands and being considerate of others. Perhaps the common mores of decency and proportion have eroded not because of diversity but because successive generations have learned what they can get away with. If people see others getting away with selfish conduct, they become cynical, and some become selfish themselves. We keep bending over backward to accommodate selfish and antisocial conduct, and then wonder why our social fabric is disintegrating.

THE ABDICATION OF LEGAL AUTHORITY

There was "a massive redefinition of freedom" in the 1960s, historian Eric Foner has observed, "as a rejection of all authority."

Our philosophy of individual rights sits high on a pedestal, bathed in the light of universal acceptance notwithstanding its corrosive effect on our culture, because it keeps authority at bay. The rhetoric of modern justice is individual rights, but its foundation is avoidance of authority. Americans can't stand the idea of some unknown jerk having the power to make decisions. With neutral justice, we don't have to give anyone authority to make choices for the common good. Almost subconsciously, we can't bring ourselves to confront the need for authority in a free society.

Avoiding authority has preoccupied legal reformers for the past half century. How to protect free citizens against abuses of authority was already an urgent topic among legal scholars coming out of the struggle against dictators in World War II. Then America's awakening on racism took center stage. In 1954, when the Supreme Court in *Brown v. Board of Education* overturned laws and court rulings supporting segregated education, it set off a chain reaction causing Americans to question their own beliefs. People in power could identify those who abused their authority by looking in the mirror. A national crisis of confidence turned up the heat on existing legal structures past their melting point.

Law lost its authority. We had been taught by judicial leaders like Benjamin Cardozo and Oliver Wendell Holmes, Jr., that law was supposed to support the mores of society, but the *Brown* decision turned the spotlight onto America's pervasively racist mores. We were taught to trust judges to do justice, but *Brown* exposed generations of judges who had been uniformly unjust to race. How could the Supreme Court possibly have sanctioned the "separate but equal" doctrine for over half a century? Who can trust judges? Most of the rest of Americans also tolerated segregation and second-class status for blacks. Can we trust ourselves? The self-doubt then turned toward the structure by which laws are made. What is law if the Supreme Court can simply reverse direction at the snap of a finger? The *Brown* opinion, viewed today as a ninety-year lag in enforcing the Fourteenth Amendment, relied on sociological facts of differences between black and white education. Where's the legal principle there?

In a famous 1959 article, "Towards Neutral Principles of Constitutional Law," Columbia law professor Herbert Wechsler agonized over the fact that *Brown* did not adhere to principle. Wechsler's article and the hubbub around it— literally hundreds of academic articles debated his call for "neutral principles"—were symptomatic of the broader crisis in authority that shook the mortar of our entire system of government.

Insulating state power from fallible human choices became the number one priority of legal reform. No error or bias could occur if officials no longer had discretion. For regulation, making law as precise as possible became the way to remove personal authority by government officials. The burgeoning regulatory state was constructed as a detailed instruction manual that admitted no human judgment. Every year, thousands of pages of detailed rules specified exactly what everyone had to do, like setting the height of factory railings at exactly forty-two inches. Regulators and factory managers walked around with their noses in the rule books, squinting at the fine print rather than trying to make sense of the particular situation. Pretty soon, the regulatory system began to function about as badly as the system of authoritarian central planning that everyone was trying to avoid.

But precise rules could not even try to address the infinite circumstances confronted by courts. How could we protect individuals against authority by judges? In an influential draft textbook, two Harvard law professors, Henry M. Hart and Albert M. Sacks, said that the central idea of justice should no longer be declaring rules of behavior but a "principle of institutional settlement." Judges would no longer decide right and wrong but would ensure instead a neutral process. "The first recourse of law in dealing with disputes," they said, "is not to seek final answers, but an agreeable procedure for getting an acceptable answer." To accommodate the "boundless and unpredictable variety" of views of a diverse society, the court should focus on the "greater importance of procedural arrangements."

Instead of looking to "considerations of social advantage," as Holmes had suggested, the new priority of law was to honor the right of each individual to make his argument. Judges lost their authority to interpret law on behalf of society. Legal philosopher H.L.A. Hart described the new individualistic philosophy this way: "The question is not 'maximization of . . . general welfare,' but a doctrine of basic human rights." Justice would be "content-neutral" and "transcend the conflict of particular views."

Diversity of belief, not uniformity of law, became the first goal of justice. In a 1957 decision, the Supreme Court admonished lower courts not to dismiss any claim unless "it appears beyond doubt that the plaintiff can prove no set of facts in support of his claim which would entitle him to recover."

The first job of judges was to be beyond reproach, disregarding, to the extent possible, even their own beliefs: to bend over backward, and then bend over some more. Judges would safeguard a pristine process, and the decision would be made by a neutral decision maker, usually a jury of citizens picked at random. Deference to the jury, a right guaranteed by the Constitution, became how judges proved their neutrality. Judges basically ignored the Constitution's indication that in civil cases "the rules of the common law" override "fact[s] tried by a jury."

The cardinal sin for a judge was to make a decision just because the judge felt it was right. Perhaps the most ridiculed judicial statement of the period was by Justice Potter Stewart, reviewing a decision in Ohio under the First Amendment to ban Louis Malle's movie *The Lovers*. He said that "perhaps I could never succeed in intelligibly" defining pornography. "But I know it when I see it, and the motion picture involved in this case is not that."

"I know it when I see it" became a kind of joke in the legal academy, a shorthand catchphrase for everything law is not supposed to be. Belief was irrelevant, or worse, a synonym for bias. The point of justice, as Professor Michael Sandel put it, became to "respect people's freedom to choose their own values."

To our modern sensibility, giving someone authority to judge right and wrong is inconceivable. No mortal, we believe, should be able to assert rulings on behalf of the state. Federal judge Charles Wyzanski, one of the country's most respected trial judges, gave a lecture in 1973 in which he stated the prevailing gospel without a hint of doubt:

> Choosing among values is much too important a business for judges to do the choosing. That is something the citizens must keep for themselves.

Entire schools of legal academics are dedicated to explaining why judges have no basis to make decisions: They're not representative enough; they must make judgments only if "entirely rationalistic." Professor Paul Gewirtz summarizes the philosophy clearly: "Judicial power involves coercion over other people, and that coercion must be justified and have a legitimate basis." Justice is neutral, or it is not justice.

Americans did not intend to eliminate rules of fairness or reasonableness. We just didn't trust any human to make these choices. Americans do not distrust government as government, Robert Samuelson has noted. "They distrust concentrated power wherever it exists." Americans may be upset that we've lost our sense of right and wrong, but we know, as clearly as we know anything, that no one has the authority to decide right or wrong. The new authority, George Trow wrote in his 1981 essay "Within the Context of No Context," is "no authority."

Striving for neutrality, however, we unintentionally removed a critical element of justice. "Legal principle," Oxford philosopher P. S. Atiyah observed, has been "rejected as a form of authoritarianism."

FINDING LAW IN UNCOMFORTABLE PLACES

Baseball is a sport familiar to most Americans. Its rules are generally known, and so are its risks. The ball is batted in all kinds of unpredictable places by people swinging as hard as they can, and thrown at high velocity to make it difficult to hit or to cut down the runner. We love the game. It's our national pastime. So let's look at why justice seems to have a hard time dealing with the accepted risks of base-ball.

When the center fielder didn't show for the Little League game, the coach moved the all-star second baseman, Joey Fort, to center field. In the third inning, a high fly came toward Joey, but Joey lost it in the sun. Usually with a run-ner in scoring position, the coach's next choices, as one re-porter put it, include bringing in the infield or setting up a special play. But Joey was injured when the ball hit him in the eye, and the coach in this case ended up hiring a lawyer. Joey's parents sued for injuries he sustained. The theory was that Joey, who had never played center field, should have been instructed about catching fly balls in the sun or given flip-down sunglasses. The coaches ended up settling the case for $25,000.

Sister Gale Rawson was on second base in a softball game when a fellow teammate hit a single up the middle. It would be a close play, but Sister Gale decided to try to score. The relay came. The catcher blocked the plate, ready to tag Sister Gale as she barreled in. The inevitable colli-sion occurred, and the catcher dropped the ball. Safe! Not quite. The catcher fell the wrong way and broke her leg. She sued. For what? Sister Gale didn't break the rules, nor did anyone else.

Getting hit by a fly ball is a common risk of baseball. So is a collision at home plate. These claims shouldn't get to first base, except maybe in a peculiar situation that's hard to imagine. There's a venerable legal principle right on point, called "assumption of risk": If the risks are well known, those are the breaks.

A legal principle by itself never quite resolves a case,

however. You can practically feel the lawyer squirming his way out of it: "Joey Fort may have assumed the risk at second base, but he had never tried center field. Not once had he been instructed about judging long fly balls." We roll our eyes, but there in the courthouse sits Joey, one eye still blurry, looking pitiful. It's hard to blame Joey.

Try to find the law in this courtroom scene. There's the injured Joey and his angry parents; the nervous Little League coaches, living proof of the adage "no good deed goes unpunished"; and several lawyers engaging in a kind of hyperbole competition. The jury then receives this enlightening instruction from the judge:

> If you find that the plaintiff knew of the risk, and voluntarily decided to expose himself to it, then your verdict must be for the defendant. . . . If you find from a preponderance of the evidence that the defendants were guilty of negligence which proximately caused the injustice to the plaintiff, you must find for him.

Now that's really helpful. The jury has no idea how to read between the lines. It must be a serious claim, if all those important people wearing suits, even one in a black robe, go on and on about it. What are the jurors supposed to do? They look at the bereft mother. The coaches could have been a little more careful. . . .

Where's the law? The law hasn't actually changed. Common law principles like assumption of risk have been around for generations. Common wisdom has it that what has changed is our diverse culture. Victims are less likely to take it lying down. Jurors are more willing to give victims verdicts. That's the way justice should work. But no juror voted for the plaintiff. The case, like most, settled. Who wants to take the risk, however slight, of a huge verdict?

Hard cases make bad law, so the saying goes. But how about easy cases? We see the just result right in front of us: A fly ball is an ordinary risk of baseball. But like someone without hands, we can't grab hold of it. It used to be, as Justice Louis Brandeis once confidently observed, that only conduct on the edges created legal uncertainty, and lawyers could readily "tell clients where a fairly safe course lies." But we can no longer rely on our instincts of what's obvious. Today, any ordinary life event, even moving the second baseman to center field, could end up in a gut-wrenching trial.

Philosophy, to paraphrase Holmes, is only words. The same is true of law. Legal principles can be argued to mean anything. In Germany before World War II, judges used legal principles that had been applied fairly for generations to send innocent people to their deaths. Describing this phenomenon, Judge Richard Posner observed that he was struck by the "extraordinary plasticity of legal rhetoric, which enables a clever judge to find a plausible form of words to clothe virtually any decision, however barbarous."

Every day, in countless arguments in and out of court, Americans experience the reality that legal principles are just words. Concepts like reasonableness and assumption of risk have been argued beyond recognition. As often as not, the law is turned upside down. The manipulation is not by judges: we solved the problem of official prejudice by taking away judges' point of view. Law exists only in hand-to-hand combat between the parties. No one has any clue where they stand.

Words only mean what someone says they mean. "Rules," a famous judge once said, "travel in pairs." A fly ball in the sun to a new center fielder can be an unreasonable risk, or it can be an assumption of risk. Which one it is depends on a ruling by someone.

So who decides? The legislature could pass laws trying to catalog what is reasonable or not, and, at this point, legislative action is undoubtedly needed in some areas. But the law books are already so thick no one knows what's in them. They would burst if a law were added for every ordinary life event. Just imagine it: This legislative session, we'll take up the risks of fly balls. Next session, whether graduation caps can be thrown in the air.

Where else can we find meaning for law? We look around the courtroom. There's the judge sitting sort of lonely up on the bench. It must be boring, parked up there all day long. We conjure up the image, basically accurate, of an aging male-type in a black robe reciting legal platitudes to an equally bored jury. There he sits, feeling half-guilty for being a male (four out of five judges), being white (ditto), getting a privileged education, and for, he's told constantly, his unavoidable prejudices that represent the views of almost no one who needs justice. For years he's leaned over backward as far as he could to avoid interjecting any personal beliefs. That's his role, so he's told. He must keep values out of it as much as possible. Law has to be neutral, not polluted by his views of right and wrong.

It might be too scary, but let's look at what could happen if the judge actually leaned forward and decided something. The judge dusts off his gavel and, interpreting the principle of assumption of risk in this case, makes a legal declaration: "A fly ball in the sun is an ordinary risk of baseball. Case dismissed." What happens? The case is over except for an appeal to make sure the decision isn't out of left field. The jury doesn't even show up. A declaration of law is pinned up on the scoreboard for all to see. Once a few more courts make similar declarations, in the common law system, people begin to feel comfortable that they know where they stand.

But how does a judge decide how to apply a legal principle? The judge knows that changing positions is part of the risk of baseball, that the argument about long fly balls is just splitting hairs. But how does the judge know? He just knows. The judge can't prove it, because it's a value judgment about the nature of the game. The judge believes, in other words, that other people believe it. To quote Cardozo, it's "not what I believe to be right. It is what I may reasonably believe that some other man of normal intellect and conscience might reasonably look upon as right."

Courts are usually criticized for what they make us do, such as activist decrees that, in the name of integration, forced children to be bused hours away from their neighborhoods. Almost no one worries about what courts don't do, or makes the connection to daily choices we no longer make. But how can Little League coaches feel comfortable unless they know a judge has authority to declare as a matter of law that fly balls or other foreseeable accidents are an accepted risk of society?

Maybe the judge deciding about fly balls wasn't so scary after all. But what keeps a judge from acting like the German judges under Hitler? The judge is subject to scrutiny for how he applies the principles. The judge is not, as Cardozo put it, "a knight errant roaming at will." He gives reasons, which are the "salutary disinfectant" against arbitrary choices. But the judge's reasons are not provable. There is no proof, because these decisions of law will always be value judgments. The judge's reasons simply allow an appellate court, or the court of public opinion, to evaluate the wisdom of the decision.

What happens if the judge decides the other way, holding that Little League coaches must take precautions to protect Little Leaguers against the sun? Everybody now knows we'd better stock up on sunglasses. Even if the rule is stupid, at least Americans know where we stand. Instead of coaching Little League, people start to go fishing.

Having no rules means that fear becomes the rule. In 1999, major-league baseball issued a directive to players that, when picking up a foul ball, they should no longer throw it to fans in the stands. There might be legal liability if someone were hurt trying to recover a souvenir. Most players, thankfully, are just ignoring the new policy. It's hard to blame MLB. Foul ball litigation is increasingly common. It's only a matter of time before the major league fields are completely screened off.

Chief Justice Roger Traynor of the California Supreme Court, a famous liberal innovator of the 1960s—he created the doctrine of strict liability for manufacturers whose products fail—emphasized the need for judges to declare rules even for the simplest accident, and not leave standards "to oscillating verdicts of juries." When a woman hit her head on an angled ceiling while walking down a staircase, Traynor insisted that the judge determine whether it was an unreasonable hazard: In that case, "the danger is so apparent that visitors could reasonably be expected to notice it." Holmes also was adamant that the judge make the value judgments presented by a case:

> Negligence . . . [is] a standard of conduct, a standard which we hold the parties bound to know beforehand, and which in theory is always the same upon the same facts and not a matter dependent upon the whim of the particular jury or the eloquence of the particular advocate.

Another renowned judge, Presiding Justice David W. Peck, in New York's Appellate Division, noted that a judge must be "mindful of the larger orbit than . . . the parties immediately before him." The judge, as Cardozo observed, must act as "the interpreter for the community of its sense of law and order."

Americans want a legal solution that's neutral, law that's served up exactly the same way everywhere, like a McDonald's Happy Meal. But no fast-law franchise exists to serve up, pre-prepared, what practically everyone knows is the right call: that a fly ball is an ordinary risk of baseball. No rule, as Wake Forest president Thomas Hearn observed, can "replace the judgment, which is required to apply principles . . . to the facts of the matter." To be effective as guides for society, legal principles must be applied as most people would expect them to be. Otherwise, law is so much hocus-pocus, and no one knows what to do.

This human stewardship of law will strike many as almost unlawful, but that's because, like most generations, we don't look to history.

THE MYTH OF TRANSCENDENT LAW

Giving authority to duly elected or appointed officials, it is useful to remember, was the organizing idea of the American Republic. The personal beliefs of these officials were considered not an evil but the essential currency of government for the Republic. Elected representatives, for example, were given fixed terms so that they would have the breathing room to act on their own personal beliefs. Their authority, in a system of separated powers, would then be checked by other officials' authority.

Personal authority for judges was similarly not considered a problem but a key part of the solution. The job of judges, as Hamilton put it in *Federalist 83*, was not to be neutral but to "interpret the laws" and "declare the sense of the law." That was the traditional role of judges in the common law system that we inherited from England, in which courts announce and interpret legal principles of social interaction. The meaning of those principles evolves over time like, as Judge Learned Hand put it, "a monument slowly raised, like a coral reef, from the minute accretions of past individual decisions."

Courts are our bastion of sanity in this constitutional system because they can take the long view, free from popular passion. To ensure their independence, federal judges were given lifetime tenure. Courts are like democracy in slow motion: Individuals of long tenure apply long-standing principles in the context of new cases and changing social needs.

In the early days of the Republic, judicial law making was not so slow. Judges immediately took the job of sorting out, under the Constitution, who had authority to do what. Did Congress have authority to establish a national bank? While the opinions of the Supreme Court in this period, like most judicial opinions, were written as if the conclusion were foreordained, these rulings were basically inventions by the remarkable individuals who were the chief justices of these courts: "It was Marshall, not law, who made the Constitution stand for nationalism. . . . It was Taney, not the writing on parchment, who made 'the police power' an instrument for control of the rising industrial system."

As the industrial revolution began transforming societal relationships, judges adapted the common law to an age of impersonal dealing. In an agrarian society, historian Arthur M. Schlesinger, Jr., notes in *The Age of Jackson,* social interactions had been "controlled by a feeling of mutual responsibility." New rules were obviously needed for a society made mobile by railroads and supplied by distant factories. A law of "contract" was invented which put emphasis on formal agreement rather than review of each agreement for fairness. The law of "negligence" was invented to resolve disputes over accidents with people who did not know each other.

The new rules generally reflected the laissez-faire bias of

the times, or, as Holmes approvingly put it, that the "loss from accident must lie where it falls." One infamous rule was the "Fellow Servant Rule," which barred recovery to workers injured on the job by a co-worker's negligence. The logic, in the words of its creator, Chief Justice Lemuel Shaw of the Massachusetts Supreme Court, was that the worker "takes upon himself a natural and ordinary risk inherent in the assignment . . . for which he is adequately compensated."

These rules would not be considered fair today any more than a Model T would be considered safe. But they were rules of society, declared by judges who, Schlesinger observes about Chief Justice Shaw, "had a very real sense of the imperatives of change" and "the requirements of the community." In the common law tradition, these rules continued to evolve over time to meet changing realities and social values.

Law has always held itself out to have a transcendent quality, better than just a bunch of people making it up. To maintain common respect for law, judicial rulings must indeed be "infuse[d] . . . with the glow of principle," as Cardozo observed, or they will not stand the test of time. But our longing for law that is immutable periodically causes law to rigidify, as judges and legislators adopt the "formalistic" approach of deciding based on abstract legal analysis instead of the purpose of the legal principle.

As the Civil War approached, the crisis over slavery drove judges toward formalism, in part as an excuse to ignore the purpose of laws. Judges like Lemuel Shaw, asked to return escaped slaves to their southern owners under the Fugitive Slave Act, found themselves in a moral dilemma.

Many, including Shaw, took the route of "seizing on minor technical lapses" to avoid enforcing the law. Judges, having reinvented law in the prior fifty years, began to take seriously again the idea that the words of law, not their own views of the law's purpose, marked the path to justice.

Formalism reached full bloom after the Civil War, when the mechanical age inspired legal thinkers to imagine that law was a "species of scientific truth" which judges discovered by careful study. Led by Christopher Columbus Langdell, the first dean of Harvard Law School, generations of late-nineteenth-century lawyers were trained to believe that any legal problem had only "one true answer": "In scientific law, the judge has no will, makes no value judgments." Although ridiculous in hindsight—a little skepticism surely must have crept into the minds of intelligent judges searching for "one true answer" in a close case—the power of accepted convention should never be underestimated. Judges flocked to scientific law in part because, in the words of Judge Richard Posner, it "shift[s] responsibility . . . to dead people." "The idea of a body of law fixed for all time and invested with an almost supernatural authority," as Professor Grant Gilmore put it, "is irresistibly attractive."

Formal law has a bad habit of elevating logic over good sense. During the reign of scientific law, a judge in Vermont dismissed a claim over a defective butter churn because, after exhaustive research, the judge could find no law specifically addressing butter churns. In 1928, Chief Justice William Howard Taft held that a wiretap on a telephone could not possibly be an unconstitutional search-and-seizure: Telephones did not exist when the Constitution was written. Professor Gilmore characterized Dean Langdell as an "essentially stupid man who pursued his one idea with the tenacity of a genius."

Oliver Wendell Holmes, Jr., started the movement toward a "realist" conception of justice when, in 1881, he famously declared, "[T]he life of the law has not been logic; it has been experience." A remarkable man whose brilliance was equaled almost by his longevity, Holmes began his career left for dead as a wounded lieutenant in the cornfields of Antietam in 1862. Over seventy years later, in 1933, he was still sitting on the Supreme Court. Holmes spent much of his career looking down on formalism of law as a parent might observe children playing, explaining why law had to weigh "considerations of social advantage," and why this was not inconsistent with the idea of legal principle.

The nadir of post–Civil War formalism came in the 1905 *Lochner* case when, over Holmes's dissent, the Supreme Court declared unconstitutional a statute designed to limit to ten hours the shift of bakers working next to hot ovens. In a triumph of formalist reasoning over practical reality, the Court declared the statute, designed to preserve worker health, conflicted with the worker's freedom to contract with his employer.

Holmes eventually succeeded in returning to legislatures power over health and safety. Benjamin Cardozo, who replaced Holmes on the Supreme Court, led the modernization of contract and tort law while the Chief Judge in New York State. Among other innovations, Cardozo abandoned the common law requirement of direct contract "privity" in order to expand duties of manufacturers to distant consumers. Until a Cardozo decision in 1923, for example, a car owner was barred from suing the manufacturer for defects causing an accident because the car, like all cars, had been bought through a dealer rather than directly from the maker.

Cardozo gave a series of lectures at Yale in the early 1920s in which he explained what judges a century earlier had taken for granted:

> The judge is under a duty . . . to maintain a relation between law and morals, between precepts of jurisprudence and those of reason and good conscience. "It is the function of courts to keep doctrines up to date with the *mores* by continual restatement. . . . This is judicial legislation, and the judge legislates at his peril. Nevertheless, it is the necessity and duty of such legislation that gives to judicial office its highest honor; and no brave and honest judge shirks the duty or fears the peril."

Holmes and Cardozo articulated the need for authority by judges that our founding fathers and their judicial appointees had assumed. But their famous wisdom was itself based on a critical assumption, largely unarticulated: Performing this role required a willingness to assert values of right and wrong. Even Dean Langdell believed that law should assert right and wrong; he just thought the choice preordained.

Every civilization has rules: Otherwise it wouldn't be civilized. Under our modern version of procedural formalism, striving for neutrality above all else, we no longer acknowledge that society needs rules which reflect a deliberate choice about what should be encouraged or discouraged. Giving someone authority to assert social values, even if accountable to us or to a higher authority, strikes us as practically totalitarian. Our neutral formalism shares Dean Langdell's goal of avoiding judicial authority, but it goes one giant step further; in the name of individual rights, it tries to avoid values altogether.

Neutrality is illusory, however. People will interact one way or another. Values don't disappear; they reflect the law. Law and social behavior are linked like birds in a migrating flock. One or the other can lead, but they must stay together. Too much or too little law can have roughly the same effect on society. If legal exposure expands too much, people start tacking warning signs all over the landscape and spend half their time worrying about possible defenses. Without adequate law, people huddle in fear or are abused, as with child labor during the industrial revolution. Some people will exploit whatever they can. That's why law is essential for freedom.

For law to be effective, Archibald Cox once observed, it "must meet the needs of men and match their ethical sensibilities" or, as Holmes put it, "correspond with the actual feelings and demands of the community." To Holmes, this was "the first requirement of a sound body of law."

But Americans no longer believe in belief. We've certainly come, or gone, a long way. Democracy used to be the vehicle by which America strove confidently toward the "perfectibility of man." "We don't expect to change human nature," reformer Jane Addams said shortly before

her death, "but we do expect to change human behavior."
It may well be, as many scholars suggest, that Americans
no longer agree on right and wrong. But the absence of
consensus only underscores the need for rules of interaction. How else do we know what's reasonable? Today,
honoring neutrality, we're too insecure to tell someone trying to avoid work because of a paper cut to go get a Band-
Aid instead.

Our founders would have been surprised. A Constitution designed to provide a government respecting common
values is now invoked to avoid all values. Justice today is
purposeless. Being purposeless is, indeed, its guiding purpose. The aim of modern justice, one scholar recently declared, is to elevate deliberations "to a level where power
goes to the most persuasive." Justice has been reconceived
as a kind of sporting contest. In Boston, the new federal
courthouse is designed so that the bench is set only slightly
above the floor. Judges are a part of a neutral process, just
"part of the furniture" as Justice Stephen Breyer quipped.
May the best lawyer win.

As with Dean Langdell's scientific justice, however, the
steady deterioration of public confidence will require
abandoning this hands-off approach. "How do we judge a
wrong," William Bennett asks, "when we have gutted the
concept of judgment itself?" Sooner or later, people have
to be "empowered," as former Harvard president and law
school dean Derek Bok suggested, "to keep watch and
make sure the process as a whole is meeting the needs of
society."

It may be "easier to conceal a diversity of values when
principles are jettisoned in favor of individualized justice,"

Professor Atiyah suggests. "But how long can this process of concealment last?"

To liberate citizens to act on their reasonable beliefs, judges must embrace a philosophy they've spent fifty years trying to repudiate, and start asserting values when interpreting rules. No issue in a case, not even how much people can claim, should be exempt from a judge's constant scrutiny.

I KNOW IT WHEN I SEE IT

In 1992, Dr. Ira Gore, a dentist in Birmingham, Alabama, bought a new BMW. He was so proud of it that, after a few months, he took it to a customized paint enhancer named Mr. Slick. There he learned the terrible truth, otherwise not visible, that the paint on his BMW had been touched up because of the effects of acid rain on its voyage across the Atlantic. Dr. Gore sued and was awarded not only damages for alleged reduction in value ($4,000) but also $4 million in punitive damages for this unbelievably outrageous conduct. The punitive damages were calculated, if that's the right term, based on Dr. Gore's argument that the jury should teach BMW a lesson by paying him another $4,000 for each of one thousand cars it had retouched in the prior decade.

The case found its way to the United States Supreme Court, whose decision was considered so noteworthy that it received front-page attention. By the tightest of margins, five to four, the Supreme Court overturned the award as "grossly excessive." The argument among the justices illustrates how far away our legal leaders are from asserting their beliefs of the legal principles that should govern our society. Justice Ginsburg's dissenting opinion accused her colleagues of a standardless decision, ridiculing their "raised eyebrow" test. Justice Ginsburg has a point. What kind of legal standard is "grossly excessive"? But why is the standard essentially standardless? Because punitive damages are inherently standardless. Why not $4 trillion?

The better question is not whether standardless judicial oversight is proper but why a rule of law tolerates wild, standardless assertions of damages. Going a step further, why in such a case should punitive damages be allowed at all? Touching up paint on a BMW is not a human rights abomination.

Making up a rule of law, whether to limit damages or to permit hot coffee, is an idea that is inconceivable to most judges today. Like a goldfish that has flopped out of its bowl, a judge asked to actually apply a legal principle is apt to gasp and feel helpless. He is used to swimming in legal process, and laying off the real-world responsibility of an actual verdict on jurors who come and go at random. It doesn't matter that the heroes of the judiciary like Holmes and Cardozo could hardly have been clearer.

In fairness, judges have always had a tendency to let claims go to the jury. When justice still labored under the fiction that law would be found under a holy grail, judges generally just let the jury find the grail. Avoiding responsibility, like avoiding risks, is a common human instinct. The judicial laissez-faire approach didn't much matter until recent decades, however, because people didn't bring lawsuits over fly balls or peanut butter. Social conventions— some for the better, some not—had the effect of limiting what people made claims for. But these social conventions, as we've seen, have broken down.

Today, almost any dispute involving an accident goes to the jury, even if the circumstances themselves are not disputed. But there's a huge difference in the impact of a jury resolving a disputed fact, like who ran the red light or who is telling the truth, and deciding the legal consequences of some ordinary activity, like whether seesaws are unreasonably hazardous. Disputed facts generally involve only the parties in the particular case. A verdict that a seesaw is unreasonably dangerous—indeed, just letting a claim go to a jury—will affect whether seesaws stay in playgrounds all across America. Letting the jury decide means that one person's claim will dictate national policy.

Damages are perhaps the area of greatest judicial deference to juries. How much a defendant should pay is certainly not a legal question. Ergo, by judicial consensus, it must be a fact question for the jury to decide. But even traditional factual issues can spin out of control until they affect society as a whole. Without judicial standards, justice has lost its credibility with society here as well.

Like weeds in a rainy spell, claims have grown ever larger over the past few decades. First it was millions that took our breath away, then tens of millions, then hundreds of millions. Now it's billions. Pretty soon, one lucky victim may own the world. Not even Huxley or Orwell imagined this would be our end.

The standard operating procedure for any aspiring litigant is to sue for the moon. A young professional at Morgan Stanley, fired after several infractions and embarrassments (including having his nude photo appear in a men's magazine and allegedly planting racist e-mails), predictably sued. It had to be racism, not that his nudie shots brought disrepute to the company, especially since the company had paid someone to try to get him to admit to the e-mails. How much did he sue for? A sum of $1.35 billion. You never know with hot buttons like race and homosexuality. Even a small percentage would tide him over until the next photo shoot.

A great thing about bringing lawsuits in modern America is that it's so easy to threaten the adversary's entire livelihood. One stroke of a finger on the lawyer's word processor, and damages go from $100,000 to $1,000,000. Three more keystrokes, and we're suing for a billion dollars. This is fun.

What kind of justice system is it that allows someone to make up an amount of money to demand? Is that a fact to be "found" by a jury? It doesn't even qualify as a value judgment, which at least is a conclusion based on facts. Damages claimed today are completely arbitrary. Just stick your finger in the air and threaten someone with any number that comes to mind.

Judges treat damage claims almost as if they are property, and only with greatest reluctance intercede. In 1987, five-year-old Gregory Strothkamp climbed up several shelves to the top of the linen closet, got an unopened box of Q-Tips, and, while trying to use them, punctured his eardrum. His parents sued the maker of Q-Tips for, among other things, $20 million in punitive damages. Whatever the merits of the argument that Q-Tips should come in childproof packaging (which would raise everyone's cost), most people probably agree that making Q-Tips is not an evil act. When the jury awarded young Gregory $20 million in punitive damages, the judge did what was obvious from the beginning and overturned the award.

The claim ended sensibly, but is this how justice should work? Sweating through trial and verdict to get to obvious justice, while the judge is sitting there the whole time, doesn't exactly instill confidence in the system. Do judges enjoy watching the Q-Tips company, or a Little League coach, or a doctor squirm on the end of a multi-million-dollar hook?

Lying dormant along the side of society is another important legal principle: that a person injured should be "made whole" by damages. Traditionally, this meant out-of-pocket losses, like lost wages or medical bills. In an unusual case, like a homemaker with no wages, claims were permitted in categories not actually calculable, like "pain and suffering." In cases of genuine evil, punitive damages were possible. Today the exceptions have engulfed the rule, with all kinds of side effects. Juries are regularly asked "to assume the baffling task of trying to place a monetary value on pain and suffering," Dean Bok observed, "although the predictable result [is] to encourage a rise in litigation and the growth of the most unsavory and deceptive practices."

Judges might concede the principle but can't imagine how to apply it; they need some objective legal post to hang on to. If $1.35 billion is too much, what is the right amount? The "exercise of judicial power is not legitimate," as one scholar put it, "if it is based on a judge's personal preference rather than law." So what do the judges do? They abdicate. Judges look up at the allegorical figure of Justice and interpret her blindfold as impotence.

But Justice is also holding balanced scales. How does Justice achieve balance but through the values and wisdom of judges? Proportion is critical to justice. Equals should be treated alike, Aristotle believed, and unequals proportionally to their relative differences: "the unjust is what violates the proportion." These distinctions, Aristotle observed, can only be made with human wisdom.

Dead people can be so smart. "[T]o speak somewhat paradoxically," Cardozo observed, there are times "when nothing less than a subjective measure will satisfy an objective standard." Justice Potter Stewart had it right after all. Judges have to know it when they see it. One billion dollars for a wrongful dismissal case is absurd. Everyone knows it. The case should be dismissed unless the plaintiff comes back with some amount he can plausibly justify.

I wonder if judges ever ask themselves why it is that damage claims have escalated to a level where they are like a parody of a dysfunctional system of justice. The answer couldn't be more obvious. Judges sit on their hands and tolerate claims that make lotteries seem like small change. The reason people bring huge claims is not hard to divine: It's a form of extortion. Why else sue for such ridiculous amounts? Being sued for, say, $5 million for a regular accident may not cause you to fold your hand, but the possibility of ruin never strays far from your consciousness. Most million-dollar claims end up settling for thousands or less. But not all. All that it takes is for a jury to get mad. . . .

At this point in the discussion, all those black robes are rising up like a human wave in a baseball stadium, hands raised in collective powerlessness. Who are they to judge? Let's respond with a question. What gives a private individual the unilateral right to invoke the court's power to coerce someone else?

I can hear the next one coming. Judges aren't supposed to be activist. For decades, judges have indeed been criticized for being too activist. The federal court in Boston caused riots when it forced children to be bused hours away from home. The federal court in Kansas City took over the school system, spending almost $2 billion to little or no effect. Like dinner-party dilettantes, judges weighed in on legislative-type judgments where they had little responsibility and less wisdom. At the same time, courts across the land were deferring to ludicrous claims by private individuals. This apparent judicial inconsistency is only superficial: Both share a common foundation of abdicating to a system of individual rights. An individual has the right to trial by jury: Don't interfere. An individual has the right to go to school in an integrated setting: Turn the city upside down. Anything in the name of individual fairness. Nothing for the common good.

Judicial activism has a bad name. Experience teaches us that judges should be loath to take over management of government. But judges have a responsibility on behalf of free society to assert standards of reasonable behavior and to prevent the power of justice from being used by private parties as a form of extortion. That's their role in our constitutional system.

THE RISKS OF JUSTICE

At a reception at the White House on April 13, 1906, honoring the formation of the Playground Association of America (Theodore Roosevelt, honorary president; Jacob Riis, honorary vice president), it was clear the association's purpose was not to amuse children. Playgrounds would divert children away from the temptation and dangers of urban streets, but their main purpose was to help children prepare for the challenges, opportunities, and risks of life. The founders were trying to create "a new equilibrium . . . between individualism and cooperation, initiative and caution."

Even the simplest playground equipment, like seesaws, was intended to cultivate both a "sense of balance and a certain feeling of responsibility." Rowland Haynes, who led the playground movement in Milwaukee beginning in 1911, stressed that team games were even more important; they would help children "build up habits of quick thinking, initiative in dealing with new situations, self-control [and] the ability to work with others in the give-and-take of group activities." Baseball was considered an ideal activity for child development. As Henry Curtis, one of the founders of the playground movement, put it:

> One boy is on first, and another is on second. A fielder gets a liner in the middle field. Shall he throw the ball to first, or second, or third? Shall he try to touch the runner and make a double play? He must decide in a quarter of a second

and act upon that decision instantly or he will never make a successful player. If his judgment is right, handkerchiefs are waved and he is generously applauded; if he makes a mistake, he is hissed and called a fool. . . . The game imparts to the mind an alertness and vivacity which are essential to any large success either in business or society.

For generations, this was the prevailing approach to healthy child development. John F. Kennedy's Council on Youth Fitness promoted the installation of monkey bars and other climbing equipment to develop children's strength and coordination.

The risks in these games were readily acknowledged, but, common sense told us, children were going to do something with all that energy, so why not make it worthwhile: "Children have always run and jumped and climbed, thrown and fended missiles, and played games. Play is the essential spirit of childhood and uses all things as its implements. Any equipment that is furnished can never be more than an incident to it."

No one supported activities with hidden dangers, such as the placement of a swing where it might strike unsuspecting passersby. But, as one of leaders of the movement wrote in 1917:

It is reasonably evident that if a boy climbs on a swing frame and falls off, the school board is no more responsible for his action than if he climbed into a tree or upon the school building

and falls. There can be no more reason for taking out play equipment on account of such an
accident than there would be for the removal of
the trees or the school building.

Lady Allen of Hurtwood, a leader of the playground
movement in Britain, dealt with the risks in a typically English way: "Better a broken arm than a broken spirit."

Fast-forward to today. Reading the pamphlets on safe
playgrounds produced by the federal government and others, it's amazing any of us survived to adulthood. As a
brochure from the National Program for Playground
Safety states: "Many of today's adults remember hours of
fun and adventure spent on the playgrounds of their childhood. But, all too often, these memories are mixed with
pain." The dangers of play include earth itself, not only
under climbing apparatus, but almost everywhere. A federal handbook advises: "Earth surfaces such as soils and
hard-packed dirt are not recommended because they have
poor shock-absorbing properties." Grass and turf are un-
desirable because "wear and environmental conditions can
reduce their effectiveness." Seesaws are not explicitly condemned, but reading between the lines, no prudent person
would keep them: "Seesaw use is quite complex because it
requires two children to cooperate and combine their actions." As a result, "there is a trend to replace [them] with
spring-centered seesaws."

In 1993 a boy climbed to the top of a jungle gym in Detroit, jumped off, and broke his leg. One mother, after
hearing of the accident, went on a crusade, finding virtually everywhere older equipment and an "almost total lack

of fall zones"—"all they had was hard-packed earth." She brought the dangers to the attention of all the schools, which, confronted with notice of a possible legal risk, jumped out of the way quicker than if a pitcher had thrown a beanball. How did they correct the problem? By removing fifty-four pieces of playground equipment.

Our modern goal is not to train children for life, including its risks, but simply to get rid of risk. New York City cut the limbs of trees near playgrounds so children would not be tempted—just the thought makes the heart flutter—to climb a tree. A school district in Southern California banned all running on school grounds. After all, someone might slip and fall. Who would be responsible then? A few years ago, to avoid perils of children interacting, a school district in Philadelphia banned recess altogether. How far can we go? Ban playing? How about children? W. C. Fields may have been onto something.

Focusing too hard on avoidance of risk, as the late Aaron Wildavsky tried to teach us, is calculated to increase the risks. Sooner or later you pay the price. Every opportunity—including safety itself—carries a risk. Safe playground equipment is boring, so children start playing dangerous games "that exceed the design limitations." Why would a five-year-old child be so interested in Q-Tips that he would climb up to the top of a closet in search of them? It turned out, although the fact was given no significance by the court, that the mother was so fastidious that she cleaned the child's ears several times a week. There is, as we know, pleasure in this activity. The opportunity carried a risk. In 1999, a mother sent a three-year-old to play on the playground and, to be safe, made sure the child wore a bicycle helmet. Tragically, the child broke his neck and died when the helmet was caught in a ladder. Risk can never be eliminated. Risk must always be judged against the opportunity.

Like playgrounds, the American system of justice also is subject to the calculus of risk and opportunity. Avoiding authority, for example, carries the opportunity of reducing personal bias and prejudice. How much is hard to say, because someone driven to a certain result, whether out of hate or influence of popular opinion, is apt to figure out a plausible way of getting there. But avoiding authority, as we've seen, also carries high risk. As Professor Robert Kagan put it:

> The spirit of distrust of authority . . . can be used against the trustworthy, too. An equal opportunity weapon, it can be invoked by the misguided, the mendacious, and the malevolent, as well as by the mistreated.

Cardozo agreed that a judge, no matter how hard he tries, can never "eliminate altogether the personal measure of the interpreter," but understood that society can't function without a ruling by someone:

> You may say there is no assurance that judges will interpret the *mores* of their day more wisely and truly than other men. I am not disposed to deny this, but in my view it is quite beside the

point. The point is rather that this power of in-
terpretation must be lodged somewhere. . . .

Americans hate the idea of a single person of uncertain
predisposition having authority to make rulings. Justice
will never be perfect, Cardozo observed, but believed that
judges who "act with conscience and intelligence . . . ought
to attain . . . a fair average of truth and wisdom." Is it better to have no rulings? With no one in authority to defend
reasonable conduct, it is difficult for anyone in society to
be reasonable. Larck Lake in West Virginia, closed for over
five years, can offer tranquillity and enjoyment, but only if
someone on behalf of society is able to accept the risk that
someone may be foolish in their use of it.

We say we honor the rule of law, not authority based on
beliefs. Imagine, we're taught, what a madhouse that
would be. In all the braying about neutral justice, however,
I don't recall much discussion about what people think
makes sense as a legal rule for, say, playgrounds.

We have the idea of justice backward. Is justice about
avoiding our beliefs in the name of neutrality, or about asserting common beliefs in the name of law? We keep looking for some way of proving correctness or, as Havel puts
it, "an objective way out of the crisis of objectivism." But
nothing important in human affairs is provable. Law certainly can't be proved. Law isn't even supposed to be provable. We "cannot be fair," Professor Lon Fuller once
noted, "in a moral and legal vacuum." Principles of law
should be based not on what we can prove but on what we
believe. That's what law is: our beliefs on the rules of society, memorialized in common law principles and statutes

and then, equally important, applied by judges who have the authority to make sense of them in accord with our beliefs. Belief isn't evil. What we believe is who we are.

The risk presented by belief is the risk of our own character: to distinguish right from wrong, to be tolerant, to be vigilant of those we give responsibility to. Taking risks used to define our national character. That's how we get anywhere. Whether in business, in personal relationships, or in justice, risk is a key component of life. Today in America, risk is also an evil concept. "You took a risk" is reason enough to get sued. Our pioneer forefathers, given a glimpse of the future as they set out across the plains in their Conestoga wagons, would have been shocked at their American descendants going through life scared of their shadows.

Only a society as wealthy and well meaning as ours could have come up with a philosophy so completely disconnected from reality. In a fit of self-indulgence, future historians will observe, Americans abandoned their self-confidence. Will Rogers once observed that Americans thought they were getting smarter because "they're letting lawyers instead of their conscience be their guide." Maybe what we need is not better leaders, but to look instead to our humorists.

The leader of the legal process movement, Professor Henry Hart, in one of his last classes at Harvard Law School, brought in a judge's decision that, contrary to ideals of neutral process, blocked local officials from prosecuting sit-in demonstrators in Little Rock. As everyone waited for the "devastating critique of which he was capable," Hart paused and finally said, "Sometimes, sometimes, you just have to do the right thing." Actually, that's what we're supposed to do all the time. Will Rogers could have told him that right at the start.

As it happens, Will Rogers came from Oologah, Oklahoma. What a field day he would have had with the removal of the double slide.

THE COLLAPSE OF THE COMMON GOOD

George Reeves, a fifth-grade teacher in Toledo, Ohio, during the 1920s, had a particular approach that his students never forgot. Whenever a student seemed ready to give up on a problem, he would turn and write on the blackboard in large letters the word CAN'T. The teacher would then ask the student, "What shall I do now?" Everyone in Mr. Reeves's class knew the response: Knock the *T* off. "You can," was his repeated message, "if you think you can." Mr. Reeves's lesson was not lost on young Norman Peale, better known later as Reverend Norman Vincent Peale, author of the 1950s best-seller *The Power of Positive Thinking*.

Almost everyone remembers teachers who influenced their lives. The financier and statesman Bernard Baruch talked about first arriving at a new school and how his teacher, Katherine Blake, sat him up front in the classroom and arranged for another boy in the class to take care of him. By her approach, the diminutive boy with nothing in common with the other students felt a proud, and secure, part of his new school. Floyd Patterson, the heavyweight boxer as respected for his dignity as for his champion's skill, gave much of the credit to his third-grade teacher,

Vivian Costen, who "gave me confidence in myself. She wouldn't accept my protest that I couldn't learn to read or write. She was so kind and considerate and understanding that I wanted more than anything else in the world to please her."

Good teachers all seem to project their own personalities into the classroom. My ninth-grade Latin teacher in Lexington, Kentucky, Hillyer Rudisill, thin as a pencil but heavy with the affectations of a Charlestonian, had a special technique for keeping adolescents attentive to ablative absolute: He threw erasers at anyone he caught daydreaming. At least two or three of us would get bopped every class. He'd probably be sued today, but we loved it. John Small at Taft School in Watertown, Connecticut, had a quiet way of looking at you that made time stand still. No one, not even the wise guys, could resist the power of that gaze. My first-grade teacher in Tifton, Georgia, Mrs. Chandler, exuded kindly but unblinking authority. There she stands in the mist of my memory, Margaret Thatcher with a southern accent, imparting the lessons of Dick, Jane, and Spot.

What did these teachers have in common? It's hard to say. One used motivational techniques, one was really kind, one had a good stare, and one threw erasers. But they all stood out as wonderful teachers. What made them each special was that each brought his or her own spirit into the classroom. Success as a teacher seems to be tied to the personality and character of the particular individual: varying measures of love, humor, sensitivity, kindliness, values, energy, all bundled uniquely into one person. The package can't be replicated, probably not even in a cloning operation. It's personal.

Professor William Sanders at the University of Tennessee has spent years studying education. He has found that no other factor—not the school funding, not the pedagogy—is even one-tenth as significant as the particular teacher. Mediocre students who spent two years with teachers known to be effective then tested above the ninetieth percentile. Ineffective teachers, Professor Sanders found, had the converse effect: Several years with a bad teacher, and students starting at the same level then tested at the forty-fourth percentile. Bad luck in the draw, and a child may be turned off to learning for years. A teacher exists in a culture, of course, and good teachers tend to be found in good schools. But, at the end of the day, it boils down to the person standing there.

The impact of a teacher is not just better academic skills but better skills as people. "What children learn formally," Professor Christopher Jencks said, "is only a small fraction of their overall education." How a teacher handles conflicts, deals with failure, and distinguishes between occasional lapses and frequent ones, all convey life lessons in how to be a responsible adult. Watching adults in action is the one lesson every child learns perfectly.

The kindergartners were shoving and pushing close to the table at the science fair to witness a volcanic eruption of vinegar and baking soda. The science teacher asked them to step back to no avail, and then loudly repeated the request. They were oblivious. With a smile, the kindergarten teacher walked over, gave a gentle hip check to the child at the end, and said in a mock stentorian tone: "We have a volcano going off here—everybody stand back." The children laughed and immediately moved away from the table.

America's system of education is also erupting, sending dark clouds across America's future. But no one will stand far enough back to see what it is that makes the age-old human enterprise of education seemingly impossible today. Professor Laurence Steinberg, after a ten-year study of twenty thousand middle-class teenagers, found that "today's students know less, and can do less, than their counterparts 25 years ago." "We have vastly increased the resources devoted to education in the U.S. in recent decades," education expert Chester Finn noted in 1990, yet "by most measures our levels of cognitive learning are lower than they were 20 years ago." Several Philadelphia schools announced in 1997 that less than 3 percent of the students were reading at grade level.

Educating America's children must be one of the hardest tasks in the history of civilization. Leaders of public education, in a kind of panic, impose new reforms on schools with such frequency and failure that they've taken on the character of fingernails scraping on a blackboard.

National testing is the latest drill. How a school stacks up against other schools certainly seems like useful information. Everyone presumably wants to know how we're doing. Testing, on the other hand, hardly seems like a silver bullet. Most schools are not, presumably, trying to fail. Uniform testing also carries with it a few problems, particularly when the test becomes the main measure of success. Teachers soon catch on and just "teach to the test."

Elementary schools become like SAT review courses, with curiosity and discovery stripped out in favor of training for the answers.

In New York City, a few schools began to show real improvements after the uniform testing was announced. Everyone was incredibly pleased. A year later, the secret got out: The test answers had been doctored by the schools. The schools had cheated. Similar incidents are popping up all over the country. In Woodland, California, science teachers got hold of the Stanford achievement test and gave out the answers. In Reston, Virginia, the teachers rigged the social studies test. Almost overnight, the national testing reform had become yet another symptom of the problem.

The pattern of reform and failure has been going on for decades. In the 1960s, central school boards took control of most city schools. Centralizing certain kinds of decisions seems sensible, like bulk purchasing or deciding whether to teach "creationism," the fundamentalist belief that earth was created in one action-packed week. But huge bureaucracies dictating rules and procedures on exactly how to do everything soon turned schools into nightmares. In the 1970s, the vogue was to decentralize large school districts. Within a few years, without central oversight, strange ideas and local greed took hold, and schools went off the tracks. Too much centralization is bad. Too much decentralization is bad. The success of every reform, as with every teacher, seems to boil down to how it's done. It takes judgment. Not too much. Not too little.

Everything in education seems to come down to people on the spot. Fostering curiosity in our children is preferable, most would agree, to turning out young robots with marginally better test scores. But how do you decide how much creativity to emphasize and how much test-centered learning? Someone just has to decide what seems right.

Teachers and principals acting on their own instincts and judgment, however, are the last thing you can find in America's schools today. Doing what's personal might as well be illegal. Teachers are given instructions "telling them what to do and when to do it, every day of the year," as if they themselves were stuck in some horrible classroom, according to Stanford professor Linda Darling-Hammond. Every choice—about students, janitors, other teachers, the lunchroom, extracurricular activities, even the next thirty minutes—is laden with instructions. There's "little room for spontaneity or that leap of imagination we called creativity," Professor Michael Smith observes, when teachers "are required to organize their entire work week according to a printed form."

Decisions like disciplining, grading, or even deciding who makes some club or team must comply with organized procedures and standards. In Gerald Grant's study of one school over two decades, *The World We Created at Hamilton High,* the principal weighed all the directives the school had received one year from the central office: The dictates tipped the scales at forty-five pounds. "It's impossible to comply with the rules," said Jules Linden, a principal in New York. "Who's against bike safety?" asked Bruce Bendt, a principal in Chicago. "But how much time should we spend on something like that?" Dreaming up a new way to inspire a class, or spontaneously deciding to focus on some world event for the morning, is not in the realm of the possible. Teachers and principals are exhausted from trying to keep up with the organizational requirements and reforms.

Public schools are a branch of government, of course. Like modern justice, we've organized schools and government departments to be squeaky clean. The goal is the same—to achieve a neutral organization, free from bias, favoritism, or unfairness. Avoiding value judgments is the operating philosophy for those with responsibility in schools and agencies, just as it is with judges. Where neutral process is a judge's mantra, organizing precisely how things are done is how teachers and other public employees demonstrate their neutrality.

Rules on internal organization permeate public institutions. Decisions that can't be dictated by a rule, like personnel choices, must comply with designated procedures and criteria similar to those in the system of justice. "Suffice it to say," as one guide for public employees put it, "value judgments should not be exercised at the work level." No one in responsibility should make decisions about anything or anyone—not a principal about a teacher, not a teacher about a student—unless it can be demonstrated to be proper. Americans want reasons. Of course we want teachers and public employees to exercise judgment—they should always use their best judgment—so long as they're prepared to show why it's proper. It's just a matter, we believe, of good organization. It is "not burdensome to give reasons," Justice Thurgood Marshall once wrote, "when reasons exist."

Accomplishing anything, however, requires choices that are unavoidably personal. Chester Barnard, a telephone company executive in the 1930s who wrote one of the great management books, *The Functions of the Executive*, observed that placing a telephone pole involves a few conscious judgments and a thousand no one notices . . . avoiding the trees, being alert not to dig into gas lines, and so forth. Getting anything done requires not only basic tools and resources but also the instinct of humans on what will work. The person on the spot must leap a kind of a chasm, using his intuition and judgment, to arrive at accomplishment. An auto assembly-line worker, interviewed by Studs Terkel, talked of the adjustments required to mount a truck tire:

> There was a trick to putting the rim in, so that it had a little click. You had to be very fine to know. So you would put this clip around . . . and I would just kick it over—boom!—in there.

The complexity of judgment expands exponentially in decisions among humans, as people evaluate personalities, character, and countless other relevant factors.

The human input needed for accomplishment has as many shapes as there are humans. But all these shapes of judgment and intuition have one trait in common: Their correctness is almost never provable in advance. "The powers of conscious reason" are limited, as Nobel economist Friedrich Hayek observed, and require "assistance from processes of which we are not aware." The ideal of neutral competence is impossible. "For practical success," Ralph Waldo Emerson observed, "there can't be too much design."

Success can be readily judged, of course. "Just walk into a school," education expert John Chubb notes, "and you can tell in ten minutes whether it's working." But the instincts that lead to success can rarely be demonstrated. Even judges can't always explain why decisions are right: " 'The trained instinct of a judge,' " Justice Cardozo quoted Roscoe Pound, " 'leads him to the result for which he is puzzled to give unimpeachable legal reasons.' "

Americans believe good government requires a kind of belt-and-suspenders approach. What's the harm of making sure each choice complies with rules and procedures? How else can we assure the requisite neutrality, or avoid backbiting later on? Better safe than sorry. But this highly organized approach has an unintended cost: It seems to supplant the human judgment and instinct needed to make anything work.

In the 1980s, the New York City Board of Education issued a directive that it would measure high schools by the percentage of seniors who graduated. A few days later, at a meeting of teachers, the principal of Walton High in the Bronx announced to all that Walton High would have a perfect showing: Poorly performing eleventh-graders would not be considered part of the senior class. They would remain juniors forever. The plan was foolproof: The assembled teachers broke out in applause. The Board of Ed's point, of course, was to measure overall achievement, not see a phony number by leaving out all the poor students. Didn't they realize that, pretty soon, Walton's eleventh grade would look ridiculous, like a lump in a python after a big meal?

If people are told that they will be judged by certain criteria, that's what they will focus on. The emphasis on uniform testing, striving to achieve objective guideposts, not only changes what teachers teach but makes them lose sight of the less tangible goals of education. Focusing too hard on tests causes education to shirk "its central task," according to sociologist James Q. Wilson, "which is to raise good citizens." Character, of course, is hard to test. So is judging which schools promote good citizenship. One thing we know for sure: Schools that themselves cheat don't exactly set a good role model.

Humans, at least most of us, don't have the ability to exercise our own judgment while working to satisfy objective criteria. It's a matter of cognitive capacity. A person "can either operate or think," management expert Peter Drucker once observed, but "no man . . . can do both at the same time." Sociologist Robert K. Merton once put it this way: "A way of seeing is also a way of not seeing: Focus upon A," and you will always be "neglect-[ing] . . . B." Make educators think about complying with the rules, in other words, and they will stop thinking about educating the children in front of them.

For longer than anyone can remember, we have been organizing and reorganizing schools. Americans want protection against arbitrary decisions. We want reliability. But judgment, viewed as a matter of provability, is almost always "arbitrary." Teachers just know, as Theodore and Nancy Sizer put it, that we "whisper to a child who is embarrassed but who needs to talk, but we also yell to get the cafeteria quiet." Real people, acting on their beliefs, figure out a way to get the job done, or not. Aristotle believed a person's prudence, one of the greatest human traits, was distinguished from intelligence, because it "cannot be apprehended by scientific knowledge, but only by perception." "Perception is not whimsical," Ralph Waldo Emerson observed. "My perception of it is just as much fact as the sun."

Today, the personal perceptions of teachers and principals about what's going on, whether about a student or a class, or what makes sense or what's fair, are basically irrelevant. Personal perception is suspect, at best a casual bystander. What matters is compliance.

Teachers, not surprisingly, are giving up. Teachers "no longer believe," Gerald Grant found, that "what they do in the hall or inside their classrooms makes any difference." Like a modern plague, teacher "burnout," a phenomenon where teachers become listless and lose their sense of purpose, has swept across America. Most teachers don't even try to deal with student misconduct. "You know what's going to happen," said one teacher, "the parents are going to get a lawyer . . . and you're going to look like a fool." One survey found a disturbing new consensus: "I'll go to school every day. I'll go through the motions. I'll put my time in. But my heart is not in it."

Everyone else in education seems to be giving up as well. In his study of middle-class high school students, Laurence Steinberg was startled by the degree of disengagement: "Classrooms are filled with dozing students whose heads lie on their desks." My Latin teacher, Hillyer Rusidill, could have solved that problem with a well-aimed eraser, but maybe not the deeper indifference. "Even the simplest questions from teachers are met with blank stares." The American teenagers averaged four hours of homework per week; in other industrial countries, students also averaged four hours, but every day. Parents, the third leg of the stool, don't feel very engaged either. A 1998 blue-ribbon report, *A Nation of Spectators,* concluded that Americans "deplore the performance of our public schools, but somehow can't find the time to join parents' associations, attend school board meetings, or even help our children with their homework." PTA participation is half what it was thirty years ago.

Spend any time in schools, and the conclusion seems inescapable: The systems in place to ensure good decisions cause failure. Schools fail because teachers can't draw on their personality and passion. Schools fail because principals can't use their judgment to distinguish the good from the indifferent, or surprise with an exception or a new idea. Schools fail because few bright people are attracted to a culture in which the beliefs of teachers and principals don't matter. The people in education have been incapacitated by the organization of it. We have taken away the human foundation of education, and wonder why the house is toppling down.

"Our subjective experience is, to an extent that seems remarkable, underestimated," said Nobel laureate Konrad Lorenz. "All current governing systems . . . abrogate the personality of the individual." "Even the Tin Woodman," one teacher wrote, "knew that without a heart he was worthless."

THE MYTH IN SCIENTIFIC MANAGEMENT

"In the past the man has been first," Frederick Winslow Taylor wrote in 1911. "In the future the system must be first."

When Taylor made this pronouncement, America had been in an identity crisis for over half a century, pulled between the individual spirit of the frontier and the institutional power of the industrial revolution. Now the frontier was gone. No longer would we focus on the individual taking risks, adapting to new circumstances, and using all of his instincts and experience to try to succeed. Americans now had to find their livelihood and character within large institutions. Organization replaced the frontier. Today, a century later, being well organized is considered a high virtue. Being wise, by contrast, is a concept too subjective to be useful.

The prophet of organization was Taylor, an engineer whose book, *The Principles of Scientific Management,* became one of the most influential books of the twentieth century. Taylor's objective was efficient industrial output, but he also believed that better efficiency would improve the lot of the worker. Industry was powered by huge machines that, literally and figuratively, devoured people, including child labor. "Industry," Taylor wrote, is "warfare."

Taylor saw scientific organization as a golden road. Careful study would reveal "one best method" to do almost anything. To establish "the science of shoveling," for example, "thousands of stopwatch observations were made to study just how quickly a laborer, provided in each case with the proper type of shovel, can push his shovel into the pile of materials and then draw it out properly loaded." Pauses and rest periods were similarly calibrated. While Taylor emphasized the importance of good relations with workers, a progressive idea at the time, worker empowerment was pretty much the opposite of Taylor's gospel. "Taylorism," as his philosophy of efficiency came to be known, had at its core the idea that people should be told exactly how to do their jobs:

> The work of every workman is fully planned out . . . describing in detail the task which he is to accomplish, as well as the means to be used in doing the work.

Taylor conducted an experiment at Bethlehem Steel to show how scientific management could increase the production of pig iron handlers. These handlers were accustomed to loading 12.5 tons per day of ninety-two-pound blocks of crude iron, called "pigs," onto railcars. Taylor picked a man who seemed well suited (Taylor said he had no doubt that he could train "an intelligent gorilla" as effectively). Having chosen what he viewed to be a good worker ("a little Pennsylvania Dutchman who had been observed to trot back home for a mile or so after his work in the evening"), Taylor then made a deal to increase his wages from $1.15 to $1.85 per day if he did the job exactly as told:

> When this man tells you to walk, you walk;
> when he tells you to sit down, you sit down, and
> you don't talk back to him.

Sure enough, the "little Dutchman" was soon loading 47.5 tons per day instead of 12.5 tons. Taylor suppressed the fact that practically everyone else quit. The story became organizational legend.

It is easy in hindsight to parody Taylor, but the idea of being thoughtful in organizing production had undeniable merit, and the basic philosophy became the dominant idea of structuring enterprise in the twentieth century. Without Taylor, as Andrea Gabor said in *The Capitalist Philosophers,* "mass production would have been impossible."

The power of organization was seemingly limitless. American industry focused on establishing ever more efficient assembly lines. Henry Ford stuck to a dictatorial model of Taylor's. General Motors, under the leadership of Alfred Sloan, innovated a multidivisional model to "find a principle of coordination without losing the advantages of decentralization."

For organizing government, Taylorism was almost too good to be true. For decades, progressives had been championing the cause of neutral administration to rid government of the taint of patronage and partisan politics. With scientific methods, we got both: Government would be pure and it would be efficient. In 1923, Congress passed the Classification Act, dividing civil servants into grades with designated tasks and assigned salaries. At last, government was all figured out: It would be like an assembly line. New York State divides its workers into 3,884 specific job categories; South Dakota, about 500. All work is divided rigidly by category. Over time, as Professor Paul Light of the Brookings Institution has chronicled, government added layers of scientific sophistication, based on models like "P.O.S.D.C.O.R.B." (planning, organizing, staffing, directing, coordinating, reporting, and budgeting).

Organizational power was on full display during World War II, when American factories retooled to turn out airplanes and tanks of high quality at a prodigious rate. In 1940, the Army Air Corps had 412 airplanes, and Roosevelt called for the construction of 50,000 new planes. By the war's end, the Air Force had 230,000 planes. This extraordinary success was made possible in part by a small group of Pentagon planners, including a young business school professor named Robert McNamara. These planners, who became known as the "Whiz Kids," developed sophisticated quantitative models that tracked inventory and deployed spare parts to make sure assembly lines never stopped. They shipped out needed mechanics so supply lines wouldn't be interrupted. They analyzed which bombers logistically delivered the most payload for the least cost. They redirected production from B-24 to B-17 bombers after finding that the B-17 was more durable. Organization helped win the war.

By the 1950s, organization was accepted as the symbol of modern society, just as the frontier had been a hundred years earlier. In the new organizational society, the assembly line was all-powerful, and administrators were modern heroes. Robert McNamara was brought into Ford and turned it around with quantitative analysis. "Under

McNamara, for the first time in more than twenty-five years," David Halberstam writes, "the company always knew where it was, how much it was spending, and how much it was making."

Having demonstrated the power of the organization to achieve national might, consumer progress, and owner wealth, almost everyone accepted as inevitable its side effect: the insignificance of the individual. Descendants of pioneers became pawns of modern industrial society. Sociologist Max Weber was as certain of the inhumanity of bureaucracy as he was of its inevitable efficiency:

> Bureaucracy develops the more perfectly, the more it's "dehumanized," the more completely it succeeds in eliminating from official business love, hatred, and all personal, irrational, and emotional elements which escape calculation.

To Henry Ford, people were cogs in a machine: "A great business is really too big to be human. It grows so large as to supplant the personality of the man." Industry, said GM's Alfred Sloan, was "designed as an objective organization as distinguished from the type that gets lost in the subjectivity of personalities." "The day of combination is here to stay," John D. Rockefeller announced. "Individualism has gone, never to return." Woodrow Wilson thought that "we are in the presence of a new organization of society. . . . Your individuality is swallowed up in the . . . purpose of a great organization. . . . The truth is, we are all caught up in a great economic system which is heartless." Frank Lloyd Wright's famous Larkin Building, designed with an interior court to maximize light, also maximized surveillance, and had seats designed to minimize movement to keep the female clerks focused on processing orders for mail-order soap.

William H. Whyte, in his 1957 book *The Organization Man,* described how the individual becomes subjugated to the group, his personality molded the way a sheet of steel is stamped. While Whyte bemoaned the anonymous conformist in the gray flannel suit, he too believed in its overwhelming efficiency. John F. Kennedy believed he was presiding over the new technocratic state, in which political values, like personal values, no longer held center stage:

> Most of us are conditioned for many years to have a political viewpoint—Republican or Democratic, liberal, conservative, or moderate. The fact of the matter is that most of the problems that we now face are technical problems, are administrative problems. They are very sophisticated judgments, which do not lend themselves to the great sort of passionate movements which have stirred this country so often in the past. [They] deal with questions which are now beyond the comprehension of most men.

Writers were holdouts from the beginning, giving vivid descriptions of this modern world where the individual no longer matters. Early works told of the nothingness of the life without individual responsibility. In *Bartleby the Scrivener,* Herman Melville describes a person who has no purpose and whose only will is to refuse to do anything, responding to every request, "I prefer not to." Franz Kafka went to work for an insurance company in Prague, where, he wrote his girlfriend, "the only true hell is there in the office":

> I'm not complaining about the work so much as the swampy viscosity of time. . . . You blame everything on your watch, which you hold constantly in the palm of your hand.

In Aldous Huxley's *Brave New World,* everything is organized: People are conceived in a test tube, preprogrammed at different levels of intelligence, put to work in repetitive cycles, and kept happy with drugs. Years are counted back to the Year of Our Ford.

Taylorism was the target of the movie *Modern Times,* in which Charlie Chaplin tightens the same bolt, over and over and over. The efficiency expert keeps speeding up the line until Chaplin goes flying into a giant hopper. The high point is when the expert creates a feeding machine to obviate the need for a lunch break. On the trial run of the feeding machine, Chaplin is fed corn-on-the-cob but the machine is miscalibrated and the rapidly rotating corn cob starts scrubbing Chaplin's face. The meal cycle finally ends, appropriately, with a pneumatically misplaced pie. Like Chaplin, George Orwell questioned whether the modern organization actually worked on its own terms. Orwell's *1984,* published in 1949, views the new order as totalitarian but not productive. The "final, most essential command" of the Party in *1984* is to "reject the evidence of your eyes and ears."

Out in real life, the smug organizational ideal strove to top its prior successes. I remember visiting a GM assembly line so long that I thought the vista to the end was obscured by the curvature of the Earth. These assembly lines were staggeringly efficient, but only at massive quantities of the same product. Might the buying public want a little more diversity in the products offered? One glitch in the assembly line or a delay in parts, and workstations up and down the line would grind to a halt. Was this really efficient? Designed for low-cost production, the Chevrolet Chevette was described by one later critic as "an engine surrounded by four pieces of drywall."

Organizational dictates began to display a bad habit of taking on a life of their own. McNamara demanded quality at Ford plants but gave managers no discretion to implement needed changes and instead ordered studies that went on for years. Like educational reformers trying to humiliate schools into better performance through standardized tests, McNamara tried to quantify quality "by assigning points for things gone wrong." But the "plants quickly learned how to rig the numbers by having a few high-quality cars on hand" for the inspectors. To avoid showing a surplus of parts at the end of a product's life, a sign of inefficiency, plant managers "dump[ed] thousands of parts into the nearby Delaware River."

A law of organizational futility began to reveal itself: If humans focused on organizational compliance instead of making sense of the situation, organization would cause failure. General Motors decided to determine increases in the next year's department budget by looking at whether people were working overtime, so some GM managers ordered personnel to stay late even if there was nothing to do. There they sat, reading newspapers and collecting overtime, to prove how overworked they were.

McNamara went to head the Department of Defense during the Vietnam War, imparting the most efficient systems available. "As America's involvement in Vietnam began to spiral out of control, the DOD kept counting: bombing strikes, energy supply lines destroyed, body bags." But, as a national security officer said later, "the excessively mechanical system of statistical reporting . . . was giving us a grotesquely inaccurate picture." The war took on a surreal quality, best summed up by the American commander who said that "we had to destroy the town in order to save it."

As America's culture began to fracture in the 1960s, brilliantly organized corporations began to fray from an unexpected source: the supposedly insignificant individual. Societal disarray plus Tayloristic organization equaled widespread indifference. Products became shoddy. General Motors had to close its plant in Fremont, California, because "nobody cared." As one worker recalled:

> The parking lot was covered with broken glass. . . . It looked like pigs lived here. People would sit wherever they wanted and read books, eat and play radios. I remember working on a car that was full of chicken bones left over from a guy's lunch. Nobody cared.

The Japanese, meanwhile, had adopted the views of management expert W. Edwards Deming, who, even be-

fore corporate America started to teeter, had figured out
what Charlie Chaplin intuitively knew: There was unavoidable variability even in the most rigorous assembly
lines, causing numerous flaws of mass-produced goods.
The only solution was to re-engage the humans. Deming's
program of "Total Quality Management," or "TQM,"
meant that workers would get together to examine results
and to figure out how to solve problems. The Japanese developed small work teams, in which one person would
have the authority to stop an entire production line if he
saw something seriously wrong. This team approach,
Konosuke Matsushita explained to Westerners in 1979,
would soon threaten all of American industry:

> We are going to win and the industrial West is
> going to lose. . . . For you, the essence of man-
> agement is getting ideas out of the heads of
> bosses into the hands of labour. . . . For us, the
> core of management is the art of mobilizing and
> putting together the intellectual resources of all
> employees of the firm.

By the late 1970s, the Japanese competitors were offering
higher quality, better prices, more diversity. Xerox discovered in late 1979 that "the Japanese were *selling* copiers
for less than it cost Xerox to *build* them" and "beat them
on quality." There was talk that America's largest car companies might go bankrupt.

Virtually overnight, American business rediscovered the
human. In an influential article in 1980, "Managing Our
Way to Economic Decline," Harvard business professors

Robert Hayes and William Abernathy blamed American business failure on "management principles which encouraged analytic detachment rather than hands-on experience." In their 1982 best-seller, *In Search of Excellence,* Tom Peters and Robert Waterman made what was then the shocking announcement that "the individual human being still counts." Trial and error, not top-down organization, was essential. Jack Welch, after a rocky start as CEO at General Electric (he became known as "neutron Jack" for the number of jobs he eliminated), soon became respected for management based on common values. Part of everyone's job was to help other people succeed. GE initiated "360-degree evaluation" where every person, including the CEO, was evaluated by subordinates as well as by superiors. Nordstrom's department store achieved success by focusing on the attitude and helpfulness of its employees. TQM was re-imported wholesale into American industry. "Continuous change" became a new mantra: If you don't make it better, someone else will. Humans can always make anything better.

Humans always mattered. The poster boy of Taylorism, the "little Dutchman" who quadrupled his output to the ticking seconds of Taylor's stopwatch, was held as a symbol of organizational success. But there's another way of looking at it. Taylor identified the strongest guy in the group and induced him to work to his prodigious capacity. Americans were taught to believe that the individual no longer mattered, but the "little Dutchman" is more accurately seen as a symbol of the extraordinary range of human ability.

For the entire century, Americans were taught that organization was king. Efficiency meant being told what to do and how to do it. In retrospect, scientific management was a useful tool, but Americans had achieved success because they had never fully bought into its mechanical philosophy. Americans still saw their main goal as getting the job done. The planes were produced in World War II not just because the Whiz Kids were good at marshaling resources but because workers cared. In the 1950s Americans still believed that doing a good job meant thinking for themselves. Holding up your share of the workload, as Whyte described in *The Organization Man,* was a part of the culture. When people, after being told for generations that they no longer mattered, began to believe it, all the brilliant organization collapsed like a house of cards.

THE LETHAL COCKTAIL: ADD INDIVIDUAL RIGHTS TO SCIENTIFIC MANAGEMENT

In his first days as a young teacher, John Fager attended a beginning-of-the-year meeting with the principal of his school in Queens, New York. He sat there, interested in hearing the principal lead a discussion of the year's goals and plans. Then, without anything having happened, right in the middle of the meeting, half of the teachers stood up and left the room. Even more surprising, no one seemed surprised. The principal just kept on talking as if nothing had happened. The whole episode seemed so strange. Later John learned that, under the union contract, teachers had to spend no more than forty minutes per week in staff meetings. Once the allotted time was up, away the teachers went. The teachers who cared enough to stay could continue discussing plans and ideas for the year.

A young principal, brimming with ideas on how to revitalize an elementary school in Boston's South End, was surprised on her first day to be cornered by a group of teachers who warned her, "Don't try to change the way we do things. We know the rules. We know our rights." Radical ideas like trying a new textbook, or supervising recess to make sure the children were all right, were dead on arrival.

Organization in modern government has a special quality, far more controlling of human action than any techniques devised by Frederick Winslow Taylor. Organization in public institutions has acquired the status of law. If the rules say forty minutes with the principal, that's the teacher's legal right, and there's nothing anyone can do about it. We expect legal standards when government is exercising its coercive powers in regulation, of course, but in deciding how to get a job done or manage an office, government exercises no more coercive powers than a private employer. But the legal dictates are the same for internal government management as for governing.

If scientific management worked as advertised, calibrating every choice without the need for human instinct and values, attaching a legal right to every organizational requirement might not make much of a difference. But scientific management, as we've seen, doesn't actually work without continual personal will and intervention. Adding legal rights to scientific organization leaves us with an odd kind of enterprise, a machine in which every human part has the right to refuse to do what's needed.

All these legal rights grew out of past reforms and political deals, some from good government initiatives like civil service laws, others from union negotiations, and still others from court rulings. Usually they were designed to protect some group or interest, often in the name of effective management. They've been interpreted and codified so many times, however, that, like bureaucratic accretion generally, no one alive remembers why they developed as they did. They're just an accepted part of government organization. What everyone knows is, because they're rights, they're untouchable.

A huge hock of mucus was dripping down the window of her classroom at Walton High in the Bronx, but when the teacher, Nancy Udell, called in a custodian, he patiently explained that the union contract requires window cleaning only on a set schedule. "Actually cleaning the window was the furthest thing from his mind," Ms. Udell marveled. "What interested him, as the disgusting glob stared at us, was how I could be so naïve as to ask." At least that custodian was polite. Down the road in Queens, when a health inspector found the elementary school cafeteria to be unsanitary, the custodian refused to mop it because the contract required mopping only on Fridays. When the principal asked if he really wanted the children's food to come out of a dirty kitchen, the custodian told him, "I don't give a damn about your health inspections," and walked away.

Students have their rights, too. Rights is the one subject area where most students, if tested, would get an A. One high school, worried about students hanging out in their cars between classes, banned visits to the parking lot during the school day. No problem: Students started parking in the driveway. When a special-education therapist in rural Pennsylvania got up from a session to talk to the student's teacher for a minute, the fourth-grader ordered the therapist to stay put: "You can't go. I'm entitled to my full thirty minutes." Students today learn their rights practically before they learn to read. In Montclair, New Jersey, a misbehaving second-grader, when caught on the arm by the teacher, started threatening the teacher with legal sanctions, including "I'll call DYFS" (Division of Youth and Family Services).

Disorder is considered by many the number one problem in schools, but it's hard to keep order when teachers and principals feel they can't do anything without tackling a hornet's nest of rights. In *The World We Created at Hamilton High*, Gerald Grant describes the frustration of a highly regarded teacher who catches a student cheating:

> I saw the kid cheating. I saw him with his open book on his lap during a test. [But] they wanted documentation. "How can you prove it?" The question now is, "We've heard John's side of the story, what's yours?" . . . Somehow it felt like I'm part of the crime.

Students' preoccupation in pushing the legal envelope is hardly surprising: Schools make a point of passing out pamphlets to students that lay out the code of conduct in excruciating detail. What happens or doesn't happen, as schools lean over backward to emphasize, will be determined in strict conformity with the stated rules and rights.

For decades, boards of education have produced thick manuals, updated constantly, that try to delineate everyone's rights and obligations. Unions negotiate detailed rights of members, down to the tiniest responsibilities of how they do their job. Under the teachers' union contract in New York, over two hundred pages of fine print, "the inclusion of cafeteria duties, yard, bus and hall patrols, and study halls is strictly prohibited." Almost any daily disagreement in schools, whether over these detailed rights or any other issue, must be resolved through a legal process.

A more diligent effort to protect everyone's rights is hard to imagine. It's also hard to conceive of a worse failure. The academic failures are nothing compared to the social failures. America's schools have a culture that more closely resembles that of a penal institution. The idea of politeness or respect doesn't exist, even in memory. "The disrespect students have . . . the name calling, it just flows off the tongue like they're saying 'good morning,' " said a Minneapolis teacher. One eighth-grader in Brooklyn insisted on calling the teacher "cu*t face" for the entire year. Instead of an atmosphere of cooperation, interaction is regularly confrontational. Honesty is replaced by a code of whatever you can get away with. In Steinberg's study, two-thirds of the students said that they had cheated in the prior year. In a 1999 survey of honor students, 80 percent said they cheated to get to the top.

Fear doesn't lag far behind the erosion of character. One-fifth of high school students say they are too scared to use school bathrooms. The breakdown of civilized order is reflected in practically every aspect of school life, including removal of doors from bathroom stalls in many schools.

Hardly a day goes by in some schools without a teacher being threatened by a student, either physically or legally.

The cornucopia of rights overflowing from America's schools probably looks good, at least on paper, to people who like legal structures that lay out everyone's place in advance. Now everyone has their very own rights. It's like handing out candy so that the children don't fight over it. But the candy seems to be poisonous. Students at least have the excuse of childhood. How could those teachers walk out of the middle of the staff meeting? It's not how humans working together behave. Why not also spit on people on the way out? Speaking of spit, why would a custodian lecture about his right not to clean it up instead of taking thirty seconds to get the job done?

Allowing ourselves to daydream for a moment, what would we want that American schools don't have? Surveys of educators note that successful schools seem to have one thing in common: a sense of shared purpose. The success of every culture, observed Lord Moulton, a respected British judge and cabinet minister in the early twentieth century, hinges not on big points of morality—there will always be issues like abortion or school prayer over which people differ—but on smaller values, like being considerate of others and pulling your weight. These values, he observed, are neither legally enforceable nor purely private, but constitute the connective tissue of people interacting in a healthy society. He called this the "world of manners":

> Between "can do" and "may do" ought to exist
> the whole realm which recognizes the sway of
> duty, fairness, sympathy, taste and all the other

things that make life beautiful and society possible.

No society or organization can long remain vital, he observed, when these values of civilized behavior are no longer shared.

The common complaint of teachers and principals, as we've seen, is that their values are irrelevant. But what can we do? In a free country, you can't force other people to be considerate. We don't like students' disrespectful attitudes or language, but remember the First Amendment. People have their rights. Rights have a power, as we've seen elsewhere, that makes people tremble before them and not even bother to argue over right and wrong. How can we?

With educators surrounded by as many individual rights as there are rules and individuals, it's not surprising that daily decisions usually focus not mainly on getting the job done but on avoiding legal land mines. As with doctors practicing defensive medicine, principals and other public managers practice defensive management. Preoccupation with the possibilities of legal entitlement has eclipsed any consideration of the common good.

But there's a false assumption here, the same as in justice. Are these rights against government decisions legitimate entitlements? We imagine a legal version of the peaceable kingdom, in which every right has its place and any disagreement is resolved by looking at who encroached on someone else's designated spot. Who are we to judge the values of a profane child? Doesn't he have a right to say whatever he wants? But, as in justice, this tidy model doesn't hold up even for one argument. Let's turn the question around: What right does that profane child have to drag a school's culture into the gutter? An adolescent can say what he wants out on the street; on a public sidewalk, people can walk away from each other. But not in school: It's a shared activity.

In shared activities, one person's asserted rights almost always affect what other people could claim as their rights. The individual achievement and happiness of your child are affected by how orderly and considerate the other students are, how good the teacher is, how clean the halls are. A student can't learn if he's scared. No student or teacher can have pride if the school and its culture are falling down around them. "Ability is not something that is possessed by an individual," management pioneer Chester Barnard observed, "independent of his environment."

We've tried to achieve a neutral system by focusing on legality: What matters is not what's moral but what anyone can argue is legal. But our value-free approach, as in justice, is not free of values. Whoever asserts their values controls the culture. Not making the value judgment means that the disruptive child is making the value judgment for everyone else. There's no way around the dilemma of having to choose. We're stuck together in the classroom. The classroom will either reflect our values or the values of the disruptive kid. Are schools today neutral? They have a moral character; it's the kind you find in a no-man's-land.

Living in a free country, we're taught, means everyone can do what he wants. People are allowed to have terrible values. Law should never use its coercive power, most of us believe, to enforce civilized values. But does that mean, for joint endeavors like running schools or public offices, that law should protect uncivilized values? Today, whoever happens to assert his rights first usually ends up trumping everyone else's, as in a children's game. Slapjack. It's my right.

If we accept values as inevitable, shouldn't they be the values of whoever has responsibility for the common enterprise? What is law doing here at all? Perhaps setting and enforcing the mores of schools or public facilities should not generally be regulated by law, except to guard against the kinds of abuses that would also be protected against in a private school or office.

Richard Riley, Secretary of Education, gave a speech in 1999 with the theme that "education was a civil right." Every American, he announced, was entitled to a good education, as a matter of individual right. In the discussion that followed, one of the panelists asked Secretary Riley whether he really meant "civil right" in the legal sense, that parents could bring a lawsuit if they thought their child's education was deficient. "If that's what it's come to," said the Secretary of Education, "then so be it."

When the national education head's idea of reform is to encourage people to sue over education's ineptness, you get the uncomfortable feeling that things are worse off than you imagined. Say you win the lawsuit. Then what happens? Do schools work better? Maybe parents collect punitive damages. Who pays for that? There go the property taxes. He couldn't really have meant it, I hope, but his speech underscores the sense of hopelessness that has overcome even our leaders.

But maybe, inadvertently, Secretary Riley has given us a

clue: When something seems intractably broken, impervious to every reform, the fault probably lies in some assumption we hold dearest. For longer than anyone can remember, the vocabulary of public management has been to detail everyone's legal rights against the institution. Everyone arrives in the morning with their fists up, literally and figuratively, determined to defend their rights.

The sum of all these rights is far less than the parts. Individuals are not more free, with all their rights, but less free, because the organization they're a part of is out of control. Adults bicker over entitlements. Nobody can be themselves. Teachers, though armed with rights, find themselves increasingly impotent. Disruptive children, riding their rights like a skateboard, have taken over. Shouldn't someone be in charge?

FROM MISTRUST TO UNACCOUNTABILITY

Americans' belief in equality, Tocqueville observed, has always made Americans "look upon all authority with a jealous eye." For over two hundred years, since our founders invented separation of powers, government reform has generally headed in one direction: to remove authority from government officials. The first century of our democratic experiment stamped an indelible distrust of public management on the American psyche.

"To the victor," as Senator William Marcy proclaimed in 1832, "belong the spoils." Under the spoils system, government was a public trough of patronage. Spoils was basically a form of campaign finance: In exchange for political support, most government jobs—postmasters, assis-

tant postmasters, customs officials, clerks—were handed
out as "patronage" to party hacks, irrespective of qualifi-
cations. In 1878, almost 75 percent of the money raised by
the Republican Congressional Committee came from federal employees. "The men who did the business last fall,"
as one job seeker, Charles Guiteau, wrote to President
Garfield, "are the ones to be remembered."

The spoils system is best remembered for its corruption. Although illegal then as now, corruption found well-
fertilized soil in a system where people essentially paid to
get jobs. While scholars disagree over whether government
under spoils was more corrupt than it was before or afterward, the stench reached unavoidable levels in the administration of President Ulysses Grant. The Secretary of War,
W. W. Belknap, was run out of office in 1876 for selling In-
dian trading posts. The American minister to Brazil fled
after stealing $100,000. The Secretary of the Treasury al-
lowed his friends to receive huge commissions on government transactions. After he resigned, it was discovered that
a whiskey ring had avoided millions of dollars in liquor ex-
cise taxes.

Corruption grabbed the headlines, but spoils was also a
terrible way to run a government. Office holders, having
paid for their jobs, were largely immune from accountability to their superiors or the public they served. General
Winfield Scott's campaign during the Mexican War was
hampered by insubordinate officers who were political appointees. Indifference and incompetence were the norm.
Since political success was tied to handing out as many
jobs as possible, the party bosses actually had an incentive

to maintain a bloated workforce. Many appointees did nothing: One forestry inspector, asked by a congressional committee if he had ever inspected a forest said, "No, sir, nothing but draw my pay."

Even at the time, spoils was notorious. The public made fun of it. After the first battle of Bull Run, New York satirist Artemis Ward attributed the vigorous retreat of the Union army to a rumor that three jobs had opened up in the New York Customs House. Political leaders probably hated spoils more than they hate begging for campaign contributions today. "Tell all the office seekers to come in at once," Abraham Lincoln is reported to have said after he got smallpox, "for now I have something I can give to all of them." But even at the height of scandal and ineptitude, the campaign by civil service reformers against spoils never quite got off the ground. "Agitation over the spoils system went on," as historians Henry and Mary Beard put it, "making ripples here and there on the smooth surface of orthodox custom." Reform would have been long in coming had not Charles Guiteau, furious that his letters to President Garfield had been unsuccessful, shot the president. Spoils finally was dethroned when, following the tragedy, public opinion mobilized against it.

On January 16, 1883, Congress passed the Pendleton Act establishing a professional civil service. The reform ideal, which remains with us today, was to purify government: "Administration," Woodrow Wilson wrote in 1887, "lies outside the proper sphere of politics." No longer would government suffer, as reformer Carl Schurz said, from "the demoralizing influence of the patronage." Instead of party hacks, the public would be served by officials with "skill, ability, fidelity, zeal, and integrity."

Virtue finally conquered corruption; that's the footnote to which history relegates civil service reform. Government would be run not by political leaders but by professionals, carefully organized to fulfill the designated tasks. "A bureaucracy devoid of political appointees," as historian Michael Nelson put it, would be "like a royal guard of eunuchs, an agency with no distracting wants of its own to impede the execution of appointed tasks."

The goal of civil service reformers was not to shift a property entitlement in public jobs from political appointees to permanent civil servants. That was the last thing on their minds: Reformers were getting rid of any idea that public jobs were anybody's private property. Hiring would be by competitive examination. With patronage eliminated, and therefore no ulterior motive to terminate good public employees, firing would remain largely a matter of discretion. The basic idea was that "if the front door were properly tended, the back door would take care of itself." As the first head of the National Civil Service Reform League, George William Curtis, put it,

> It is better to take the risk of occasional injustice from passion and prejudice, which no law or regulation can control, than to seal up incompetency, negligence, insubordination, insolence and every other mischief in the service by requiring a virtual trial at law before an unfit and incapable clerk can be removed.

Government employees would get and keep their jobs on the basis of merit. That became its shorthand name: the merit system.

Civil service had its critics. Opponents described the idea as "snivel service," filled with detached experts doing what they, rather than the public, wanted. But these critics were party hacks, ignored or derided by those devoted to good government. After a few years, however, observers began to note an alarming truth in this critique, but not exactly for the anticipated reasons.

Civil service became permanent patronage. Congress initially "classified" only 10 percent of federal employees as professional civil servants, leaving it to the executive to decide whether to increase the ranks. Presidents Cleveland and Harrison made their usual political appointments and then "blanketed in" the party faithful by simply redesignating their patronage jobs as civil service. By 1900, more than seventy thousand party hacks had become proud members of the merit system, representing three-quarters of all civil servants, virtually all without competitive examination. President McKinley, under pressure from their burgeoning ranks, then perfected this alchemy of civil service into super-spoils by closing the "back door" to give political supporters lifetime tenure.

Reformers who had struggled for the "merit system" barely knew what hit them. Teddy Roosevelt, a longtime civil service reformer, "tried to increase presidential control over federal employees by, among other things, making dismissals for cause easier to obtain." But at this point, federal employees had become their own political force. In

1913, the Civil Service Commission formally announced that part of its mission was to protect public employees. A new die was cast. Paul Van Riper, in his history of civil service, characterizes this as a "revolutionary" event: Civil service, devised to eradicate the idea that public jobs were private property, was now a property right.

As the original reformers faded from the scene, the age of organization provided perfect cover for additional organizational mechanisms that, in the name of fairness and efficiency, added layers of insulation for public employees against managerial discretion. Accountability disappeared, and with it, a key tool of leadership. In 1921, Secretary of Labor James J. Davis noted that policy changes were basically impossible to implement:

> The simple fact is that I am powerless to enforce changes which I desire because I am powerless to put in charge of these places individuals in sympathy with such changed policies.

How civil service mutated into a monopolistic guild never made it to the red zone of the public consciousness. The only lesson from civil service reform that has stayed with Americans to the present is that the key to managing government is to remove authority. The abuses of the spoils system a hundred years ago are a far more vivid fear in the modern mind than the bureaucratic inertia that slowly drains our national vitality. What Americans know is that political authority has been removed, and that is good. As children of the age of organization, we have this vague belief that public employees are organized into systems that, if managed properly, will run government like a machine, neutral and uniform: to "straighten the paths of government," as Woodrow Wilson put it, and "to purify its organization."

. . .AND BACK TO MORE MISTRUST IN THE NAME OF ACCOUNTABILITY

In the 1960s, the Supreme Court led a new and broader assault on public authority, this time aimed not at politicians but at all public officials. In the wake of the civil rights movement and the Vietnam War, as we've seen, Americans no longer trusted anyone to decide anything. The new idea—now America's public philosophy of fairness rather than a bureaucratic mutation—was that no decision in the public sector that affected anyone, including decisions about personnel and student discipline, should be within anyone's official discretion. The mechanism devised for checking official authority was brilliant in its simplicity: Government employees or students who disagreed with decisions about them could bring a lawsuit under the Constitution's due process clause. Self-help by any aggrieved individual would ensure fairness in government.

Until then, except in egregious situations, the Constitution's protection of due process—no person shall be "deprived of life, liberty or property, without due process of law"—had not been applied to government operations. Law made a distinction between a *right*, like your freedom or property, and a *privilege*, like your good standing as a student or employee. Government couldn't interfere with someone's private life (his rights), but government could, for example, freely revoke government benefits (like a job or public education, which were considered privileges). This distinction was famously articulated by Oliver Wendell Holmes, Jr., in a case brought by a Boston policeman: "Petitioner may have the constitutional right to talk politics, but he has no constitutional right to be a policeman."

In an influential 1964 article in the *Yale Law Journal,* "The New Property," Professor Charles Reich advocated that the benefits provided by the government should not be considered a privilege but a "new property" protected by due process. Reich's thesis reflected a philosophy that, to preserve individuality in a world dominated by huge institutions, advocated giving individuals legal priority over social interests. As David Riesman, author of *The Lonely Crowd,* asserted in 1954: "No ideology, however noble, can justify the sacrifice of an individual to the needs of the group."

For welfare benefits, Reich's new property rights had undeniable merit, since the wards of the state had nowhere else to go, and the Supreme Court accepted Reich's framework. But the right to sue soon spread. We have "witnessed a due process explosion," federal judge Henry Friendly observed in 1975, "in which the Court has carried the hearing requirement from one new area of government action to another."

The right-privilege distinction for government employees was overthrown in a case involving the termination of a professor at a state university who refused to certify in a loyalty oath that he was not a Communist. The logic, according to Justice William Brennan, was that due process protection was needed to preserve the teacher's "free play of the spirit":

> It would be a bold teacher who would not stay as far as possible from utterances or acts which might jeopardize his living. . . . The result must be to stifle that free play of the spirit which all teachers ought especially to cultivate and practice.

In dissent, quoting an earlier case, four justices feared a world in which people running schools would no longer have the authority to judge character at all:

> A teacher works in a sensitive area in a schoolroom. There he shapes the attitude of young minds towards the society in which they live. In this, the state has a vital concern. It must preserve the integrity of the schools. That the school authorities have the right and the duty to screen the officials, teachers, and employees as to their fitness to maintain the integrity of the schools as a part of ordered society cannot be doubted.

Professor Reich had not suggested that ordinary personnel decisions, like dealing with someone who doesn't show up to work, should be slated for constitutional scrutiny. But the Supreme Court assumed that allowing anyone who is upset to have a hearing, like a mini-trial, would be like a *Good Housekeeping* seal of approval. What's the harm?

The prospect of purifying decisions throughout government, even in mundane personnel choices, proved irresistible. The "opportunity for the employee to present his side of the case is recurringly of obvious value in reaching an accurate decision," Justice Byron White wrote in one decision, because dismissals "often involve factual disputes."

Student discipline was an obvious target, since managing our children has the ring of regulation, even though when disciplining students, schools don't impose fines and in the harshest sanctions just send students home, not to jail. The first case arose in the charged context of the First Amendment: the suspension of five students in Des Moines who wore black armbands to protest the Vietnam War. Justice Abe Fortas declared that public schools would not be "enclaves of totalitarianism": Students do not shed their "constitutional right[s] . . . at the schoolhouse gate."

But the Supreme Court did not draw the line on students' rights at political speech. In 1971, a student disrupting a class in the school auditorium in Columbus, Ohio, was ordered to leave, and refused. When a police officer came to escort the student out, the officer was "physically attacked" by four other students. The principal, who witnessed the incidents, suspended the students immediately. The Supreme Court overturned the suspension with the broad holding that "suspensions without notice or hearing" are unconstitutional. The Court's logic was that "the disciplinary process" is not a "totally accurate, unerring process," and any "risk of error" was unacceptable.

The due process revolution deeply divided the Supreme Court. Justice Lewis Powell, in dissent with three other justices in the case of the brawl in Columbus, tried to warn his colleagues of the dangers when classroom choices "are so formalized as to invite a challenge to the teacher's authority—an invitation which rebellious or even merely spirited teenagers are likely to accept." Justice Hugo Black, normally the staunchest defender of individual rights, warned that the unintended effects of allowing individuals to sue over daily management decisions might be to hurt the intended beneficiaries by discouraging the needed decisions and benefits altogether.

The Supreme Court majority assumed that it satisfied all concerns of practicality, however, by holding that due process required only "some kind of hearing" that was appropriate under the circumstances: "the opportunity to be heard . . . 'at a meaningful time and in a meaningful manner.' " No one had any idea, faced with a real dispute, what might be argued to be a "meaningful" hearing. But the theory sounded good: Just make sure you can prove you've been fair.

Due process by the mid-1970s had become a kind of legal air bag, inflating instantly to protect students and public employees. These changes in constitutional law, as the *Harvard Law Review* observed, "blur[red] any distinction between the government as regulator and the government as employer." Losing your job or being disciplined in school had become a deprivation of basic rights, in a similar category as being sent to jail.

Secretary of Education Riley, in advocating education as a civil right, hardly shocked an American audience used to hearing that practically any failure violates someone's rights. He gave the stock sermon of modern political discourse. Americans believe in individual rights, particularly against government. Letting students and public employees challenge decisions that affect them is considered as American as apple pie. Who trusts government? Go ahead and sue the bastards. Even a reform leader like Diane Ravitch, who regularly appears before Congress to discuss the sorry state of education, always reaffirms steadfast adherence to due process for teachers. Protecting fairness for individuals is best achieved, we have been taught, by letting individuals protect themselves. The individual against what? Authority, wherever it lurks.

Contemporary American democracy, taking our founders' skepticism of state power to a new level, now rests on a foundation of an almost perfect mistrust. We don't trust political leaders to make decisions for the common good. We don't trust teachers and other public employees to assert values on how to manage schools and government. We don't even trust public employees to judge one another. Government today is organized as kind of a Möbius strip, with mistrust flowing round and round. Letting people make decisions that affect other people is an almost archaic concept, unnecessary in a modern government in which everyone's rights and obligations have been laid out in advance.

POWERLESSNESS CORRUPTS

On the evening of his inauguration, former New Jersey governor Tom Kean went to his office and discovered the lightbulb in his desk lamp had burned out. He called the state trooper on duty and asked if he could find a replacement. Five minutes went by, then ten. After almost half an hour, the trooper called back to report. He had found the custodian with the lightbulbs immediately, he told the Governor, but the custodian wouldn't release a bulb without an authorized requisition form. The trooper also determined that the official with authority to release lightbulbs had left for the evening. So the trooper couldn't bring one up.

Being Governor is hard, probably harder than we appreciate. The difficulty comes not with the enormous responsibility, however, or with difficult policy choices. Being Governor is hard because the government, supposedly under your charge, doesn't respond when you call. Chances are you'll get back a reason why it can't be done. The Governor pushes the button, and nothing happens.

Common wisdom is that government fails because it has no profit motive. But most people in the private sector just work for a salary. Moreover, some government agencies, like the United States Attorney offices, have an esprit de corps that is the envy of private enterprise. Every so often we read about an inner-city school that, like a biblical miracle, actually teaches with energy and pride. The lack of market discipline is obviously a problem for government— a private company would long since have gone bankrupt— but it doesn't explain a system where people don't feel they can replace a lightbulb.

The culture of any society or organization, like a strong tide, pushes people toward predictable responses in certain situations. After over one hundred years of organizational brainwashing, the culture of modern government also leads people to react predictably. In this culture, doing the job is not anyone's job. What matters most is compliance. The custodian obviously felt it wasn't proper to release the bulb. This is the trained instinct of our public employees, like a matter of conscience. The custodian, indeed, may have been demonstrating his virtue: to refuse to perform the job, no matter how obvious, except in punctilious adherence to the rules.

Labor has a highly effective technique, which the French call *grève du zèle:* to "work to the rule." By meticulously following the letter of every rule, nothing gets accomplished, and the factory slows to a crawl. In successful ventures, by contrast, the organizational structure hovers above the people, who bob and weave to get the job done. In American government, public employees operate as in a huge labor strike, except they're not trying to strike. They simply believe that accomplishing the purpose of their job is only coincidentally related to their own role. They feel powerless to do anything else. Public employees, on the edge of a gaping bureaucratic maw, close their eyes and fall in.

Taking a trip into the operations of contemporary government is like descending into Dante's rings of hell, ever darker and stranger as we get farther away from the sunlight of the outside world.

From a distance, the large white columns make government look almost idyllic, the image of stability and wisdom. But we know better, and soon we start seeing the clues that something's wrong. Near the entrance there seem to be people doing this and that, but most stay close to the shadows and look furtive as we approach. These, it turns out, are people who believe in getting the job done.

They talk in whispers, because they're constantly ignoring or breaking the rules. "You have to cheat to do your job," said one official in New York. A few flaunt their attitude, standing in the sun smiling, as if asking to be fired. These mavericks seem to be viewed by the others as leaders. A 1999 study of successful inner-city schools found they had one thing in common: "these people had to break a lot of rules." "I break every rule in the book," said one teacher proudly.

Going inside, you immediately know where you are because of the difficulty in finding anyone to take responsibility. One of my researchers tried calling the New York Board of Education to find the regulations governing schools and was transferred fourteen times. High-level appointees live this frustration all day long. "It took me ten months to get authorization to get a key to the elevator so I could work on weekends," notes Linda Schrenko, state superintendent of schools for Georgia's Department of Education. "Then it took seven months to get someone to hang my pictures on the walls." Superintendent Schrenko soon figured she could reorganize and consolidate her office, saving the state millions of dollars in rent. "But I could never get authorization to reconfigure the cubicles in our other space to make it happen."

Moving past the lobby into the bureaucracy itself, the complexity immediately overwhelms you, with regulations and numbers all around, even painted on the floor. Every discussion impresses the complexity upon you. The language is foreign and always capitalized. Nobel laureate physicist Richard Feynman, no stranger to technical terminology, found his job of investigating the space shuttle

Challenger explosion impeded by "the crazy acronyms that NASA uses all over the place: 'SRMs' are the solid rocket motors. . . . the 'SSMEs' are the space shuttle main engines." This "one-directional" language, as Professor Ralph Hummel notes, makes it almost impossible for outsiders to understand or communicate with government.

The expertise sounds impressive but, as we stop to watch, nothing much seems to happen. "We have a silo system," said one bureaucrat in Virginia. "Each memo goes to the next level." "If you can't make a decision," said another official, "then hold a TQM meeting." When the teacher from a parochial school joined a public school in a suburb of Chicago, she was amazed: "Meetings were held over *parking spaces*." "Meetings are a perk," observed former New York City deputy transportation commissioner Sam Schwartz. "It gives people something to do for the entire afternoon."

As we continue downward, a critical element to human accomplishment seems to be missing: Public employees don't have willpower, at least not the willpower to get the job done. In the early 1980s, walking into the cavernous Metropolitan Transit Authority barn where subway cars are repaired in the Bronx, Robert Kiley, then the new head of the MTA, was immediately struck by the cooking odors. Amidst the railcars in various stages of disassembly, men were huddled around camping stoves and half-size refrigerators. Paying little heed to their new boss, the workers seemed almost like refugees who had wandered into some evacuated factory. The performance was equally miserable. Subway cars broke down, on average, every thirty-five hundred miles, or once every week or so.

You expect to see rats in dark places, and, sure enough, they were infesting rest stops in Georgia's park system. But the commissioner, Randy Cardoza, learned that no one could put down rat poison because the regulations prohibited it. ("Did they think people were going to eat rat poison?") At one rest stop, however, a stray cat wandered by and took the matter into its own paws. But the cat's success meant that it was also soon out of food. The cat's natural instincts were not matched, unfortunately, by the bureaucrats. They looked, but there was no line in the budget for cat food. How hard can it be to find a few bucks for cat food? There may be a thousand ways to skin a cat—that's the genius of America's success—but inside American government they couldn't find one way to feed a cat. As so often happens in government, the rats win again.

As we get deeper, energy starts to wane. Motion is casual in the offices, as if passing the time until, you know, the inevitable. Middle-level employees spend time selling real estate in their cubicles or reading books, while clerical workers wander around selling hair care products or the like to co-workers. Public employees obviously feel stuck. "Each job is a dead end," as Thomas Dydyk, a legislative analyst in Syracuse, New York, put it. "To advance to another position you almost have to wait until someone dies." Why don't they bail out? The inevitable, as it turns out, is retirement with a pension. "I can retire in four years and twenty-five days," said Paul Belliotti, an IRS agent. A big payday—usually an 80 percent pension after twenty to thirty years of service—keeps everyone holding on. "When you talk to anyone, they're figuring out their pension or how many years they have," said Mary Tese, a supervising inspector of amusement rides and ski lifts in New York State. "That's the nice thing about this job, you know there's a time you can quit." As one teacher told a principal, "Only twenty-two more years to go."

Trapped people rarely feel loyalty, and so, arriving at the next level, we aren't surprised to find public employees dripping with cynicism. They see the government as the enemy, to be taken advantage of whenever possible. "We schedule meetings at night to accumulate comp time," admitted a town planner in North Carolina. "It's shamelessly abused." One federal clerk, interviewed by Studs Terkel, described how she deliberately sabotaged work so that no one would come to her again:

> I would type a paragraph and wait five or ten minutes. I made sure I made all the mistakes I could. It's amazing, when you want to make mistakes, you really can't. So I just put Ko-Rec-Type paper over this yellow sheet. . . . Oh, I did it up beautifully. (laughs) He got the dictionary out and he looked up the words for me. . . . Well, I didn't finish it by noon. . . . I decided I'd write him a note. "Dear Mr. Roberts: You've been so much help. . . . I hope this has met with your approval. Please call on me again." I never heard from him. (a long laugh)

We begin to see why government decisions, supposedly extruded uniformly out of the bureaucratic machine, are so erratic. There's no reality check from the group around you. "At large meetings, there's often one person who

cares about the issues," said a former New York commissioner, "and nobody else challenges them." At the
economic development agency in Oakland, California, a
self-proclaimed socialist would drag her feet on big projects because, as she said, "I try not to help people who
have too much money already."

The physical surroundings reflect the absence of pride.
Offices are often decrepit and dirty, as if whoever was in
charge died a long time back and was never replaced. A
few years ago, I walked up the main stairway of Queens
Borough Hall in New York under dim lights, with candy
wrappers, trash, and dust filling the corners of the steps.
The water fountain at the top of the stairs, a metallic
model with a bar to press, was obviously broken, the bar
askew, half in and half out. Judging from the accumulated
dust, it had been that way a long time. This is the main
stairway for the seat of government for almost two million
residents.

The unemployment office in southern Georgia was
housed in a former motel, where the unemployed were received in offices that "had old carpet rolled against the
wall and were overrun with infestation." "If working here
was what it was like to have a job," former Georgia official
Joe Tanner observed, "I think most people probably
thought they were better off staying on unemployment."
Even "the temple of justice," as Judge Hiller Zobel observed, is "a pigpen." At the Massachusetts Superior Court
in Boston, "stairways were stained, littered with cigarette
butts, Styrofoam cups, and an occasional dead rodent. The
elevators, when able to function, . . . [were] frequently
odorous." Schools get fixed up only when the conditions

become scandalous, as when bat droppings started dripping from the ceiling at Mullins Elementary School in Pike
County, Kentucky, at the beginning of the 2000 school
year.

Many schools and offices are like museums of outdated
furniture and equipment. About 320 New York City
schools, or 25 percent of the total, are heated by coal-fired
furnaces. "At the same time we are talking about bringing
high-tech to schools," said Harold O. Levy, chancellor of
the New York Board of Education, "we have workmen
stoking boilers with coal as if it were 19th century England."

Only halfway down in our journey, we realize that the
idea of working toward any common goal, even cleaning
up the office, has disappeared. "When men do not choose,
do not will," Chester Barnard observes, "the very stuff of
cooperation dissolves." From here on, we're warned, any
notion of a common purpose is pushed aside by obsession
with personal entitlement. When Senator Max Cleland
was Georgia's Secretary of State, an employee in his office
filed a grievance for unlawful discrimination when she
didn't get a raise in the middle of a statewide salary freeze.

Like animals dozing, bureaucrats are quiet but not indifferent to what happens near them. Each person has a designated spot, zealously guarded, with each responsibility
and right carefully delineated. Federal secretaries have a
seventy-three-page manual that lays out precisely what
they have to do and not do. Helping out is definitely on the
"not do" list, because it might require working "out of
category." "My job is WordPerfect, not Word," one New

York secretary responded as she refused to type changes in a letter.

Get too close or try to dislodge these entitlements, or make a negative comment on an evaluation form, and they snap back, often viciously, with a legal "grievance" proceeding. Public employees value the right to be left alone above all others. No one can make demands on them. This is a philosophical tenet of the culture that values organizational status instead of accomplishment. A school in a poor neighborhood of Boston introduced a breakfast program, but the principal needed adults to supervise. Several teachers were happy to help, but the teachers' union rep at the school described her reaction when she learned what was going on:

> The teachers started doing breakfast duty, and I got wind of it, and I said, There is no breakfast duty. In the last contract, it didn't come up. We didn't negotiate it. There IS NO breakfast duty. I don't care who wants to do it, there is no breakfast duty.

Union newsletters trumpet the good news whenever they discover a public employee helping out beyond his job category: "Clerical's Out-of-Title Grievance Yields $8,000" is one headline underneath the photo of a smiling public employee and union official.

At New York City's housing department, a worker filed a grievance because another worker took on responsibilities higher than his job classification. The supervisor had the choice of promoting him, with a higher salary that was not in the budget, or demoting him. The diligent worker was demoted. "So here this guy took a leap of faith," said a program consultant who observed the dispute, "and in the end he should have stayed on the job and done less."

One reason for the squalor is that public employees don't have the *right* to clean up their own offices. A new staff lawyer at the Securities and Exchange Commission, with permission from an office supervisor, repainted his dingy office one weekend. All hell broke loose; that's apparently covered by a union contract. He was confronted by an official who told him: "We know you repainted your office. We have masking tape as evidence." After months of controversy, the supervisor ended up footing part of the tab for the union to repaint the freshly painted office.

Getting near the bottom now, there's a human quality we've never seen before. Bureaucrats' eyes often look dead, like someone cut the nerve to the brain. Many people do nothing. "Look around this office," said a middle-level manager at the New York Board of Education. "Half the people aren't doing anything. There's one guy who, when you ask a question, looks up, pauses, and then says 'I don't know about that.' It doesn't matter what the question is. He always says 'I don't know about that.' Not 'why don't you try over there?' Or 'have you thought of this?' Just 'I don't know about that.' " At an office in the Department of Agriculture in Minnesota, one woman "logs in to the computer but she doesn't work. She just sits there."

Other bureaucrats do nothing about the bureaucrats who do nothing. One principal, confronted with an audit showing that a person on his payroll had not come to work for seven years, knew exactly what to say: "If he was missing for seven years, this was a mystery to me." The principal had evaluated the phantom worker each year as "satisfactory," which, in relative terms, may not have been far off.

Sometimes entire departments do nothing useful. When Joe Dear became head of the Washington State Labor Department in the late 1980s, he learned that a department, supposedly processing numbers for budgeting unemployment claims, for years had produced data that were useless to the actuaries. They knew it was useless—everyone knew the data were useless—but that's the way they had always done it. Until Joe Dear came along and flipped the switch, that's what they kept doing.

In the worst departments, it's like a neutron bomb dropped and destroyed the human spirit; everything is grim and slow. People shuffle back and forth. At the claims administration office in Washington State, as described in a Harvard case study, "the first thing that struck me when I got off the elevator was that I'd see people in the hallway and nobody talked. Nobody. There was no laughter. It was incredible. . . . They just looked at the floor and no one spoke." One federal doctor with the National Health Foundation, after a disagreement with his supervisor, was given no assignments. Every day he would come to work with nothing to do. He spent years building castles and arches out of Styrofoam cups in his office.

People can get away with almost anything as long as it's not theft or political incorrectness. A lab assistant in a New York environmental agency had a "tendency to make animal sounds in the laboratory and to sneak up behind people" but succeeded in getting an official reprimand against a co-worker who, to get him away, moved his personal bag out to the hall. A secretary at the Office of General Services in New York would scream at people for no reason and become hysterical in the middle of the day. Everyone just tried to avoid her.

Treading carefully now, we trust no one we encounter. "People forced to live a life which goes excessively against natural impulses," Bertrand Russell once observed, "show strains of cruelty." In 1995, investigators discovered that employees at the New York Board of Ed food service were providing school cafeterias with meat and vegetables that were almost two years old. The petty food resale scam came to light after dozens of children came down with food poisoning. Stooping too low is not a relevant concept in a culture disconnected from social norms.

Standing in near darkness, we realize that many of these bureaucrats, though human, can't be considered participants in our society or, indeed, in any sort of civilization. This culture is not one born of human aspiration but is more like the type that grows in biology labs or damp cupboards. All sorts of pathologies grow out of the hopelessness. One particularly high-strung purchasing officer in New York looked up one day to see two others standing at his door, just staring at him. When he asked what they wanted, they just glanced at each other and smiled. He begged them to go away. Finally, one said, "We just wanted to see what it's like for someone to work."

At last, we arrive at the door to the bottom level, expecting a den of thieves or worse. Opening the door with trepidation, we're practically blinded by the brightness of artificial lights, like on a movie set. We don't see boiling cauldrons or bodies writhing but just the opposite. Well-dressed men (it's mainly men on this level), with handkerchiefs in their suit pockets and every hair in place, strut back and forth, talking in the language of capitalized letters. Back and forth they go, like windup toys, but doing nothing. These, it turns out, are the people in charge. They know they're doing nothing; you can tell by their self-conscious glances to see if anyone's watching. Their job is to pretend that someone's in charge.

People from the outside come to them all day long, most seeking selfish favors. The people in charge make no moral judgments—who are they to judge right and wrong? They simply calculate whether it is possible to do nothing and get something. Given what's above them, they know they can't deliver anything out of the ordinary. Most issues, happily, involve someone who wants the status quo. That's the formula for success: no change, no responsibility, nice to see you.

When a decision is required, they don't change their pattern. They just go to meetings until the issue disappears or someone drops out from exhaustion. Picking the colors for the air-traffic control tower in the new Denver airport was one of these intractable problems. The meetings continued for six years, union officials disagreeing with FAA officials, until finally the newspaper wrote about it. In a culture where no one is in charge, media intervention is the only way to get a decision. The sunlight of public exposure is intolerable to those who preside over a culture of darkness.

Government has failed for so long that the public accepts failure as the status quo. Most of us can't tell if it's gotten worse since, in the real world, we're not trained to evaluate degrees of failure. The people in charge have a perfect technique that gives the appearance of trying to fix things and, so far, satisfies the public. They point the finger somewhere, usually at a regulatory scheme or a department, then, wagging the finger really hard, devise some new bureaucratic mechanism to institutionalize the distrust. Taking away everyone's right to decide doesn't solve anything, but it's the foolproof approach to appease the public. Getting sensible decisions out from under the accumulated distrust is nearly impossible, as Christopher Jencks describes:

> The school board has no faith in the central administration, the central administration has no faith in the principals, the principals have no faith in the teachers, and the teachers have no faith in the students. Decision-making is constantly centralized into as few hands as possible rather than being decentralized into as many hands as possible, in the hope of reducing errors to a minimum. Of course such a system also reduces individual initiative to a minimum. . . . Distrust is the order of the day.

One official in New York posed the problem this way: "How do you decide who to trust in a dysfunctional agency?"

The power of government, we realize now, has been transformed into a collective powerlessness. Every wire is crossed; overlapping rules and rights short-circuit every person and every aspiration. But everyone in it has a secure job. Taking a cue from Frederick Winslow Taylor, bureaucrats have discovered one best way to avoid blame: by creating systems in which no one has the ability to do anything.

It's not a good life. Americans think working for government is easy street, but it burns people out, because, as Professor Ralph Hummel observes, the system "tears from them their conscience." A study of civil servants in Britain showed far more stress and coronary disease than in the private sector. As Professor James Scott describes in *Seeing Like a State,* in tightly controlled cultures humans feel powerless to do their job and fall victim to

> an institutional neurosis marked by apathy, withdrawal, lack of initiative and spontaneity, uncommunicativeness and intractability. The neurosis is an accommodation to a deprived, bland, monotonous controlled environment that is ultimately stupefying.

The Twentieth Century Fund found in the late 1980s that the morale among public employees was "alarmingly low," but the word *morale* itself implies a foundation of common purpose. "At the core of bureaucracy," sociologist William Swatos observes, "is the evisceration of anything distinctly human."

We decide to do a few exit interviews on the way out and are struck by the self-awareness of public employees who see what's happening to them but can't imagine how to break out. "People didn't come here saying, 'I can skate for twenty-five years,' " said a career senior official at the Occupational Safety and Health Administration. "Worker safety is important. I wanted to do something useful with my life. But the system drags you down. The most basic decisions are nearly impossible. You have to go to God to get supplies or hire someone or get someone fired. No decision is possible without running a gauntlet of forms and meetings. After a while you just put in your forty hours. Don't rock the boat." "I can't imagine a worse working atmosphere," whispered a town planner in Chapel Hill, North Carolina. "The best thing to do is sit at your desk and shut up."

Many people go into government with enthusiasm. But the inability to get anything done, or done properly, soon takes its toll. "I feel very unimportant," said a social worker in Chicago, who confided his secret ambition to Studs Terkel: "Success is to be in a position where I can make a decision." "With each new employee, we have a pool on how long it will take to break their spirit," said an official in the public affairs department of the United States Fish and Wildlife Service. It's easy to see how it happens there: Twenty-one signatures are required for each press release. By the time everyone signs off, there's no news to report. "It's so discouraging. Why try? It doesn't matter what you do."

Americans don't exactly hold government in high regard, but the reality is probably worse than they imagine. Public employees become almost half-human. "Can't you see it?" asked David Maloney, a career public servant who was a top aide to former Florida governors Lawton Chiles and Buddy McKay. "Look around you. These people are depressed. They learn they can't make a difference. So they give up."

Normal people like you and me, being purposeful creatures, will do almost anything to stay away from this weird underworld. It holds a certain anthropological interest, like a giant experiment in severing humans from their pride. Still, it's repellent; it makes you want to take a shower. How could humans so lose their grip on the purpose of the endeavor around them? A television network could probably do a *Survivor* series inside a municipal bureaucracy, with hardy volunteers trying to make things happen in the dark world of burned-out civil servants and teachers. Maybe the most discouraging aspect, as we look around at broken fountains and dusty corridors, is that the failure seems perpetual, like hell itself.

ABSOLUTE POWERLESSNESS
CORRUPTS ABSOLUTELY

Government didn't used to be like this. No golden age of government ever dawned in America—democracy is too sloppy for golden ages—but there was a time, in my life, when top graduates wanted to go into government and teaching. I remember being proud, after we moved to Kentucky, that John Sherman Cooper was our senator, and I would push my way up to the front of the crowd on Court Day in Mt. Sterling to be near such a distinguished leader. In an interview in 1993, Barry Goldwater recalled his early days in the Senate, when credibility and wisdom were tools of leadership:

> When Jack Kennedy and I went to the Senate in
> 1953, we had what we called "giants": senators
> like Walter George and Richard Russell of Geor-
> gia, Bob Taft, Lehman of New York—very intel-
> ligent, honest men. When they went on the floor
> to make a speech, damn near every member of
> the Senate went to listen to them.

This was a period when people like Howard Baker, Pat
Moynihan, and Colin Powell decided to make their careers
in public service. In 1960, over three-quarters of Americans had confidence in government. Americans never felt
government was a model of efficiency; but it worked, and
it was ours.

Today, top graduates scoff at the idea of public service.
The trust of Americans has fallen off a cliff, from 76 percent in 1960 to 24 percent in 1996. Most eighth-graders
don't know who their senators are, and many adults don't
either. When he resigned from the Senate in 1992, Senator
Warren Rudman expressed his frustrations with trying to
serve in a government that was "not functioning" and
"out of control," and in a Senate where colleagues force
votes on frivolous amendments because they're "eager to
make statements for the papers back home." "How many
times should we have to count the yeas and nays on Robert
Mapplethorpe and the National Endowment of the Arts,
or on flag burning," asked Senator Tom Wirth, who also
resigned in frustration, "Meanwhile, the real issues get
lost."

"Over the last twenty years I've worked for the government," said a civil servant in Delaware. "And I'd have to

say that government has gotten worse and worse." Many new teachers now come from the bottom of the class from colleges that can be fairly described as institutions of lower learning. These teachers, longtime union leader Albert Shanker conceded a few years ago, "wouldn't be admitted to college in other countries." While the pool of potential teachers diminished when job markets were finally opened to women, that alone cannot account for the precipitous drop in talent. In 1998, 60 percent of those applying for teaching jobs in Massachusetts, all college graduates, could not pass proficiency tests required of tenth-graders in English and math. Their command of English, observed Dr. John Silber, chancellor of Boston University and former chairman of the Massachusetts Board of Education, was "material for Jay Leno," such as the apt answer that this "should not be aloud under any cercumstances."

The power of democracy, supposedly, is that citizens exercise control over government through the ballot. But Americans don't exactly feel that power. Most Americans have given up on anything to do with government. Voter turnout has steadily declined. In local elections, indifference sometimes reaches terminal proportions. In one school board election in New York, the turnout was not even 2 percent. Whoever shows up wins.

Social commentators criticize Americans for our apathy. But the sermons don't explain what exactly we're supposed to do. Why the public sector is grinding to a halt may not be readily apparent to us, but one thing we know for sure, without any doubt or reservation whatsoever: It's beyond our control. You're "not going to make a difference. . . . Why go to the trouble?" an Atlanta woman asked in a survey of American attitudes. "Your voice is not going to be heard." A national survey found that citizens were "unable to imagine what a functioning public, or a society of citizens, would look like or do." As a friend put it, "It's hopeless. What can anyone do about it?"

Hold on for a second. That's odd. American citizens sound just like those depressed public employees. We feel powerless. Teachers, principals, and bureaucrats, as we've seen, also feel powerless. Is it a coincidence that the public feels the same way about government that public employees do? Maybe there's a link. Is it possible that we feel powerless *because* public servants feel powerless?

Government is just too big, we believe, for a citizen to make a difference. Too many layers of unknown officials lie between us and the things that bother us. But is it really size that separates Americans from government? How about the school principal or the bureaucrat who refuses to be helpful? They're in your face. Maybe it's not the size of bureaucracy but the powerlessness of everyone within it that makes us powerless. If the governor has trouble getting a lightbulb, how can the governor respond to what we want? If the principal doesn't have authority over a teacher the parents think is inept, what good are the parents' views?

Alan Wolfe found it "odd that people who believe so much in personal accountability seem to take so little responsibility for what they see as wrong with their society." But how can we take responsibility? Democracy is supposed to be a chain of responsibility, but the links in the chain are broken. Everyone feels helpless to make a difference, even union officials:

> We are the ones who toil in dilapidated, poorly
> maintained buildings; who do our jobs despite
> being stifled by multiple layers of management;
> who face a public often frustrated and angry.

Governors, principals, teachers, janitors, citizens all throw up their hands. What we believe doesn't matter because what public employees believe doesn't matter.

Our culture today is about each of us individually, no longer all of us together. We're "bowling alone," to use Robert Putnam's metaphor. We don't like what we see in schools, in Congress, or in society. The loss of morality tops the list of American's concerns in recent polls. But our views don't matter. Is this the inevitable condition of a modern society? Or, like bureaucrats, have we been trained to believe society is not ours?

Personal powerlessness is not the only thing we have in common with those repellent bureaucrats. Like them, instead of viewing freedom as the opportunity to accomplish things, Americans now conceive of freedom, as Robert Bellah found in *Habits of the Heart,* as the right to be left alone. We too have reverted to Number One, making demands on schools and public resources without regard to the effect on others. Even the meanness seems to have infected us. Americans now find sport in ridiculing the escalating failures of the society around us, taking "perverse pleasure," Alan Wolfe found, "in powerlessness."

Americans go through our days working like mad to keep up in a demanding economy. We reach for meaning in fundamental religion or obsessive consumerism, occasionally pausing to wonder why students in middle-class communities like Littleton, Colorado, are driven to armed violence. There is little sense of being together in a great society, not to mention a society with the future of the earth more or less in our care. We don't *feel* that power.

We don't have that power. We lost it when we took away the authority of those with responsibility to make judgments and replaced it with bureaucracy. There's no longer any effective mechanism by which anyone can do what they feel is right for the common good. Daily management choices become legal tangles. "When every American must think like a lawyer," Eugene Kennedy and Sara Charles wrote in *Authority,* "no American can [live] naturally, spontaneously, or freely." If what a teacher, or principal, or governor believes doesn't matter, then what we believe doesn't matter either. As Vaclav Havel observes:

> If politicians have no authority at all, the state
> and its various constituent parts can have no au-
> thority either. This, in turn, has an adverse effect
> on society.

Democracy itself is threatened, management expert Peter Drucker has noted, when the centers of power lack authority and accountability. When people are denied the role of their own beliefs, bizarre side effects are inevitable. Havel tried to warn us:

> The more systematically and impatiently the
> world is crammed into rational categories, the
> more explosions of irrationality there will be to
> astonish us.

We didn't intend to destroy democracy. We just wanted to organize it carefully to make sure decisions were on the up-and-up. Public institutions would be neutral, sanitized from human idiosyncrasy and error, like a hermetically sealed silicon-chip factory. Everyone's rights would be laid out neatly without room for unfairness. But we succeeded mainly in killing government's ability to function, and killing our own ability to influence it. We got a kind of freedom: We cut ourselves loose from the society around us. Our powerlessness has now made us numb, and our eyes dead, to our role in a larger culture. Like public employees who tolerate dirty offices, we've come to tolerate a common good that's no longer any good.

At this point, it's hard to imagine how we would ever start to take back control.

THE ONE ESSENTIAL CHOICE
FOR ALL COMMON ENDEAVOR

Nick, a fifth-grade teacher in New York, had an "impatient and irritable manner." Parents accused him of "verbally assaulting" their children with aggressive gestures and angry remarks, and they pleaded with the principal to pull their children out of his class. The principal almost persuaded Nick to resign, but then Nick "changed his mind when he talked to his union representative."

The next year, Nick was transferred to teach first grade and agreed to work with an "intervenor," a teaching coach who sat in Nick's classroom one day a week. But, even with first-graders (and with a reporter and the "intervenor" present), Nick couldn't seem to control his temper.

He yelled at one six-year-old for not properly cleaning up after a leaf-rubbing project, ordering the boy to "get on the mat in the middle of the room and stand up and face the class." Diverted for a minute by another task (putting checks by names of children who had misbehaved), Nick then turned and scolded the boy for standing in the middle of the room. "Bingo. That's it," Nick announced to the child. "You get a check" for misbehaving. As reported by Pam Belluck of *The New York Times:* "Stunned, the boy looked as though he would burst into tears."

Nick was hardly the worst teacher she had worked with, according to Gail Seiden, Nick's "intervenor." Because Nick had tenure (earned with three years as a computer skills instructor), there was not much she could do for the impressionable children under Nick's erratic charge. Instead, Ms. Seiden viewed her job as one of positive reinforcement for Nick: "It takes a lot of courage for a tenured teacher to say . . . 'I can't do it.' " For his part, Nick was convinced teaching was right for him: "I belong teaching kids."

There we have it: Exhibit A on why Americans mistrust public employees. The Tin Woodman is starting to look pretty good. No sensible person would want to empower Nick to do what he thought was right.

On the other hand, whoever conjured up all those systems to control public employees didn't do so well either. The levels to which government has pushed the idea of organization would surprise even Frederick Winslow Taylor, like the idea of organizing bad personalities with "intervenors." The concept of personality intervention is more Huxley than Orwell, I think, with its presumption that anyone can be duped (or doped?) into being someone other than who he is. Government is filled with jobs and departments with similar *Brave New World* names that cajole and instruct public employees who aren't any good. The Board of Education sends out troops of "Staff Developers" who basically try to make schools "teacher-proof" by imposing a more or less rote instructional program. Some principals, whose efforts at leadership have failed so miserably that they can't make it in a system where failure is the norm, are relegated not to the job market but to time at a "Professional Development Center." How would you like to spend a week with that group? The federal government has PIPs, or "Performance Improvement Programs," for unproductive employees. Some people spend their entire careers in PIPs. What is your job? PIP. All these organizational systems, for reasons obvious to every truck driver, don't seem to be doing us much good.

A more obvious truth lies before us. Nick is who he is. Nick just doesn't seem cut out to be a teacher. His instincts for dealing with children are horrible. Acting on this truth solves both our mistrust and also the need for fancy organizational intervention. Why not, as gently as we want, show Nick to the door? Nick's probably a nice guy, underneath it all, and he could probably find a job somewhere else, far away from young children. No one would need "intervenors" if we could decide who is doing the job and who isn't.

But telling Nick that he should go elsewhere is not in the cards. Discussing termination is not a fruitful topic. Why waste our time? Virtually no one loses his job in government. Terminating a public employee is rare, about as infrequent as the death penalty. Between 1991 and 1997, only 44 out of 100,000 tenured teachers in Illinois were dismissed. In California, 62 out of 220,000 tenured teachers were dismissed during a five-year period. "In my twelve years here," said a Veterans Administration official in New Orleans, "I've seen one person dismissed." "Public employees," Professor Bruce Buchanan observed, have a "virtually impregnable position." Whether good, bad, or indifferent, public employees keep their jobs.

How public employees came to enjoy immunity from accountability is an ironic history that starts, as we've seen, with our mistrust of them. But there's a greater paradox, far more consequential than even a government that tolerates employees not fit for their jobs. Focusing on terrible employees, as with egregious jury awards, diverts us from a broader impact, hidden from us only because it's so large that it blocks the horizon.

Why is everyone powerless? Reformers are always changing the rules, and streamlining procedures. But every time we try to take one more step, we find ourselves in a bureaucratic fog once again. Why do we always end up with our nose in a rule book when we're trying to get something done?

We're not fixing the right problem. The world doesn't accomplish anything by following rules. The world works, as Emerson reminded us, by individuals making it work. It's not rule books but people, with willpower and good judgment and ingenuity, who can respond to what we want. The smallest effective unit of organization is a person. Nick is not an effective teacher. Hillyer Rudisill, my eraser-throwing Latin teacher, was. People know how to make these distinctions.

Not being able to make judgments about people starts a cycle of escalating bureaucratization. The millions of words of bureaucratic rules that clog our schools and government agencies are the result not of the world's stupidest central planners, although that's what it looks like. Who would actually want a department of "intervenors"? The clumsy, ineffective effort of bureaucracy to tell people how to do things is the inevitable consequence of not otherwise being able to distinguish who's doing the job and who's not.

Bureaucracy, at least for internal management, is mainly our substitute for making judgments about people. When people can't be judged, human instinct and initiative are replaced by red tape. As the rules proliferate, everyone then loses the capacity to make judgments about anything. Unless people can "be held responsible for the results of their efforts," Friedrich Hayek observed, they cannot be "allowed to act as they see fit."

Bureaucracy has billowed like black smoke since the due process revolution drove in the final nail sealing off judgments about people.

Because the principal can't make judgments about teachers, formal evaluation programs are initiated in an effort to hold teachers accountable by neutral criteria. But evaluations also entail the potential for unfairness, so we get another bureaucratic control: Teachers have a right to file "grievances" to challenge evaluations. Principals are reluctant to spend half their time arguing over an evaluation that's not provable and not usually important. "Avoid giving an opinion, however firmly held, that can't be backed up," advised one trade journal for public managers, especially on issues of "character."

The effect is predictable: 99 percent of teachers in Georgia, Superintendent Linda Schrenko found when she took office, received ratings of "satisfactory" or higher. In 1998, only 14 of 7,000 teachers in Duval County, Florida, got less-than-positive reviews from their principals. On paper, success of public employees is a landslide. In the federal government, 99.6 percent of federal employees got a rating of "full satisfactory." These evaluations bear no relation to reality, of course. As a former head of the United States Office of Personnel Management admitted before Congress, "People we rated 'outstanding' . . . are not very functional."

With ratings meaningless, what little accountability that is built into the system disappears. So educators start looking for other surrogates for accountability. Rigid teaching protocols are imposed as a substitute for human judgment. But teaching protocols stifle the personal spirit needed to be an effective teacher, so we try to get teachers who are trained so well that their personality doesn't matter; many states now require teachers to be "certified" with special programs, and some require graduate degrees. But we also have a "desperate need" for new teachers, and these requirements exclude bright liberal arts majors who, with mentoring from experienced teachers, might prove to be excellent teachers. So new bureaucratic programs are initiated granting exceptions to "uncertified" teachers, to try to attract bright young college grads. But what bright person would want to jump into this airless cage?

As education continues its slide, the black bureaucratic smoke billows. Uniform testing sweeps across the country like wildfire, overwhelming classrooms with new materials and pressures and tests, all in the hope that objective criteria will humiliate everyone into better performance. But teachers and schools start cheating on standardized tests. So new rules and protocols are enforced to stem the cheating.

"Intervenors," staff developers, politicians, newspaper reporters all wander school halls, kicking the carcass, wondering what's wrong. Meanwhile, educators are deprived of the one ingredient needed for better performance: the ability of humans to infuse their personal spirit and initiative into schools, starting and ending with the ability to decide who's doing the job well and who's not.

Fighting our way through the dense bureaucratic smoke, now filling every corner of schools and government, we finally arrive not at a volcano but at a tiny fire that is the main source of the bureaucracy we hate. It's stoked not by the idea of organization, which chokes us mainly because it fills a vacuum. What stokes that deadly fire is the inability to judge other people.

The ability to make judgments about people is far more important than dealing with whatever the rules happen to be. Keep most of the rules, and if people are judged on how well they do the job, they'll figure out how to get around the rules. Rules that get in the way will be like logs in a river, to be avoided but not impassable. Conversely, eliminate 90 percent of the rules, and if unable to judge people, the friction or fear of people bickering will impede progress and soon bring the rules back again.

It is ironic that a legal structure dedicated to individual rights would end up with everyone powerless. Preserving individual rights against big government was our goal, not rendering everyone impotent and lost in a bureaucratic fog. But freedom to make judgments and exposure to being judged are two sides of the same coin. "The more we try to solve our problems by increasing personal autonomy," Philip Slater wrote, "the more we find ourselves at the mercy of these mysterious, impersonal, and remote mechanisms that we have ourselves created."

When individual authority to judge people was trumped by individual rights, the resulting bureaucracy rendered everyone powerless to act for the common good.

FINDING FREEDOM IN SOMEONE ELSE'S AUTHORITY

As soon as you walk into the main office of Public School 6 in Upper Manhattan, you feel like you're in a colony of busy ants. Two fifth-graders are sorting mail, teachers are checking through files, and a boy brings a piece of birthday cake to the diminutive and energetic principal, Carmen Farina. P.S. 6, formally a mediocre school for "children of doormen," has become one of the most sought-after elementary schools in the city under Mrs. Farina's leadership. To outsiders, the school looks like, well, what a school ought to look like. Tidy and freshly painted, the school is bordered by small grounds that are carefully planted with flowers. Classrooms are well kept, each displaying the personality of the students and the subject or grade. To the teachers, however, the difference is their own feeling of importance to the enterprise.

"You can do things here," said third-grade teacher Medea McEvoy. Every teacher we talked to immediately volunteered a special project they had a hand in creating. Several years ago, after expressing an interest in children's writing, Barbara Rosenblum was encouraged by Mrs. Farina to participate in a program called the "Writing Network." She then brought the ideas back to the school, which now encourages its youngsters to write, often about something familiar. Some are poignant. One student wrote about the death of his father. Another confronted her fears about relatives in Kosovo. Another innovation is "Zero Period," in which students who need extra help come a half hour early rather than miss regular classes. This means teachers must come early, but they wouldn't consider not doing it because, as one said, "it's obviously so much better for the children."

Before Mrs. Farina came, "everything was mandated," according to Alice Hom, another teacher; there was "no camaraderie, no sharing." Teachers ate alone and saw colleagues only at mandatory staff meetings, where they barely spoke. Today, teachers regularly lunch together, and according to Ms. McEvoy, it's "like eating lunch with friends."

Parents are also involved in almost every aspect of P.S. 6's anthill of activity. Several parents got the idea of creating a garden club, and before you knew it, there they were, a whole troop of parents and children with gardening gloves and trowels in hand, creating a storybook entrance. Another parent thought it would be useful for children to learn basic economic ideas, and started the Purple Pencil, a school store open after lunch that sells pencils and other supplies. The Purple Pencil is staffed exclusively by students under a parent's supervision. The PTA enjoys over 80 percent parent participation, and its executive board (which includes two teachers) sits down every month to go over issues with Mrs. Farina.

Public School 6 is like a human power plant, generating energy in everyone involved. Everyone agrees that Carmen Farina's leadership has made the difference. "Many parents move to the neighborhood," according to *The New York Times,* "just to be near P.S. 6 and Mrs. Farina."

But what does Carmen Farina's leadership entail? We tend to think of leadership as involving personal strength, which Mrs. Farina obviously has, but she also provides something more ordinary, unique enough in contemporary public life, that is common to all successful managers: She is willing to make decisions. Stated differently, Mrs. Farina has assumed the authority needed to run a school.

The third-grade teachers at P.S. 6 generally liked a new math program but, after getting together to discuss the details, concluded it was a little light on the fundamentals of arithmetic. So they decided to create their own two-week program teaching basic computational skills. Approving that project would have taken years of bureaucratic runaround at the Board of Education. But Carmen Farina doesn't seem to worry much about the rules. With Carmen Farina, it took only a few short discussions.

Authority, the mere mention of the word *authority,* gets

Americans' backs up. We're a free people. No one can tell me what to do. The idea that someone might be "in charge" evokes images of Al Haig after President Reagan was shot, making everyone nervous by nervously assuring us he was in charge. In frontier days, Americans unhappy with local authority could just move west and chop down some more trees. But now we're stuck together, sharing schools and paying over a quarter of our wealth in taxes for common services. How to make those common services work again, and to make our voices heard, is the dilemma that confronts Americans today.

We no longer understand the meaning of freedom, philosopher Hannah Arendt observed, because we no longer understand the meaning of authority. It sounds like a contradiction, I know, to say freedom depends on authority. Authority, we're taught, is a zero-sum concept. If someone else has it, you don't.

But opportunity for individuals basically does not exist in joint activity unless there's someone around like Mrs. Farina to approve or ratify the ideas. The standard complaint of public employees, as Tracey Harrell from the United States Department of Agriculture in Minnesota put it, is that "people have good ideas but they can't change things." But P.S. 6 overflows with projects and ideas from teachers, parents, and students, from the Writing Network to the Purple Pencil to the flowers around the school's outside border. What's the difference? There's someone who can make decisions.

Individual freedom has been measured by the absence of authority since the rise of nineteenth-century liberalism, an extension of John Stuart Mill's idea that freedom is the absence of state power: A government that values liberty should never exercise authority over people, Mill suggested, except to "prevent harm to others." That binary formula, freedom versus authority, is true enough for private choices—I'm either free to speak my mind or I'm not. But for common choices, the opposite is closer to true: Authority acts as a kind of hub or clearinghouse, permitting choices to be made.

No American likes the idea of traipsing up to someone to get approval. Some might prefer, although I don't, big meetings that go on all day long. Infatuation with "consensus" fades quickly when one obdurate person refuses to budge. Authority offers a larger benefit, however, than having someone who actually makes a decision.

Having someone around with authority offers advantages that ripple through all of your daily choices, particularly if you trust the person. The availability of authority—not an actual decision—liberates you to act on your own best judgment. No approval required, no traipsing up to anyone. All you need is confidence in your own sense of right and wrong.

At P.S. 6, the art teacher organized a student mural in the front hall that became controversial among certain parents accustomed to the standards of the nearby Metropolitan Museum. A whole brigade of parents came after the project. Mrs. Farina was happy to take the heat. That's her job. The art teacher continues to thrive.

Competent authority empowers everyone around it. With authority in the background, teachers can stand up to a pushy parent, or make an exception, or deviate from the course plan. Do you have a good reputation? That

THE COLLAPSE OF THE COMMON GOOD   149

alone will take you most of the way. If someone later starts taking potshots, you know there's someone who knows you who can stand up for you. No need for a grinding legal hearing or objective proof.

But what about abusive authority?

An awful monster, perspiring in anticipation of the demeaning tasks it will force upon us, hides just around the corner in our imagination. It may send out benevolent emissaries to lure us on, like Carmen Farina, but these could be tricks. "Carmen Farina" even sounds like a trick name, too sweet to be true. Its real name, Authority, says it all. Troops of mini-dictators lie in wait in the wings.

Before jumping back into the maw of bureaucracy, consider, however, what we're talking about. Authority is not unaccountable power but conditional responsibility, available only as long as others permit, to make choices for the common good: "just powers," as the Declaration of Independence put it, derived "from the consent of the governed."

Authority does have a scary side, however, which is the ability to make decisions about people. What if there's a disagreement over the fairness of that judgment? The potential for dispute is undeniable: Almost every decision negatively affecting a person is unfair from that person's point of view. But this negative side of authority may be the most beneficial, because, paradoxically, the resulting anxiety energizes everyone and infuses the joint endeavor with mutual trust: You know that others around you will do their part.

Judith Bardwick, in her book *Danger in the Comfort Zone,* draws a bell curve in which one end represents too much pressure, leading to desperation, and the other end too little pressure, ultimately leading to lethargy. Anxiety is an indispensable ingredient in healthy human relations, whether in a marriage or a school. "Reducing anxiety absolutely," philosopher Martin Heidegger believed, "is the absolute denial of the prime human condition." Opportunity is not enough. Dangling a carrot in front of someone who is already full, for example, doesn't usually work. It doesn't matter if our stomachs are filled only with gruel. Full is full, and without pressure, most people won't move.

One of the most passionate advocates of putting more pressure into schools was the late Albert Shanker, longtime head of the American Federation of Teachers, who noted:

> High school students quickly discover that they will graduate from high school no matter how little they do. . . . Since they can get what they want without working, it's no surprise that youngsters . . . do very little work and achieve at very low levels.

His realistic assessment of human nature is directed to students, of course, but the same obvious point can also be applied to teachers, principals, and everyone else. The mother of an adolescent who went to a charter school that clearly asserted academic and disciplinary values was overjoyed by the positive impact on her son: "They don't let him get away with anything. It shook him up a lot." Fear can be bad or good, but it's a vital ingredient to human growth. As Vaclav Havel explains:

Fear of our own incompetence can evoke new competency; fear of God or of our own conscience can evoke courage; fear of defeat can make us prevail. Fear of freedom could be the very thing that ultimately teaches us to create a freedom of real value. And fear of the future could be exactly what we need to bring about a better future.

When Carmen Farina came to P.S. 6, the fifth principal in five years, teachers were skeptical that she would be able to reinvigorate the culture. But she identified teachers who seemed enthusiastic and those who felt content with their roles. One teacher "just preached for the whole period. I couldn't even understand what exactly the children were supposed to be learning." Another teacher was punitive, calling some youngsters "morons" and occasionally striking them. One senior teacher was mediocre, just boring and unenthusiastic. In her early years, Mrs. Farina spent almost half her time building bureaucratic records. With each written comment, a teacher has the right to file a grievance and then, with the aid of a union lawyer, appeal it up two more levels. The boring teacher filed twenty-three grievances against Mrs. Farina, who at times spent most of her week in a bureaucratic struggle with this teacher. Undaunted, Mrs. Farina won the battle of attrition, and the teacher finally left.

Other teachers got the message: Either get on the program or go elsewhere. After eight years, 80 percent of the original teachers had left. Even today, Mrs. Farina spends 40 percent of her time and the full time of two other employees keeping records, just in case someone decides to go to the mat. Her authority is real because she keeps it that way. The pressure, as Carmen Farina sees it, gives teachers a choice. "Once you create a climate in the building that is hardworking, people will find out whether they are comfortable or not," she said, "and they have decisions to make." Today P.S. 6 has one of the lowest teacher-turnover rates of any school in New York. That's because everyone shares its goals. "The ability to hire and fire," Mrs. Farina observes, "is an incredibly powerful management tool."

Americans equate authority with *authoritarianism,* a term invented in the late nineteenth century and used as a synonym for totalitarianism or dictatorship. The concept of authority is not created by power, however, but by mutual assent. That's its role in every culture. In ancient Rome, authority was contrasted with power and referred to someone who, like an "author" of wisdom, had the respect of others. "Authority," in a description Havel attributes to Confucius, "derives from the holder's heightened responsibility" and "is lost when a person betrays that responsibility." Authority is considered an instrument of freedom because it is a delegation to someone to make group choices—"an obedience," as Arendt puts it, "in which men retain their freedom."

Authority does not exist, as Arendt explains, if it requires either force or argument with one disgruntled person:

> [A]uthority precludes the use of external means
> of coercion; where force is used, authority itself

has failed. Authority, on the other hand, is incompatible with persuasion, which . . . works through a process of argumentation.

Because authority is grounded in consent, whoever coined the word *authoritarianism* (probably some misguided disciple of John Stuart Mill who believed that authority was the archenemy of freedom) should be condemned to a lower circle of bureaucracy for linguistic desecration. " 'Moral authority,' " Chester Barnard concludes, "is the only effective authority."

Having authority reside in known people reaches to the heart of the bureaucratic dilemma: using human personality to transcend that horrible enforced sameness, for example, when central boards of education stamp heavy protocols onto everyone to maintain consistency.

It's been so long since anyone had authority that we probably can't even imagine what we're missing. One is change for change's sake, just to spice up life. One day Mrs. Farina suggested to an excellent fourth-grade teacher, regarded as one the best teachers in the school, that she change grades the next year. She was "too good at it." After a little discussion, the teacher got excited about the idea. For the sole reason of making herself "a little uncomfortable," she switched to the fifth grade. She is loving the challenge of teaching at a slightly different level. A science teacher, nearing retirement, also seemed out of challenges, so Mrs. Farina asked if she would like to take on a project of reconfiguring the science room. After a year of looking at other schools, she came up with a plan to transform the science room into an Amazon rain forest. With support from Chase Bank, arranged in part by Mrs. Farina, the Amazon moved to Manhattan.

Authority is the missing link to individual freedom in a world dominated by huge bureaucracies. Only when humans have authority can we escape, Havel observes, "the dreary standardization and rationalism of technical civilization."

In the few instances where government has reclaimed personal authority away from bureaucratic protocols, the liberating impact on the department has been almost immediate. Georgia's Office of Planning and Budget went off the civil service system in a 1992 pilot program. The immediate change, according to former head Bill Roper, was the "need for less supervision, dramatically improved performance and more camaraderie." All of a sudden, what everyone thought mattered. "We started," he observed, "having fun." In 1996, Georgia governor Zell Miller eliminated the merit system for all new hires and for any new position or promotion for existing employees: "Despite its name, our present merit system is not about merit," said Governor Miller, saying the unsayable. "It offers no reward to good workers. It only provides cover for bad workers." The reform caused great trepidation but, since the change, an atmosphere of cooperation and accountability has started to rub off on existing civil servants. "I can't remember," one Georgia official notes, "the last time we had a grievance."

We resist authority as undemocratic when, in fact, authority is the indispensable tool of our republic. As James

Madison stated in *Federalist 10,* American government should be run by "a chosen body of citizens, whose wisdom may best discern the true interest of the country." The rest of us, being governed, then have the authority not to second-guess their every judgment but to judge the people with responsibility. "If I weren't doing the job," Mrs. Farina puts it simply, "I would be out of here in a flash."

THE FATE OF THE INDIVIDUAL

FAIRNESS TO EVERY INDIVIDUAL is the billboard that hovers over American society. Dismantling it to permit judgments about people to be freely made by those with responsibility will be done with the greatest reluctance. Why can't we ensure both the common good and individual fairness? The vision of some mistreated public employee or student appears before us, like a hurt puppy with a club about to come down on it.

Nobody could get away with that kind of abuse, of course. Due process is probably less of a deterrent to awful behavior than exposure to the personal judgment of people like you and me. The gamesmanship of litigation appeals to bad people. But the mistrust is overwhelming: "We need due process," said a teachers' union official in California, "as long as there are people who might fire you because they didn't like what you wore that day."

Requiring proof in an adversarial legal proceeding, however, is not the only way to protect people. Authorizing a third party to approve major personnel or disciplinary decisions could guard against arbitrary or vindictive decisions, while preserving the ability of supervisors to act on their best judgment. Economic safety nets can soften the blow of dislocation; retraining programs can help someone readjust to a new position.

But due process, we believe, practically *guarantees* fairness. The self-help aspect of it appeals to us. It allows each and every one of us to take on the system. It also allows us to avoid having to stand up for right or wrong ourselves when dealing with co-workers. Oh, that's terrible. Why don't you get a lawyer?

In the cozy den of our preconceptions, we imagine due process as a kind of fountain of truth, automatically bestowing accountability and fairness in equal measure. In practice, applying due process to internal decisions is more like pouring acid over the culture. It may be hard to comprehend how one of our most hallowed constitutional protections could possibly work such mischief, but consider the effect if you had to prove your position every time you disagreed with, say, one of your children. Due process for ordinary management choices basically ensures the corrosion of the common good. Let's start with the most obvious effect: decisions not made.

Maria Tuma, an elementary school art teacher in south Florida, was a little unbalanced. The problem surfaced in 1983 with complaints that she was bringing her evangelical beliefs into the classroom, handing out Bibles, preaching and otherwise acting inappropriately—for example, cutting a lock of a child's hair as punishment. Formal warnings were followed by required psychiatric evaluation. There were more meetings with school officials, at which Ms. Tuma promised she would stop. But Ms. Tuma couldn't help herself, and in 1986, the principal "strongly recommended" that she be dismissed for her "gross insubordination." Instead, probably trying to avoid the extensive legal proceeding, the assistant superintendent directed her to "cease and desist all proselytizing of religion in the classroom" and "not to advise students with regard to powers of the devil or hell." Things were quiet for a while, until a new principal came and began hearing complaints, and the formal warnings began again. On one, Ms. Tuma wrote back that "all I said was: 'the devil came to kill, steal & destroy.' " More hearings followed, resulting in medical counseling and therapy.

Ms. Tuma transferred schools in 1993 and developed a fixation on the unsuspecting principal, Dr. Jeanne Friedman, who recounted that Ms. Tuma told her "that I had eyes beautiful like Jesus. . . . She would take pictures of me and she would stand in the hallway and look at my pictures. Now that would send off signals to other people. . . . She would just shower me with all kinds of gifts." Her performance in the classroom was also inappropriate, altering children's work, lowering grades of children she didn't like, and saying that children and parents who complained were "liars." In 1996, "having exhausted all avenues of assistance" to Ms. Tuma, the school board suspended her and initiated dismissal proceedings. Nine months later, after hearings that included the testimony of three principals, one associate superintendent, and five other senior school officials (including two who had since retired), Ms. Tuma was dismissed. Thirteen years had passed since serious problems had arisen, during most of which Ms. Tuma had been teaching young children.

When the Supreme Court extended due process to daily managerial choices, it seemed to assume that, of countless choices made every day, only a few, in which there was real possibility of injustice, would give rise to genuine dispute. Due process was conceived by the Supreme Court as a warm cloak ensuring fairness to everyone. In practice, it incites conflict.

The employee always sees himself as the victim, not because he's selfish but because people are wired that way. As Robert Wright in *The Moral Animal* observed:

> One might think that, being rational creatures, we would eventually grow suspicious of our uncannily long string of rectitude, our unerring knack for being on the right side of any dispute. . . . Time and again—whether arguing over . . . a promotion we never got, or which car hit which—we are shocked at the blindness of people who dare suggest that our outrage isn't warranted.

Self-delusion gets worse as competence declines, as two Cornell professors found in a 1999 study: "When people are incompetent, their incompetence robs them of the ability to realize it." "The only one who doesn't know," as one specialist in disciplinary problems wrote, "is the incompetent teacher."

Emotions run high when personal worth is put on trial. It's one thing to lose a job, but it's another for the employer to be proving your incompetence. Imagine having to prove someone's lack of virtue before a panel of third parties. That's what due process shoves in everyone's face. Disciplinary hearings turn into name-calling affairs that cause normal people to want to be fired themselves rather than have to endure. Firing someone isn't literally impossible, but it often takes years—literally years—of building a record and then enduring an awful proceeding of laying out, in gory detail, why someone isn't any good. Even if you win, there go months of no sleep. It's ordeal by trial.

The thirteen-year delay in dismissing Ms. Tuma is just one symptom of the bias against decisions of any kind. Supervisors believe "it is simply not worth the effort," according to a 1995 federal report. *Washington Monthly* founder Charles Peters put it this way:

> Imagine yourself a supervisor of a person who does nothing but read the paper and take coffee breaks. Thinking of firing him, you might turn to Title 5 of the U.S. Code and peruse parts 752.101 through 752.402 and 772.101 through 772.404, which describe one hearing and appeal after another. By the time you reached the end of 772.404, you'd say the hell with it and toss him the sports section.

"Dismissing a tenured teacher," one California superintendent observed, "is not a process, it's a career."

No cost is too great to guard against unfairness, some believe, fearing the odd case where someone really good is nonetheless let go. Aside from the fact that good people generally land on their feet, failure to act can be more harmful to people than acting unfairly. How about the children under the care of inept or unbalanced teachers? "My daughter, who used to love school and wanted to be a teacher," said a Seattle parent, now "cries on Mondays" and "complains of stomach aches."

Although we don't like to think about it, failure is a reality. Even in the best of organizations, with the most selective hiring, a certain number of people will not succeed. The amazing variability of human conduct is only compounded by group dynamics. A teacher who is effective at one school may not be successful at another school for reasons entirely beyond his control. Failure of a few can drag down an entire department. Decisions must be made. In most situations, being subjected to others' negative judgment is not a death sentence but a life lesson that helps direct a sensible individual down more productive paths.

All humans fail at some things. This reality can't be avoided. How people fail has as many causes and variations as how people succeed. Just think of the possibilities.

Some people, like Nick the irritable teacher, don't have the right personality for the job. Others lose energy and enthusiasm. Surveys of school administrators suggest that 15 to 20 percent of America's teachers are marginal or worse and not fit to teach. A student stringer for *The Seattle Times* described a science teacher who would "write the assignment on the board, and just leave":

He did not love teaching; it showed in his tired
eyes, his illegible handwriting, and the total lack

of life in his voice during the few lectures he
gave. This "anti-teacher" had the ability to
make minutes seem like millennia.

Bad personalities and burnout are only two of the ways
people commonly fail. Some people, for whatever reason,
have a bad habit of being careless. On February 9, 1998, a
New Jersey Transit commuter train ran a stop signal and
collided with another train in the marshland of Jersey City,
killing the engineers of both trains and injuring scores of
passengers. The careless engineer, as it turned out, had a
history of running stop signals.

Some people aren't team players and let selfishness get in
the way of their responsibility. One teacher in Louisiana
took thirty sick days a year, always, her colleagues observed, on either side of a weekend. Once one person starts
abusing the privilege, it's hard for others not to. In Framingham, Massachusetts, public works employees taking
sick days became an epidemic, with almost half the workers taking twenty or more days per year. When some employees don't pull their weight and get away with it,
everyone else gets discouraged. "I guess some people," said
a disheartened fellow teacher in Louisiana, "can just turn
their backs and walk away."

Some people are (as we used to say) crazy. Willie Woods,
a radio technician for the city of Los Angeles, was paranoid about people trying to get him. He would sometimes
get a violent look in his eyes, as if he were about to attack
someone. This sometimes translated into real violence.
During a discussion of his job performance one year, for

example, he picked up a chair and smashed it against the wall. People in the office avoided him as best they could.

Alcohol and substance abuse have to be near the top of the list of ways to fail. Jay Dubner, a special-education teacher in Brooklyn, supported his drug habit by selling cocaine from the school office, often packaged in Board of Ed envelopes. He was finally arrested when caught selling half an ounce to another teacher.

In Hamden, Connecticut, the superintendent had a reputation for being erratic and temperamental, with a record of drunkenness. But the students didn't know how erratic until he was arrested, really drunk, coming out of a porn shop dressed as a woman. The local newspaper did not ignore these events, and the superintendent skipped town in the middle of the school year.

Due process assumes that we can prove in an adversarial legal proceeding who's fit to keep the job. But how do you prove someone has bad judgment? Or doesn't try hard? Or has a vicious look in his eye? Or wasn't really sick every other Friday? To try to catch the worst sick-day abusers, government investigators sometimes tiptoe around backyards taking pictures of absentees *in flagrante gardenia*. But you can't take a snapshot of an unhelpful attitude or of burnout. Judgments about who is doing a good job, more than most, are essentially unprovable.

None of the people just described, for example, lost his job.

The New Jersey Transit engineer with a record of moving violations had never been suspended. Inquiry showed that a small percentage of engineers of the area's commuter railroads had most of the violations (9 percent of New Jersey Transit engineers had 54 percent of the serious infractions, and at the Long Island Railroad, 2 percent had 39 percent of the infractions), but in the prior eight years only one engineer had been let go for moving violations.

Willie Woods, the paranoid radio technician in Los Angeles, finally exploded. He came to work one day and shot and killed four of his co-workers.

The cross-dressing superintendent who skipped town showed up in Hamden a few weeks later, after the town fathers had appointed a replacement and thought they had put this behind them, and sued to keep his job. The town ended up paying him over $200,000 to get him to leave the job he had just left. Two hundred thousand dollars is a whole neighborhood worth of Hamden property taxes, but it's not as bad a deal as you might think. In New York State, it costs an average of $194,000 to terminate a teacher, not counting the diverted time and energy of principals and others. Detroit has reported a seven-year process.

Officials thought it would be easy to terminate Jay Dubner, the teacher who used Board of Ed envelopes for his cocaine sales, for "conduct unbecoming a teacher." But after Mr. Dubner was allowed to work under the prison work-release program, he challenged the dismissal. As required under civil service and union rules, a three-person arbitration panel was picked. Eight hearings, eight hundred pages of transcript, and fifteen months later (during which Mr. Dubner was paid), he was officially dismissed.

But Mr. Dubner had a right to appeal to the education commissioner. Is it really fair to single him out when so many incompetent people keep their jobs? Presented with evidence that Mr. Dubner was rehabilitated, the commissioner overturned the dismissal and instead suspended him for two years. At the end of the suspension, Mr. Dubner, now out of jail, began negotiating for which job he should hold in the public schools. As he put it, "I can return any time I want."

The other teacher in the cocaine bust, Mr. Dubner's customer, was also convicted of a felony. But he was not tenured and had no civil service right to challenge his termination. So he went to court and also won a ruling overturning the dismissal. No one else is dismissed for personal transgressions. Why should he be?

Due process, striving to ensure fairness to individuals, has a side effect when applied to cooperative activities like running schools: It basically kills the culture. In his 1993 article, "Defining Deviancy Down," Senator Daniel Patrick Moynihan observed that "we have been re-defining deviancy" and "also quietly raising the 'normal' level in categories where behavior is now abnormal by any earlier standard."

How do we keep standards up? We can't, because due process looks not to excellence but to the minimum acceptable standard. The bias of due process is to prevent government from acting: Government shall not "deprive . . . except by due process of law." If you're a supervisor, how do you know where the minimum level is?

The values of due process, almost necessarily, are relative: What happened in the last case? That drug dealer was allowed to come back to his job, why shouldn't this one? Who wants to litigate it? The floor of acceptable behavior keeps dropping.

Senator Moynihan suggested that a " 'society that loses its sense of outrage is doomed to extinction.' " But dealing with the worst teachers, observes Professor Donald Fuhr, is not the main problem. The ones "just doing enough to get by" are the ones who "turn kids off to school." A system that looks to the minimum has no chance against mediocrity, however. The downward slide continues.

In one short legal phrase, transported from the entirely distinct context of state coercion, our aspiration for excellence in schools and government is replaced by forced acceptance of almost anything.

Due process cannot be applied to daily supervisory judgments without causing failure. Its proper role is to check exercise of government's coercive power, not apply that power against non-coercive common choices.

I can practically hear the whimpering for the hurt puppy. By what right does the group, or its representative, make judgments about another person? In his personal life, they don't. But in joint activity, judging and being judged is the natural flow of freedom. Natural selection, Robert Wright observes, doesn't care what you think of your own arguments, nor will people be long fooled by someone "whose merit," to quote Edward Gibbon, "is loudly celebrated by the doubtful evidence of his own applause." What's important in the world is not what you think about yourself, but what others think about you. Making these judgments is an aspect of everyone else's freedom. "I think him so," wrote Shakespeare in *Two Gentlemen of Verona*, "because I think him so."

Due process is supposed to support everyone's freedom,

not provide an immunity against the demands of joint activity. Albert Camus wrote, in *The Fall,*

> Once upon a time, I was always talking of freedom. At breakfast I used to spread it on my toast, I used to chew it all day long, and in company my breath was delightfully redolent of freedom. With that key word I would bludgeon whoever contradicted me; I made it serve my desires and my power. . . . I didn't know that freedom is not a reward or a decoration that is celebrated with champagne. . . . Oh, no! It's a chore, on the contrary, and a long-distance race, quite solitary and very exhausting. . . . Alone in a forbidding room, alone in the prisoner's box before the judges, and alone to decide in the face of oneself or in the face of others' judgment.

Exposure to the judgment of others is freedom's condition for the opportunity it affords. A generous society can cushion life's dislocations and disappointments, but it can only destroy the overall fabric of fairness and freedom by shielding people from others' beliefs.

WHO'S IN CHARGE AROUND HERE?

In April 2000, a New Jersey school suspended four kindergartners for pointing their fingers at each other as if they were guns. This act violated one of the "zero tolerance" policies which have swept across the country. No drugs are allowed under zero tolerance, so a girl in Houston is suspended when found with a bottle of Advil. But nothing could be done about a teenage boy with a metal spiked ball designed to maim people because, Kay Hymowitz reports, it wasn't "on the superintendent's detailed list of proscribed weapons."

Most Americans can distinguish between Advil and marijuana, kindergartners playing cops and a teenager carrying a weapon. But deciding to discipline one, and not the other, requires giving someone the authority to draw the line. Educators today don't have that authority. The inevitability that someone will occasionally be unfair has caused us to retreat to a system where no one can make the judgment at all. It's either law in black and white, or anything goes.

Americans want proof. But almost nothing important in human affairs is provable. "If it can be measured," observed Bill Coats, who runs The Leona Group of charter schools, "then it's probably not very important." Even measurable academic success is ultimately a function of unmeasurable human inputs. Good judgment is certainly not provable, which is why the authority to judge people is the heart of democratic institutions, just as it is in any joint endeavor. People get the job done, or not. They're fair minded and have sound character, and try hard, or not.

Still, we don't want to release ourselves into some dog-eat-dog world where people act on their beliefs. Like bureaucrats, we feel our vitality draining. But, like them, we can't see leaving the protection of the legal cage that promises safety and sameness. Just one whisper in our ears about a possible abuse causes us to lock the gate, preventing everyone from doing what they believe. Recently the ACLU opposed a standard of conduct for Denver schools that would ban immoral conduct, because of concern with "the vagueness of the term *morals*." Vague it is, like every other important aspect of life. But we're not putting anyone in jail for immorality, just trying to run a common enterprise that values decency for our children.

Maybe, as we're demanding tests of students, we should test the legal system we've stuck them in. A basic ACLU principle is that "students and their schools should have the right to live under the principle of 'rule of law' as opposed to 'rule by personality.' " This philosophy sounds wonderful, so high-minded. But does the absence of personal authority imbue schools with fairness? Unfairness, even fear, is the status quo. Students have not learned a "wholesome sense of the place of the citizen in American society," as advertised. Students have learned a lesson that is the exact opposite of what reformers intended: Life is a game of what you can argue and get away with.

Neutrality was our goal. Tracing the path back past the due process revolution, the racial awakening, and the rise of public unions, we arrive at the civil service reforms over one hundred years ago. To cure spoils, we decided to create a neutral government. But the reform went far beyond guarding against spoils. By removing politics from the administration of government, it set off a chain reaction of powerlessness in which public institutions began to take lives of their own.

The civil service reformers, according to historian Henry Steele Commager, had "no real faith in democracy." Who else is going to hold the bureaucrats accountable but those we elect? What happens when a value judgment needs to be made? Almost every decision—indeed, even the timing of a decision—involves the exercise of personal judgment and values. "The idea that a 'public interest' exists somewhere as a kernel of true knowledge, untainted by politics or self-interest, is an attractive thought," historian Alan Brinkley notes: "But it is also a myth. We cannot identify a public interest outside of politics."

Sooner or later, the collapse of the common good had to come, because no one was making the value judgments needed to make anything work. As columnist Walter Lippman put it in 1914:

> The confusion of public life [comes from] insisting upon looking at government as a frame and governing as a routine. Politics has such an unreal relation to actual conditions. Feckless— that is what our politics is . . . it has been centered mechanically instead of vitally. . . . We have hoped for machine regularity when we needed human initiative and leadership, when life was crying that its inventive abilities should be freed.

The idea of neutral civil service, historian Paul van Riper observed, ultimately "carried with it the seeds of its own destruction." Instead of neutrality, we got the pathology of a democracy purged of the beliefs of its constituents.

What replaced our beliefs was the self interest of the new institutions intended to guard against self interest. Designed to purify government from politics, civil service (together with the teachers' union and other public unions it spawned) has become perhaps the most powerful political force in the country. Almost twenty million people—one out of six working Americans—works for government. During the 1960 election, John F. Kennedy made promises to public employee unions that then resulted, by Executive Order 10988, in "the greatest personnel add-on of all times," as unions secured new layers of work rules and grievance procedures. One out of ten delegates to the Democratic National Convention in 1996 was a member of the teachers' union. Teachers' unions are the top-spending lobbyists in New York State, making it "virtually impossible" as Diane Ravitch and Richard Viteritti observed, for "an education bill to emerge without the union's support."

Every decade or so, a blue ribbon panel calls for civil-service reform. Education leaders repeatedly call for an overhaul of the teachers' union contracts to permit accountability. Yet each proposal disappears without a trace, as if public employees exist in a kind of Bermuda Triangle.

These huge interest groups, surrounded by a vast desert of failure, huddle desperately around the political system, succeeding mainly in entrenching the failure. No one can do anything. Accountability is dead. A committee of school superintendents discovered in 1998 that "in the state of Pennsylvania only thirteen teachers have been dis-

THE COLLAPSE OF THE COMMON GOOD   171

missed for incompetence since 1957." Purpose is lost in bureaucratic prehistory. In New Jersey, the teachers' union organized a boycott of Pepsi products when the bottler had the nerve to offer underprivileged students scholarships to private schools. How dare Pepsi think of students first and impugn the quality of public schools?

Bureaucratic systems bring out the worst in people. Instead of looking to do what's right, people use the logic of the structure to advance their inevitable instinct for personal security. Even after the goals get turned upside down, systems perpetuate the failure because they provide cover to the people within them. The public sees the system, not a person. Who's at fault for the failure of the schools? Precisely. The system brilliantly disperses all fault among countless people and departments that, like drops of water on a pane of glass, have a seemingly random connection to each other. What we get, as Arendt noted, is "the rule of Nobody, which is what the political form known as bureaucracy truly is."

One question is the litmus test for any healthy organization or culture: Who's in charge here? If you can't identify a live human being who has authority to solve your problem, then the enterprise can't succeed for you or for anyone else. Returning authority to individuals returns their personal exposure to the judgment of others. Only then will the self-serving logic bred by systems wither under the sunlight of others' opinions. "I believe in face-to-face contact," Havel concludes, not in watching officials "move in a giant inhuman theater . . . for which nobody is responsible."

Giving people authority, to choose and be chosen about,

is the only way to release the human spirit. It's also the only known antidote for bureaucracy. That's how P.S. 6 got turned around. "The more we did things our way, the more successful we became," Carmen Farina noted as I was leaving P.S. 6. With an afterthought, she smiled. "We got better and better."

THE LEGAL WEDGE IN THE
RACIAL DIVIDE

Darnell Williams worked his way up from the projects in Gary, Indiana, to the Air Force, to college, and then to Aetna Insurance Company, where he started out as an underwriter working with insurance agents to decide which contracts were worth the risk. He knew he had a steep learning curve compared to others. ("They hit the track running while I was trying to tie up my shoes.") Mr. Williams then encountered problems with agents, who "would be telling my manager that they wanted their book of business to be transferred to a different underwriter." But he couldn't have an honest discussion about what was wrong, and whether the fact that he was African-American was affecting his relations:

> My manager would suggest there was something wrong with my communication style or method of customer service, but I felt he was not being straight with me. . . . I understand my managers were tense about the issue because of discrimination suits, but that tension was making it so we couldn't have open discussions about my situation and how I could get to the next level.

Sometimes silence is the most definitive behavior.

Reading through personal accounts of blacks in business, there's a pervasive sense of nonbelonging. Black executives feel they're not part of the flow of the workplace, as if half out and half in. As one young investment banker quoted by Stephan and Abigail Thernstrom in *America in Black and White* put it: "The subtle part is unspoken. It's inflections . . . , it's all the nuances people feel that suggest 'you're not welcome here.' " A law professor noted that "often . . . people will simply avoid talking to you."

Granting private citizens broad powers to bring lawsuits, as we saw earlier, has cascading unintended effects. The mere availability of a lawsuit, not actual claims made or threatened, changes the way millions of people go through the day. Removing authority of those with responsibility for a school or office also has cascading effects, ultimately making powerless those intended to be protected. While venturing onto the hot coals of racial debate is something I hesitate to do, for fear of diverting the focus away from these structural flaws of modern society, I believe these same legal mechanisms, applied to protect individual African Americans against unfairness, have been similarly counterproductive, impeding black progress and racial healing.

Objective measures of black progress, like income and education, show huge strides since the walls of segregation started being dismantled in the 1950s. It's hard to imagine that barely fifty years ago an all-American baseball and football player at UCLA was barred from the big leagues. Jackie Robinson (also a champion golfer at UCLA) was reportedly as surprised as anyone when the Dodgers' Branch Rickey asked him if he had the courage to break the major league color barriers. Today, to remind ourselves, Colin Powell, Tiger Woods, and Oprah Winfrey are national role models. White Americans feel pretty good about how progressive they are, studies show, and view the burgeoning black middle class as proof of their declining prejudices.

Blacks, the same polls show, feel almost exactly the opposite. In a survey of black executives published in the *Harvard Business Review* in 1986, 98 percent believed prejudice pervaded their companies, and 84 percent believed that race "worked to their disadvantage when it came to ratings, pay, assignments, recognition, performance appraisals, and promotion." The situation, black leaders believe, is not improving. Racism "is worse today than it was in the '60s," Benjamin Chavis, former executive director of the NAACP, has said. Professor Jennifer Hochschild found that "African Americans increasingly believe that racial discrimination is worsening," even as "whites increasingly believe that discrimination is lessening." Some middle-class blacks, Alan Wolfe discovered, were "so angry that they could barely articulate reasons." Blacks know that overt patterns of discrimination have broken down. But that's because, blacks say, whites have learned to cover their prejudices. Commentator Carl Rowan in 1996 asserted that "racism has not been as virulent throughout America since the Civil War, with short fuses burning on a thousand powder kegs."

Black self-consciousness is not hard to understand. Constant indignities remind blacks that they are dealt with differently because of their skin color. The stories are legion: the woman professional who was mistaken for a cleaning person; the senior law partner who was blocked in the hall by a young white associate wanting an explanation for why he was there. How would you feel if, as a successful black professional, you were stopped by police for the sole reason that you're driving a new car? The fact that one-quarter of all black males aged fifteen to thirty-five are in jail or on probation would be little consolation. We all want to be treated as individuals, not weighed down by stereotypes.

The widespread bitterness among middle-class blacks is reinforced not merely by indignities in dealings with strangers but, even more, in dealings with people they know. Blacks in corporate America see that they are slotted into jobs with little opportunity for further advancement. Even the less observant probably have noticed that black executives don't tend to get jobs on the front lines of business, but get placed in human resources, public outreach, legal, and other "soft" jobs. As diversity consultant Verna Ford put it:

> They give them titles, but not the plum assignments. You have these highly paid, well-educated, polished people in top corporate jobs twiddling their thumbs and looking for work to do.

The natural conclusion of these executives, as one told Ms. Ford, is that "racism plays a part in the unchallenging projects that are assigned to him."

In *The Rage of a Privileged Class,* Ellis Cose recounts a conversation with a *New York Times* editor about how a black editor would probably not get a chance at a vacant high-level editorship because the *Times* "would have to think hard . . . for they could not afford to have a black journalist fail in such a visible position." What else could it be, Cose suggests, but prejudice: "Failure at the highest level of the *Times* was a privilege apparently reserved for whites."

Daily encounters seem to confirm further blacks' view that covert racism pervades the workplace. Studies by psychologist John Dovidio and others show that many whites, while believing that they are being solicitous and encouraging, proclaim by their body language an entirely different message: that they're not being candid and, indeed, are uncomfortable dealing with minorities. Blacks find themselves constantly wondering whether decisions affecting them are racially motivated or not.

The one thing that almost never occurs, either in the workplace or in public debate, is honest discussion about race. There's hardly a more sensitive subject. Just mention a racial issue in mixed company, and all the oxygen drains out of the room, leaving whites shriveled up and helpless, and blacks seething with righteous indignation. President Clinton tried to host a national dialogue on race in 1997, but the staged events were platitudinous, the usual pattern of blacks indignant and whites patronizing. "We do not converse," David Shipler notes in *A Country of Strangers,* "across the racial line."

"The wall between the black and white worlds," Professor Cornel West observes, "is getting thicker and thicker." Black distrust of whites is almost perfect: Experiments by psychologists show that blacks tend to attribute positive remarks by white supervisors as patronizing, but attribute negative remarks as evidence of racism. But people just can't bring themselves to talk it out, or indeed, to talk at all, leaving everyone's imaginations to concoct new levels of resentment. Hovering over every workplace disagreement, even over ordinary choices like who does what, is an unspoken suspicion of discrimination.

It is hard to see any path through the accumulated resentments. Like bureaucracy, the situation feels impenetrable. But taking it down to the most elemental level, what's involved is one person dealing with another person. Is there some structural barrier that keeps people from being honest and bottles up everyone's worst assumptions and preconceptions? Affirmative action is a hot button with many whites, but giving preferences doesn't stop people from talking. There's one structure, however, that almost no one ever questions.

Discrimination law sits squarely in the center of modern workplace relations, always available if someone feels he has been discriminated against. Discrimination law has proved to be among the most effective laws ever passed, breaking down most of the obvious barriers of exclusion within a decade of the original 1964 Civil Rights Act. The landmark cases of this era were class actions, designed to break down employment barriers against blacks as a group, mainly in hiring. For the last two decades, however, virtually all discrimination cases have been not class actions over hiring practices but claims by individuals who believe they were treated unfairly once on the job.

The right of every American to bring a claim of discrimination is considered practically part of the Bill of Rights. Almost no one approves of discrimination, so we assume that having as strong a law as possible, enforceable by any aggrieved person, is the right and just way to rid society of the cancer of discrimination.

The more relations seem to fracture, the harder people push for tougher discrimination laws. Congress regularly expands the scope and penalties of discrimination laws. In 1991, Congress gave plaintiffs the right to a jury trial and to attorneys' fees. The general idea, laid out in the legislative history, is that expanding relief is "necessary to encourage citizens to act as private attorneys general to enforce the statute":

> Monetary damages simply raise the cost of an employer's engaging in intentional discrimination, thereby providing employers with additional incentives to *prevent* intentional discrimination in the workplace before it happens.

The law certainly worked to expand litigation. As one employment lawyer put it, getting a jury trial was like "manna from heaven." Discrimination-type employment claims increased threefold between 1990 and 1998, and both the success rate and damages awarded increased significantly. That's only the tip of the iceberg, of course, and does not include claims threatened and settled.

Harder and harder, we keep pushing law to eradicate the prejudices that we know exist in our society. In response to the revelation that federal employees were seven times more likely to file discrimination claims than employees in private business, the equal opportunity officer of the Department of the Interior had the ready answer: "There are some people who just haven't gotten the message."

But maybe people have gotten the message. The prospect, or fear, of a charge of racism hangs over black-white relations like a gun with a hair trigger. Discrimination law is obviously still needed, but in what kinds of situations and enforceable by whom? It's reassuring, I guess, that everyone places such faith in our system of justice. We assume, as we do with litigation generally, that claims will be brought only when they can be proved, and justice will take its course. That idea is valid enough when we're dealing with patterns of discrimination, like Wendy's restaurant turning away one black customer after another, but how does someone prove, or disprove, discrimination when the angry person in the next office hurls a charge of racism in his direction?

Legal systems, as we've seen, have a bad habit of taking on a life of their own when divorced from human judgment. Put law or any other formal structure in the middle of daily dealings, and people will start looking to the law instead of to one another. Is it possible that the cure for discrimination has become a wedge keeping us apart?

WALKING ON EGGSHELLS

For decades now, whites have been trained in the supposed art of dealing fairly with minorities. Like political indoctrination, managers are trained not to trust their instincts. Elaborate protocols are devised that practically guarantee that no honest feelings or beliefs come out. Who knows what subconscious prejudice will be revealed? The "effect is to neutralize the language itself . . . destroying almost all spontaneity," as people "pick their words as though traversing a minefield." Jokes are especially dangerous. The proper mind-set is guilt, with "white males encouraged to think of themselves as oppressors or recovering racists." At one sensitivity training session in Detroit, the sensitivity trainer, when told that a participant's father had just died, remarked that the death "removed one more racist influence" from his life.

This new sensitivity is pretty heavy-handed, but the guilt of most white Americans leads them to tolerate it as a kind of psychological reparation: Okay, they'll be extra polite no matter what they think of someone.

Blacks' distrust of whites, in other words, is fully warranted. Whites aren't being honest. The goal was to respect blacks, but the effect is that whites have clammed up. Instead of healthy give-and-take, "everyone walks on eggshells," as diversity expert Verna Ford observed, "concerned about what they should or shouldn't say":

> It's one thing to give a person positive emotional
> support, . . . it's another to give a good, swift

kick in the butt when they aren't performing
well.

Observers have noted cultural disconnections that cause
blacks and other minorities to founder because they don't
"know the ropes." Honest evaluation, candid tips, and
sometimes critical words are indeed essential to personal
growth, but blacks don't get the mentoring needed to succeed, neither the arm around the shoulder explaining how
things really work, nor the hard criticism required for
growth. "You can make adjustments if you have direct
feedback," said Darnell Williams, now a diversity manager
at Massachusetts General Hospital, "but if you don't have
direct feedback, you're making presumptions. . . . It puts
thoughts in your head."

Why do whites keep blacks at arm's length? It's possible,
I guess, that racist whites have a new scheme: to be polite
instead of nasty, and to revel in withholding comments.
But Ms. Ford has another explanation: "Sometimes people
are so afraid of lawsuits that they won't give minorities
constructive feedback."

Do you think whites are afraid of discrimination claims?
Frozen with fear is more accurate. As sociologist Orlando
Patterson observed, "No Euro-American person, except
one insensitive to the charge of racism, dares say what he
or she really means."

But why should anyone be scared if he doesn't discrimi-
nate? Let's look again at what's required for a person to
bring a discrimination claim. Basically, it involves one person's anger at what he perceives to be an unfair personnel
decision. The proof is the personnel decision itself, plus a

collage of real or imagined slights that are supposed to underscore the evil intent. Human nature has wired the aggrieved employee, as we've seen, to always think the worst.

There's no other claim like it. Lawsuits over hot coffee or seesaws, by comparison, look like mathematics theorems. At least they require a value judgment that ordinary people can make. But a charge of discrimination by one person hinges on a charge of evil motive. Like a claim of heresy, it challenges what's in the supervisor's soul. Nobody, not even the supervisor himself, really knows what lurks in his psyche. All he knows is who he believes is doing a better job. It doesn't even matter if he could convince someone that he truly believes he's right; we're told we don't know our own prejudices. Shine the spotlight on the angry employee. Listen to the arguments about how he's better than the other guy who got the promotion. Basically, as Professor Shelby Steele observes, "whites have to prove a negative: that they are not racist."

Discrimination claims that have merit are usually settled quickly, but, managers say, so are many claims that just use discrimination law for personal gain. As their courtrooms "are becoming flooded with employment cases," several federal judges have noted the small percentage that seem to have merit. United States District Judge Stanley Sporkin suggested that the law allows "almost anyone not selected for a job to . . . maintain a court action."

Abuses of discrimination claims, as with outrageous lawsuits, travel over the informal wires with lightning speed, like that of the British arts administrator fired for allegedly using a racial epithet two years earlier in the presence of no one except her accuser. The availability of the race card is genuinely terrifying to whites. As a general manager of a tool factory told Professor Alan Wolfe, "You could've done everything that you thought was right for the last twenty years, and you can be ruined over one statement that was taken out of context." "Career-enders," in the words of a former federal administrator, is what these claims often become.

In government, racial threat is so common that Harvard's Kennedy School of Government has case studies showing how managers consciously make wrong decisions to avoid dealing with a militant employee. In one case study, in order to avoid a discrimination claim, a manager promoted a black secretary despite the fact that her "lack of performance had already led to other clerical employees resenting the mere toleration ... of her poor performance." Morale within the department sank immediately. One manager explained why his secretary refused to do some work because she was so upset about the promotion: "It was one thing for me to turn down her requests for promotion, but quite another to see a promotion go to the worst employee in the place."

Most people don't abuse the race card, of course. Lena Parker, an Atlanta teacher interviewed by Alan Wolfe, "simply cannot understand why white employers fear black workers":

> If you hire me you're hiring a good person. . . .
> You're hiring a Christian person, one that has values, one that will stand for no nonsense and will give you an honest day's work for an honest

day's pay. I will be loyal, . . . now why wouldn't
you hire a person like that?

Everyone would want Ms. Parker on their team. But failure and disappointment are inevitable in the workplace,
for whites as well as blacks. Just as there's no X ray to
show someone's prejudice, there's no X ray to reveal who
will interpret any disappointment as a possible discrimination claim.

Let's look again at why black professionals are usually
slotted into corporate positions like human resources, or
community outreach, without a path to the top. Is there a
nationwide conspiracy to save every "plum" responsibility
for a white person? That's what it looks like. What's the
risk of giving a black the chance at a leadership job, like
running a division? People are given jobs all the time that
don't work out. But there's another risk to giving that shot
to a minority. Remember what experts on human nature
tell us: Almost no one ever thinks that failure is their fault.
A discrimination claim by an angry high-level executive
might make headlines. People in charge don't want legal
fears to influence how they deal with their most important
managers. It's hard to imagine a more powerful disincen-
tive to black advancement than white apprehension about
discrimination claims. In lower-level jobs, or "soft" jobs
like human resources and law, success and failure are less
important and usually do not require decisive personnel
moves. And so black executives "twiddle their thumbs"
while never given the opportunity to show their stuff.

Martin Luther King, Jr., dreamed of a world in which

people would be judged "not by the color of their skin but by the content of their character." Today whites feel they can't judge African Americans on any basis. It's understandable why blacks like to have the awesome power of a discrimination claim in their holster, unilaterally available. But now many whites deal with blacks as if in a Kabuki play, wearing phony faces and making artificial gestures, but not being real. Blacks, meanwhile, find themselves in a kind of isolation chamber, left to their imaginations as to what's really going on.

RACE IN ISOLATION

In 1999, trying to secure regulatory approval for a large merger, Ameritech Corporation proposed to sell its wireless telephone business to GTE and a small financial firm run by successful entrepreneur Chester C. Davenport, who was reported to have a personal net worth over $100,000,000. The idea behind the participation of Mr. Davenport, who is African-American, was that the transaction would have a better chance of regulatory approval with minority participation. With such a high-visibility deal, Mr. Davenport was probably not surprised when *The New York Times* called to organize an interview. But the *Times* reporter seemed surprised at the torrent of injustices that came flowing out:

> I think if I were white, I would own one of these damn telephone companies, O.K.? . . . All the time I've spent here, whatever money I have now, if I were white, doing everything I've done,

> I would have 100 times more money than I have
> now, O.K.?

Mr. Davenport's public relations consultant, also taken aback, asked if he were joking, to which Mr. Davenport replied several more times, for the record,

> I would have 100 times more money than I have
> now, and I think these guys know that. . . . If I
> had that network, the network these guys were
> operating in, I'd have 100 times more money
> than I have now.

Getting worked up is easy when sitting around with your pals, and I'm sure Mr. Davenport, like all African Americans, could write a book on the indignities he's faced. But this was an interview with a reporter. The intensity of Mr. Davenport's belief that he has been held back financially by his race suggests that it's worth pausing to consider his perception of reality. Let's see now, 100 times $100 million would be $10 billion or, to put it in upper-middle-class terms, $100,000 per year for 100,000 years. Most tycoons know (or at least pretend to know) how many twists and turns of fate are required to amass a huge fortune. Mr. Davenport's own success, according to the *Times*, is partially due to getting cut in on deals where businesses felt they needed a minority partner. The fact that Mr. Davenport got some breaks does not necessarily diminish his accomplishments—we all get breaks where we can—but it does make his resentment over his financial situation look, well, misplaced.

Robert Wright in *The Moral Animal* seems to have understated the characteristic of human nature that drives us instinctively to come up with whatever self-serving rationale we can get away with:

> The human brain is . . . a machine for convincing others that its owner is in the right—and thus a machine for convincing its owner of the same thing. . . . Like a lawyer, the human brain wants victory, not truth; and, like a lawyer, it is sometimes more admirable for its skill than for virtue.

Political philosopher John Locke, whose ideas on freedom inspired our Founding Fathers, made a similar observation over three hundred years ago:

> Men being partial to themselves, passion and revenge is apt to carry them too far with too much heat in their own cases.

People have their imaginations kept in check in dealings with the outside world, particularly in the workplace. "It is through his work," as social scientist Elliott Jaques put it, "that a person maintains his primary sense of reality." When race enters the picture, however, reality checks are as hard to come by for blacks as they are for whites.

At first no one thought there was anything inappropriate when the Buffalo school superintendent, James Harris, was asked to appear before the school board to explain how his office in 1999 managed to miss a filing deadline that cost the schools $8.9 million in expected state aid. But Mr. Harris was apparently upset at this assertion of the school board's authority, and he tendered his resignation "in a huff." Perhaps to his surprise, the school board accepted his resignation. Then the dispute quickly took on a different color. Mr. Harris is black, and several local black leaders quickly accused Helene Kramer, the school board head, of "racism" and of conducting a "witch hunt." The fact that Ms. Kramer, a veteran of the civil rights movement, had been married to a black professor and named their two sons after Marcus Garvey and Malcolm X was of no import. Throwing the "vile epithet" of racism "as lightly as a Frisbee," as one observer put it, the deputy speaker of the state legislature, Arthur Eve, compared criticizing Mr. Harris to the Attica Prison killings in the 1960s. Most people in Buffalo probably knew that race had nothing to do with the issue, but trying to argue back was like walking into a flamethrower. Ms. Kramer's call for accountability just showed her bias, according to another local black leader, Warren Galloway: Some people "have trouble dealing with strong, highly educated black men."

As honest discussion recedes beyond the horizon, the scope of perceived racism keeps expanding. When Bosnian refugees were resettled in Utica, New York, a long-depressed small city on the western edge of the Adirondacks, their energy and excitement at being in a free country sparked a revival of the entire economy. Industry moved back to take advantage of the eager labor pool. Old neighborhoods were fixed up. New stores opened. Existing residents looked on in amazement, and most joined in. To the local black leadership, however, it was a textbook case of racism, notwithstanding the fact that until the Bosnians came along, neither whites nor blacks in Utica were successful in creating new jobs. The fact that white immigrants were received so enthusiastically was evidence enough. As one black leader told a reporter, they don't "let us know what jobs are available." Another saw Bosnian success as "acceptance for the refugees that isn't there for people of African-American descent."

A kind of frenzy greets any perceived racial insult or slur. In 1999, during a budget discussion among three Washington, D.C., municipal officials, one of them, David Howard, said that he would have to be "niggardly with this fund because it's not going to be a lot of money." His black colleague "stormed out" and promptly got the new black mayor, Anthony Williams, to force the resignation of Howard, who was the mayor's first openly gay official. Calmer heads noted that, while other phrasing might have been preferable, the word *niggardly* comes from a fourteenth-century Scandinavian term for miser. Both H. Patrick Swygert, president of Howard University, and civil rights legend Julian Bond weighed in on the side of Mr. Howard. As Mr. Bond put it,

> You hate to think you have to censor your language to meet other people's lack of understanding. . . . This whole episode speaks loudly to where we are on issues of race. Both real and imagined slights are catapulted to the front burner.

But Keith Watters, a prominent black lawyer, disagreed: "Do we really know where the Norwegians got the word?"

The reluctance to ridicule these charges, given our history, is understandable. But reality is useful, if for no other reason than to maintain credibility needed to wear down the many hurdles that still exist for blacks. Today, controversies on race often resemble comedy routines.

Blacks have become almost as paranoid as whites. Ordinary mannerisms of whites grate on the black consciousness. David Shipler in *A Country of Strangers* tells how Roger Wilkins, a Pulitzer Prize–winning journalist, saw racism in the fact that Senator John Danforth, after meeting him, instead of using the honorific *Mr.*, said "nice to meet you, Roger." Shipler then tells how, when he met Senator Danforth for the first time a year later, he was greeted as "David." Senator Danforth calls everyone he meets by their first name. It's correct that blacks (and immigrants) used to be demeaned by being known only by first names. But wouldn't it be just as patronizing today to make an exception from normal conversation? ("It was very nice to meet you, *Mister* Wilkins.") This is not a dilemma that's either solvable or, in the scheme of things, particularly important. But trivial perceived slights have apparently become a preoccupation of some African Americans. In *It's the Little Things*, Lena Williams catalogs subtle racial slurs, such as a white woman flipping her hair. Is somebody flipping her hair really something that a normal person, whether black (or bald), should take offense at?

Blacks use similar trivial acts to get back at whites. One

way to go on the offensive, as a friend described, is for blacks not to cooperate in the joint protocol of accommodating each other on the sidewalk, a game of sidewalk chicken in which one side sees vindication and the other sees rudeness.

Without honest feedback, people in this country have let their imaginations spin into outer space. Whites are as tight as clams, assuming mediocrity or worse without giving blacks a fair chance. Some blacks have let rhetoric and resentment escalate beyond reason, getting the attention of the press and driving whites further into their shells.

THE WEDGE IN THE WOUND

At the FAA's air traffic control center in Hilliard, Florida, in the early 1990s, racial tensions had begun to emerge out of a program called "train to succeed" that, in an effort to increase the number of minority controllers, allowed trainees repeated failures of certification tests. Controllers began to resent the fact that some trainees, at it for more than a decade, were making more money than certified controllers. One trainee, Ozzie Watson, had "washed out after five years at a Memphis facility" but claimed discrimination, and was reinstituted. After several years at Hilliard, however, he still couldn't pass the test. A controller training Mr. Watson would watch as he sent planes on odd routes that disrupted "the efficient flow of air traffic," but the trainer couldn't interfere "unless the plane was at risk." As the trainer put it, "He drives me nuts." To Mr. Watson, his failure to win certification was clearly due to racism. "I can't do anything," as he put it, "to please the guy." Some controllers began to refuse to participate in training on the grounds that people "can train until they retire."

Tensions kept mounting, and in 1993, a controller named Gregory Harris organized a group of black controllers. White controllers wondered "what . . . the blacks need a group for" and unsuccessfully sought FAA approval to form a group for whites. They then tried to attend a meeting of the black group, which was supposedly open to all controllers. Within minutes, however, they were forced to leave.

A few weeks later, Mr. Harris announced that he discovered a large racial epithet written on the bathroom wall. In any sensible society, the graffiti is painted over quickly, without any fuss, and then someone noses around to identify the sickie. But in modern America, a racial epithet is like an exploded bomb. The manager at Hilliard, Ed Drury, had the bathroom sealed off and called in a team of FAA investigators from the central office. Mr. Drury had recently reprimanded Mr. Harris for verbally abusing a pilot in the middle of a commercial flight, and suspected that Mr. Harris himself had written the epithet. The FAA investigators never determined that Mr. Harris was the culprit ("A minority," Mr. Harris said, "would never have done that"), but the investigators did conclude that he was "out of control." The investigators also did not find any rampant racism, but because of the high racial tension, recommended that a black be given the top job.

Mr. Drury was dismissed and replaced by an African American who, over the next three years, elevated minorities to top positions. But morale deteriorated further as controllers perceived his choices as unfair and racially motivated. Operational errors increased, to 50 percent higher than under Mr. Drury, and much higher than in other flight control facilities. In 1998, the black manager who had replaced Mr. Drury was reassigned to headquarters, and a new manager was given the job of trying to repair a facility that by now had almost melted down under racial tension.

What's missing here? No one, black or white, profited from the meltdown at Hilliard. Antipathies in the workplace are not uncommon and generally can be managed. But none of the actions needed to defuse the situation at Hilliard was available. No one felt they could terminate Mr. Watson, or paint over the epithet, or tell Mr. Harris to cool it or else. Disputes involving race are, literally, out of control. What does this pattern remind you of?

Discrimination law insulates blacks in the same way that bureaucracy insulates bureaucrats, and creates risks that drive whites, like defensive doctors, away from their best judgment. Because of fear of violating someone's civil rights, no one has authority to do or say what he actually believes. The unilateral power of any individual to bring a discrimination claim has deprived everyone of an essential condition of free interaction and understanding. One person's racial anger can start a cycle of resentment and recrimination that virtually destroys the culture.

All the bureaucratic pathologies are present. Blacks are protected from criticism but walled off from opportunity. When in doubt, blacks are left alone. Managers tolerate widely disparate performances and attitudes, even ones destructive to the common purpose.

Giving individuals the power to make a claim of unfairness, even if rarely used, transforms every worker into a shadow lawyer, concerned as much with legal status as accomplishment. The smallest nuance becomes possible evidence. "Each meticulous gesture," as sociologist Everett Hughes once described the bureaucratic pathology, "bursts with symbolic meaning." At the forefront of the thoughts of whites and blacks is not the merits of the project or judgment but whether it might have racial implications. Blacks and whites focus on legal rights instead of on one another. Just as the custodian of Governor Kean's lightbulb was obsessed with the absence of proper authorization, how a white person flips her hair becomes the concern of some African Americans. Everyone is off balance, as preoccupied with race as bureaucrats are with rules. The workplace is a minefield.

Professor Orlando Patterson, in making the case for affirmative action, draws a distinction between law that helps a group and law that affects a particular individual. Policies and funding for a group enable many people to advance, he argues, but do not interfere with anyone's freedom in one-on-one dealings. "In our face-to-face interactions," Professor Patterson observes, "Afro-American and Euro-American people should treat each other exactly alike," not with "any special set of sensitivities."

This same wisdom requires a change in discrimination law. Discrimination claims must be viewed not as a vehicle for personal vindication—a high proportion of claims, we now know, are too unreliable—but mainly as a group concept, requiring patterns of discriminations that can be challenged by class action. The unilateral power by any individual to bring a discrimination claim is too destructive of daily relations. The cost of freezing honest interaction among millions of people is far greater than the harm from isolated incidents. Egregious individual abuses will occur, but the right to bring individual claims should be entrusted to an unbiased third party, such as government.

Minimizing personal vendettas will enhance the employer's incentives, putting the onus on the employer to investigate and deal with valid complaints. Employers will have an incentive to fire unfair supervisors rather than defend them in order to avoid liability. But the employer would also know that failure of particular black employees, even bitter conflict, could not itself give rise to a claim. This change could thus unlock the quarantine on opportunity that, because of fear of a lawsuit following black failure, now impedes opportunity for black success.

Honesty may bring disagreement and conflict, but conflict over how to do things is an important aspect of joint endeavor and personal growth. As management expert Linda Putnam has observed, "Conflict in organizations balances power relationships, promotes flexibility and adaptiveness, and prevents stagnation."

Legal conflict, on the other hand, is a surefire formula for divisiveness. It takes away the authority of people to act on their beliefs.

The realization that anyone can transform a personality clash or personal judgment into a federal case has driven a wedge not only between blacks and whites, but, to a lesser degree, between everyone in the workplace. It's hard to imagine a more perfect mechanism to engender distrust and bitterness. A survey of racial tension in the armed services revealed an "intriguing symmetry": "the more minorities perceive discrimination in a unit, the more white males perceive reverse discrimination." Ed Drury, the former head of the FAA's Hilliard facility who was dismissed in a fruitless effort to smooth racial tensions, sued for reverse discrimination. In 1997, a jury found that "the FAA dismissed him because he was white." The recriminations are potentially endless.

Professor Harold Laski once observed that we must "judge an institution not by its purposes but by its achievement . . . of those purposes." Discrimination law has few rivals for high purpose. Conducting every personal interaction against the backdrop of a high-noon legal showdown, however, does not achieve those purposes. The difficulty of distinguishing between a valid and an invalid claim is driving blacks and whites further apart.

Law can go after patterns of discrimination, but law can't make a person successful or respected. Succeeding in work or any joint endeavor requires not the "right" to succeed, but the ability to convince those you work with how good you are. Fair or not, that's the way the world works, and freedom also. As Professor Glenn Loury has observed:

> Black Americans cannot substitute judicial and legislative decree for what is to be won through the outstanding achievements of individual black persons.

"Freedom does not last long when bestowed from above," Arthur Schlesinger observed in *The Age of Jackson*. "It lasts only when it is arrived at competitively." Exposure to

others' judgment, as we've seen, is the condition of freedom. Without it, there is little meaning, or distinction, to
an individual's character and accomplishments.

Freedom requires that each of us has the authority to
deal honestly with one another. Whites need to be able
to be honest in their evaluation and criticism. Blacks need
to know they're being dealt with honestly, not being pa-
tronized, and to engage whites frankly on issues of race.
"It's really hard," as Darnell Williams, who is now also
president of the New England chapter of the NAACP, puts
it, "to overcome silent discrimination."

"If each side were allowed room to make small mistakes
without instant condemnation," David Shipler suggests,
"we might feel safe enough to have the dialogues we need
to have."

THE SECRET TO FREEDOM

A distinguishing trait of Americans, Tocqueville found, was our ability to join with others, whether in barn raisings or town meetings, to create what individuals alone could not: "[I]f an American were condemned to confine his activity to his own affairs, he would be robbed of one-half of his existence."

America's power would only increase, Tocqueville believed, if we cultivated "the art of associating together," which he considered the "mother of . . . progress." For much of America's history, that's exactly what happened: Grange Halls and Masons, then Elks, Lions, Rotary, Kiwanis, Optimist and Shriners, Boy Scouts, Girl Scouts, Brownies and Cubs, VFWs and DARs, the Playground and the City Beautiful Movements, PTAs and Little League. Even the National Civil Service Reform League.

Americans know how to get together to make things happen. It's in our bones. Just look at the technology revolution, almost like a modern renaissance. But we can't make our schools function. Our link to the common good is so attenuated that Americans today can't imagine how to participate. A man moderating forums in Portland for a nationwide study on civic engagement said, "I've had almost every person come up to me afterward and say, 'Okay, so now what do we do?' And I'm not sure what to tell them."

Reading through the chronicles of civic engagement in American history, you can practically feel the determination as like-minded people got together to get something done, just because that's what they believed was important. What was different? They weren't lone rangers out on the frontier. They were creating and sustaining institutions for a common good, some huge, that maintained their vigor for generations. What did they have that we don't?

They felt free to act on their beliefs. The paradox of an individualistic society building joint enterprises, Tocqueville understood, was the pursuit of "self-interest rightly understood." That's where the energy came from; people did what they believed. They shared a passion for the particular cause, but they also had something more mundane: They were free to make the countless judgments needed to make something happen.

Americans no longer feel free to do what we believe is right. Ordinary choices are burdened with legal fear and argument. Cooperation of all kinds has become risky. Daily interactions are imbued with distrust. Is the doctor free to act on his best judgment? Does the teacher have authority to run the classroom? Are you free to say what you think?

Tocqueville considered the authority to make daily choices the most significant aspect of freedom:

> For my own part, I should be inclined to think freedom less necessary in great things than in little ones. . . . Subjection in minor affairs . . . is felt by the whole community indiscriminately. It does not drive men to resistance, but it crosses them at every turn, till . . . their spirit is gradually broken.

Feeling free to do what you think is right is the source of human accomplishment and personal pride. Each reinforces the other. "No one has a greater asset for his business," management pioneer Mary Follet observed, "than a man's pride in his work."

Americans are told we're freer than any citizens in history, lucky to live in a society that protects individual rights. We're certainly free when planning our lives, like where we work and who our friends are. But, out in society, we're not free to be ourselves. Maybe the best description is that we're half-free, able to pick our route through life but not able to do it our way. Throughout America's offices, hospitals, schools, courts, and public agencies, in roughly ascending order, people have been deprived of the authority to do their jobs as they believe is right and reasonable, and to judge and be judged on that basis. We've lost the ingredient Tocqueville considered essential to our national character: the freedom of spirit that comes from the authority to act on our beliefs.

At this point, Americans are so out of practice that we no longer know what we believe. Our self-confidence has evaporated: Who are we to judge? In 1998, a blue-ribbon commission's report on the decline of civic involvement, "A Nation of Spectators," concluded that Americans "lack confidence in our capacity to make basic moral and civic judgments."

The villain is an oppressive legal structure that sprawled away from core principles of the Constitution, common law, and social justice to scrutinize almost any individual choice or event that anyone cares to complain about. Law has abandoned its mantle as the protector for society as a whole, and instead has become a vehicle for individual attack and entitlement. Law looms over daily choices, demanding proof by objective criteria. In public institutions, all the important personal virtues—character, drive, judgment, morality, courage—have become optional features, nice but not central to any objective evaluation. "Spontaneity and instinct," which Emerson considered to be "the essence of genius, of virtue and of life" have virtually disappeared in public life, and increasingly in private life as well, shoved aside by anxiety over compliance with some legal checklist or a possible lawsuit. Who might complain? We don't know, but we'd better go slowly. Everyone starts tiptoeing through the day.

No pride exists in any culture where the people don't have the authority to do what they feel is right and reasonable. That's what freedom is supposed to offer: the authority to act on your beliefs. "Our freedom depends at least as much on the character of life within . . . institutions as on the principles" of government, political scientist Larry M. Preston observes: We must "support our freedom to choose," not accept "a paltry life of routine and petty choices."

Reclaiming this authority to act freely requires, however, abandoning some of our most deeply held preconceptions, particularly about individual legal rights and about the authority of those, like judges and political leaders, who run our common institutions.

THE FLAW OF MODERN INDIVIDUALISM

Since the dawn of modernism, one of our highest national priorities has been to preserve individual freedom in a society dominated by huge institutions; to "salvag[e] the individual," as historian Henry Steele Commager put it, "within an economy dominated by vast, impersonal and largely imponderable forces." Like waves gathering force with each decade, reforms exposed and then battled abuses by social and political institutions, first spoils, then exploitation of labor, then racism. As the twentieth century evolved, the battle lines were clearly drawn. The institutions of society were the enemy. Enhancing individual rights became the goal of all right-thinking people.

Social relations organized around individual legal rights, we believed, would be like the free market, where, as Professor Donald Black noted, "each citizen will voluntarily and rationally pursue his own interests, with the greatest legal good . . . presumptively arising from the selfish enterprise." Freedom for all would be enhanced if each person could use law to preserve his own freedom. Law, however, is not a free-market instrument. Whoever wields law has power over everyone else. Almost without our noticing how it happened, the regime of individual rights began threatening our freedom instead of protecting it.

Our system of individual rights, as it turns out, has a structural flaw: It unintentionally transfers power for common decisions to self-interested individuals. Individual rights, girded with legal powers against institutions, has become an intimidating institution itself. This new institution of individual rights, however, doesn't have any common enterprise in mind. Nor is it readily accountable to the common good. It exists only for the aggrieved individual.

In a society that honors individual rights, we imagine, the innocent inhabitants coexist peaceably and happily, like in a petting zoo; a "perfect whole," as philosopher Isaiah Berlin observed, "in which all good things coexist." But in the real world almost every choice, as Berlin explained, "involves a collision of values." Giving a disruptive child another chance may be best for that child, but it may have harmful effects on the other twenty-nine children in the class. How do we decide? Professor Carl Bogus argues that the current litigation system "is one place where the average citizen can battle the powerful on nearly equal terms." But whom does that average citizen represent? What if most of the rest of us would prefer traditional playground equipment? The world is not "a crossword puzzle," as Havel observed, "to be solved in one correct way—the objective way." Social judgments, from minute-by-minute choices in a classroom to judicial decisions that determine presidential elections, are inevitably laden with value choices.

Wringing our hands, we exhaust ourselves trying to satisfy everyone's individual rights. But because pleasing everyone is impossible, the prudent course usually is to avoid deciding anything. In bureaucracy, as we've seen, not deciding is standard operating procedure. With issues like affirmative action, debates go on forever, like a stuck record, because rightswise they are literally imponderable. Professor Lani Guinier, trying to find a solution for affirmative action, proposed that universities set a minimum academic threshold, and then admit students by lottery. At last the ideal freedom: eliminate free choice.

To organize decisions in society, Hegel conceived a dialectic between competing forces, where the person in authority needs the cooperation of those down the line, and they in turn need a person in authority to make common choices. Marx thought that this mutual dependence would eventually shake its way down to one level until, at last, all people would be equal in a dictatorship of the proletariat. In our quest for a perfect government that gives every individual what he wants, we have landed closer to where Marx predicted. By replacing authority with individual legal rights, we achieved almost perfect equality in common dealings: Most people are scared to do much of anything. Instead of dictatorship of the proletariat, what we got was a dictatorship of one proletarian: One person, any individual, can assert his own perceived interests and basically bully the rest of society.

INSTITUTIONS ARE US

We don't trust government or, for that matter, any institution. Our pervasive distrust is hardly groundless, given the many failures and abuses of the institutions that sit atop society. It is easy to feel that the people who run them are our antagonists. Even without individual rights to challenge institutional decisions, most Americans would probably support tight controls. Every dispute, every failure, is reason to pile on more legal dictates.

The more our common institutions fail us, the more Americans want to limit their authority. Through a downward cycle of distrust, legal controls, worse failure, and heightened distrust, we drive Americans' governing institutions further into the bureaucratic maw. We don't care anymore. Just keep them away from us. "The gulf separating individuals from the institutions and processes that govern" our lives, as historian Alan Brinkley observes, "grows ever larger."

Giving anyone in these institutions authority to decide anything is not exactly our first instinct. But there's a difference between guarding against use of government power—for example, when government imposes new regulations on private citizens—and putting shackles on internal management of government. How can government respond to us if it can't manage itself? There's also a difference between a judge tossing you in jail, which obviously requires all the safeguards of juries and due process, and a judge setting limits on use of legal power, for example, whether someone can sue over seesaws. Without the protection of someone drawing these lines, how can we feel comfortable in making reasonable choices?

America's prosperity makes it easy, and perhaps inevitable, for us to forget that our freedom only exists on a platform of institutions that provides common services and makes common choices. Our lives are cloaked in

choices made by these institutions: about justice, education, medical care, the range of products available at the
store, the lakes available for recreation, the air we breathe—
how, indeed, we interact with each other.

Even as our common good declines before our eyes,
Americans take it for granted, the way children take their
parents for granted until, of course, one day they're no
longer there. Our forebears didn't. "There is no private
life," to quote novelist George Eliot, "which is not determined by a wider public life." The metaphor of play is
again useful, in the words of playground movement founder
Luther H. Gulick, Jr.:

> We are only beginning to learn what freedom
> means. It is not the privilege of doing, irrespec-
> tive of everybody else, what one wants to do.
> That would make the tramp the ideally free
> man. Freedom lies in the recognition and joyful
> acceptance of relationships. In organized play,
> where every child is a unit on a larger, mutually
> responsible whole, all reach a higher and more
> significant freedom than is possible [with] the
> unorganized free-for-all. . . .

Which is more rewarding, playing in a pickup game where
the players are bickering, or in an organized league? The
latter requires coherent rules that people abide by and a
referee with authority to make the calls. Which is preferable, a system of medical care dominated by fear and selfishness, or one that encourages doctors' best judgment?

The latter requires, not a cacophony of contradictory rights, but a reliable mechanism for professional judgment that guides and protects everyone involved.

Institutions are not the enemy. The authority of justice, schools, and government is directly linked to our own authority to act on our beliefs. How they are organized makes the difference between feeling secure to do what's right, or just avoiding the responsibility altogether; between an effective medical system, or one fraying and nearly bankrupt; between having good teachers educating our children in clean schools, or having teachers as burned-out as the schools are decrepit; between a culture dripping in cynicism or one looking towards a brighter future.

But institutions have a bad habit, as we've seen, of taking on a life of their own when cut loose from control by the humans on the spot. Like black magic, legal structures intended to prevent human error transform themselves into defenses against accountability. High legal walls surround each public employee, making accountability and accomplishment equally impossible. Is anybody in there? It doesn't matter: They couldn't do anything anyway.

Busy with our daily lives, all the public sees are the opaque walls of a system that we know doesn't work. By removing human authority, we hoped it would work better. Everything is neutral. Anyone can bring a legal claim. Why doesn't it work better? We cling to the hope that someday, somehow, its promises of bureaucratic regularity and individual rights will result in a smoothly functioning machine.

Tocqueville suspected that we would fall for a system

that, in the name of uniformity, would eliminate our freedom to make common choices. Setting out everything in advance has an irresistible comfort. Nothing tomorrow will be a surprise. Everyone will be treated exactly the same. This new regime would not be despotism, but something new, which Tocqueville said "I cannot name":

> It covers the surface of society with a network of small complicated rules, minute and uniform, through which the most original minds and the most energetic characters cannot penetrate, to rise above the crowd. The will of man is not shattered, but softened, bent, and guided; men are seldom forced by it to act, but they are constantly restrained from acting. Such power does not destroy, but it prevents existence; it does not tyrannize, but it compresses, enervates, extinguishes, and stupefies a people, till each nation is reduced to nothing better than a flock of timid and industrious animals, of which the government is the shepherd.

Tocqueville saw the dark cloud of bureaucracy coming over the horizon, but he did not see that we would try to preserve our individuality against it by giving each individual the power to reject its decisions. The notion that anybody could use law to single-handedly block common decisions probably would have been unthinkable in Tocqueville's time. But he would have identified the flaw in this new system immediately. Pit individual legal rights against bureaucratic decisions and we get bureaucracy to an exponential power, with new rules and procedures trying to cover every individual situation. Sagging under the weight, our common institutions gradually slow down, and decay, dragging our freedom down with them.

THE SECRET TO FREEDOM

Shortly before Halloween a few years ago, Frank Mickens, the principal of Boys and Girls High School in Brooklyn, who had brought this "notoriously violent school" under control, decided to clean out all the lockers to avoid any disruption. Cleaning lockers was too big a job for one person, and so, although not within their job description, several teachers pitched in to get the job done. "How can you stand there with your arms crossed and watch the principal clean up?" noted Tony LoCastro, a computer teacher. "A teacher cannot teach in an environment that's out of control," Amateka Morgan, a math teacher observed: "If we don't do it, who will?"

This small episode, not extraordinary in any way, embodies personal virtues needed to make anything work. On display here were good character and dedication to a common purpose, with the principal trying to do the job even if no one helps and the teachers pitching in even when the rules say not to. What they got out of it was the personal pride that comes from a job well done, and a school made successful by their efforts. Their attitude seems natural, just the way things should work.

But today it's newsworthy. Their behavior cuts against the grain of American public life. The conduct is not required by any rule; indeed, in the case of the teachers, it violates union rules. Nothing in the incident is readily organizable in advance, since it's a once-a-year problem. Rewarding the teachers would be out of the question: someone would have to use subjective judgment to allocate merit pay. Pretty soon the headline that shocks us may read like this: EXTRA. EXTRA. SOMEONE TRIES TO DO THE RIGHT THING. OTHERS HELP OUT.

For over a hundred years we have been erecting elaborate systems designed to avoid human judgment. Objective criteria would provide neutrality and uniformity. But objective systems exclude the context, and lack the illumination of human perception. That's why they fail.

No system of law, nor any organizational system, can succeed unless humans have primacy over ultimate judgments at every level of responsibility. Only humans make things work, applying their beliefs, instincts and experience to applicable guidelines. Humans will either succeed or not. Humans, not any objective system, must be the focus of any structure of government.

All the legal protections erected to avoid human authority—the right to bring a lawsuit for almost anything, the detailed rights of the civil service system and teachers' unions—need to be overhauled or dismantled. Viewing every social choice through the narrow perspective of individual rights is a utopian fantasy that has produced a society scared of its shadows and mired in legal bickering.

Taking off the blinders won't be easy. Isn't individual rights what freedom is all about? But letting individuals use legal power against others' free choices, as we've seen, is a funny way to run a free society. With every dispute, law puts a magnifying glass on the one complaining party, leaving only a small and distorted image of everyone else at the edges. Who's protecting us?

Freedom, it turns out, is not just an individual concept. Our own freedom is intertwined with everyone else's; every decision about one person affects another person nearby. The whole class is affected by the inability to remove the teacher who doesn't try. Every American is injured by the legal fear paralyzing the medical profession. The complexity of these interrelationships, however, makes any objective legal formulation impossible. Where do you draw the line? The people with responsibility must have the authority to make these common judgments.

This is the secret to freedom. Each person must be able to freely choose, equal to the scope of his responsibility, or else all lose their authority to act on their beliefs. Instead of guarding against others' beliefs, we have to insist on their beliefs. Only if those with responsibility are free to choose what's right and reasonable can we be free to do so. That's how our reasonable choices are affirmed, and how abusive conduct gets rejected.

Social structures have a concentric quality. Every constraint or limitation on one person has an effect up and down each ring of responsibility. Take away the personal authority of the teacher to act on his best judgment, and the students' suggestions can't be implemented. The teacher's lack of authority causes the principal to lose his authority—how do you blame a teacher who is just following the script? Over time, schools inevitably decay.

The greater the responsibility, the more reducing authority will detract from everyone's freedom. Remove a judge's authority to assert his views of what's right and reasonable, as we've seen, and the entire society starts acting like a nervous wreck.

Americans "feel they have lost the distinction between right and wrong," Alan Wolfe found, "and desperately want it back." Our moral compass is broken not because we need indoctrination, but because our beliefs require affirmation of right and wrong. If anyone can get away with almost anything, whether in a school, a courtroom, or a bureaucracy, then what are we supposed to believe? Our freedom, even our values, hinge upon the authority of those with responsibility to make common choices.

EVERYTHING IS PERSONAL

For decades, leaders have sought to restore American character and good sense by returning responsibility to local citizens. Robert F. Kennedy in 1966 observed that the modern organizations, particularly government, are "so large and powerful that individual effort and importance seem lost":

> Bigness, loss of community, organizations and society grown far past the human scale—these are the besetting sins of the twentieth century, which threaten to paralyze our capacity to act. . . . Therefore the time has come . . . to bring the engines of government . . . fully under the control of the citizens.

Ten years later, Ronald Reagan called for "an end to gi-antism, for a return to the human scale—the scale that human beings can understand and cope with . . . It is this activity on a small, human scale that creates the fabric of community."

But these cries for human engagement can't get past the first hurdle: giving people on the spot the authority to do what they think is right. Any choice that affects someone else had better be justifiable in a legal proceeding. This is where most reforms get bogged down. Without personal beliefs, the institutions of law and bureaucracy inevitably become our masters. They tell us what to do, not the other way around. Whether centralized or decentralized, what we get, as Chester Barnard put it, is "a purely passive or bovine kind of association."

Some evolutionary weakness must account for the human tendency to build new systems that try to fix problems once and for all. We long for something more reliable than people who, we know, are fallible. But that system, in any form, is the road to ruin. "The belief that adherence to the external forms of judicial procedure will preserve the rule of law," Hayek observed, "seems to me the greatest threat to its preservation." "Men are misled into a reliance on institutions," Emerson noted, "which, the moment they cease to be the instantaneous expression of devout sentiment, are useless."

What's always needed are personal decisions of right and wrong. Hannah Arendt, in *Eichmann in Jerusalem*, explained that Eichmann, after all, "acted in accordance with the rules" of the Hitler regime. His amoral rationale, Arendt emphasized, is all too familiar: *"Who was he to judge?"*:

THE SECRET TO FREEDOM

> What we have demanded in these trials . . . is
> that human beings be capable of telling right
> from wrong even when all they have to guide
> them is their own judgment.

"Arendt linked totalitarians and technocrats together," according to Professor Leah Bradshaw, "by saying neither think." Fairness is achieved not when law is complied with, but when, under legal principles, we think people are acting fairly and honoring the law's purpose.

What Justice Benjamin Cardozo wrote about judges deciding law applies to the countless daily choices by everyone:

> We seek to find peace of mind in the word, the
> formula, the ritual. The hope is an illusion. . . .
> We think we shall be satisfied to match the situa-
> tion to the rule . . . [but] there's nothing that can
> relieve us of the pain of choosing at every step.

Success or failure, morality or immorality, prudence or extremism, all boil down to personal judgment and character. Identifiable people, guided but not shackled by law and organization, are what keep society in balance. "In the long run 'there is no guaranty of justice,' " Cardozo observed, "except the personality of the judge." What "keeps the law in any reverence and power," Emerson concluded, "is always at last the virtue of some men in society."

This is the idea of leadership, as important in a classroom as in the White House. George Washington, asked how to manage government, immediately got to the point: "Find men esteemed and honored by their neighbors." Washington knew leaders would make mistakes, but also understood that striving too hard to eliminate error is the perfect formula to achieve error. "No man is a warmer advocate for proper restraints . . . than I am," Washington wrote in 1787, "but I have never been able to discover the propriety of placing it . . . out of the power of men to render essential services, because a possibility remains of their doing ill."

This is the hard part. Our distrust reflexively boils to the surface. Some principals are unfair; some doctors are inept. Do you trust anyone in authority? Of course not. Protecting ourselves from bad decisions, however, requires the same approach as trying to make good decisions—to rely on some other human's judgment. We can load up schools and courts with checks and balances. But effective second guessing also requires personal judgment by someone with that responsibility. Otherwise, as with individuals asserting rights willy-nilly, the "neutral" checks against abuse will become the vehicle for abuse.

Relying on personal beliefs seems old-fashioned, like using a horse and buggy. But what's our alternative? Law can't think. Good values and good judgment aren't provable. Zero tolerance, stupid warning labels, paranoid doctors and burned-out teachers are all just symptoms of a legal system that doesn't allow personal belief.

Everything is personal. A fair system of justice requires constant value judgments: Americans won't be free to do what's reasonable until judges take the responsibility of deciding who can sue for what. Running the institutions of democracy is uniquely dependent on the particular people: Schools will continue to deteriorate until we replace the system of bureaucratic rights with personal judgment and personal accountability.

You may wonder, as Bertrand Russell once put it, "what can one humble person do" to change the faceless institutions of modern society. The answer is everything. Only a popular movement can succeed in breaking the hammerlock that vested interests have on the system. Trial lawyers who pit Americans against each other so that they can feed on the carnage preserve the status quo by filling the pockets of political and judicial candidates. Union leaders brandish millions of votes in the face of politicians to ward off any challenges to the lifeless security of public employees. Civil servants and teachers trudge along towards retirement, their spirits crushed and woefully underpaid. But nothing will get them to voluntarily change their ways, not even dangling money. They've never seen the sunlight of free choice, or felt its heat.

To get back the authority needed for real freedom, we have to take it back. That's how democracy works. We get together, in the way that Tocqueville so admired, and demand it. The institutions of government look powerful, but the walls are long-weakened by the absence of anyone's beliefs of right and wrong. A government used to being cowed by any individual threatening a bogus legal claim won't long stand up to a coherent force of public opinion. "There is an amazing strength," Tocqueville observed, "in the expression of the will of a whole people."

There's only one catch: We have to keep asserting our beliefs. Otherwise our new system will derail as well. The beliefs needed are not mainly about liberal and conservative differences—we can save these for election day—but our beliefs in day-to-day relations. We need to speak up if we think the principal was unreasonable when disciplining a student, or believe another parent is being too pushy. In a free society, these responsibilities are supposed to belong to us, not to an anonymous legal proceeding. There's an upside, of course, and it's boundless. Our future, and our relation to the society around us, will be limited only by our reasonable beliefs of what's right and good.

Looking back at recent history, steeped in racial guilt and a culture of public failure, it is understandable why "we've learned," in Vaclav Havel's words, "not to believe in anything." But it's impossible, as we've seen, to do anything without a point of view. We don't really have a choice. Look around and take stock for yourself. As a homemaker in Atlanta commented in one survey, at some point "you've got to stand for something."

NOTES

CHAPTER I. THE LOST ART OF DRAWING THE LINE

3   The double slide in Oologah: John M. Wylie II, "Slide Moves to New Rural Home," *Oologah Lake Leader,* February 2, 1996.

3   "I knew it": Linda Martin, "Fear of Liability Win Over Pleas for Slide," *Tulsa World,* February 9, 1996.

3   Other facts on double slide: Conversations with Susie Merrell, town clerk and treasurer; Bill Higgins, Esq., attorney for Oologah; John M. Wylie II, publisher and editor of the *Oologah Lake Leader;* Judy Ashwood, who petitioned to keep the slide in the park; and Charles Montgomery, who bought the slide.

3   All across America: Frank Donze, "Lakefront Play Spots Closing for Good: Financial Woes, Lawsuit Blamed," *The Times-Picayune* (New Orleans), March 18, 1999; Jack McCallum and Jack O'Brien, "Monkey Barred," *Sports Illustrated,* May 27, 1996; Linda Wilson Fuoco, "Swings, Slides to Be Dismantled," *Pittsburgh Post-Gazette,* June 8, 1994; Marianna Riley, "Playground Safety Thrust Is Seesaw's Downer: Park Stables Vanish Under New Guidelines," *St. Louis Post-Dispatch,* December 27, 1993; Marcia Chambers, "Whatever Happened to the Sandlot?," *The National Law Journal,* April 22, 1991.

3   Bristol, Connecticut: Carolyn Moreau, "Playground Collision: Fun vs. Liability Lawsuit Fears Cast a Chill on a Public Recreation," *The Hartford Courant,* May 10, 1997.

3   seesaws: Donna Premes, "Playground Perils: Must Creativity and Safety Concerns Be in Conflict?," *The Washington Post,* May 30, 1996.

4   The new equipment: Douglas Martin, "That Upside-Down High Will Be Only a Memory," *The New York Times,* April 11, 1996.

4   Additional facts on playground equipment: Discussion with Lauri Macmillan Johnson, associate professor of landscape architecture, University of Arizona.

4   Park City, Utah: Karl Cates, "Litigation Fears Put Brakes on Bike Program," *Deseret News* (Salt Lake City), July 17, 1996; interviews with participants.

4   Larck Lake: John McCoy, "Promising Recreational Lake Kept Closed by Abuse, Fear of Litigation," *Charleston Daily Mail,* February 20, 1998; interviews with participants.

5   hugging: June Kronholz, "Chary Schools Tell Teachers, 'Don't Touch, Don't Hug,' " *The Wall Street Journal,* May 28, 1998. See also Gerald Grant, "Children's Rights and Adult Confusion," *The Public Interest,* Fall 1982, pp. 92–95.

5   "Ultimately, we came": McCoy, "Promising Recreational Lake Kept Closed by Abuse, Fear of Litigation"; interview with Fred Stottlemyer.

6   "It's a shame": Linda Martin, "Fear of Liability Win Over Pleas for Slide"; interview with Charles Montgomery.

6   $2.9 million verdict: Andrea Gerlin, "A Matter of Degree: How a Jury Decided That a Coffee Spill Is Worth $2.9 Million," *The Wall Street Journal,* September 1, 1994; "McDonald's Settles Lawsuit Over Burn From Coffee," *The Wall Street Journal,* December 2, 1994.

6   Christopher Sercye: Patty Davis, "Just Outside Hospital, Teen Lay Bleeding to Death," CNN interactive, May 18, 1998; Lola Smallwood, "Witnesses Say Hospital Refused to Help Dying Teen," *Chicago Tribune,* May 18, 1998; AP, "As Dying Teen Bleeds, Nearby Hospital Staff Stays Inside," *The Washington Post,* May 19, 1998. See also Robert Pear, "Hospitals Told Not to Delay Emergency Room Treatment," *The New York Times,* December 1, 1998.

7   A new medical school graduate: Discussion with recent graduate.

8   "You can't touch me": Interview with Jane Parshall.

8   "morally neutral judgment": Michael Sandel, *Democracy's Discontent: America in Search of a Public Philosophy* (Cambridge, Mass.: Belknap Press, 1996), p. 77.

9   "Everyone's views": Thomas K. Hearn, "Social Regulation, The Rule of Law," *Vital Speeches of the Day,* January 15, 1999.

9   "an eleventh commandment": Alan Wolfe, *One Nation, After All: What Americans Really Think About God, Country, Family, Racism, Welfare, Immigration, Homosexuality, Work, the Right, the Left and Each Other* (New York: Viking, 1998), p. 54.

10   "but the investigation": Kronholz, "Chary Schools Tell Teachers, 'Don't Touch, Don't Hug.' "

10   "everyone's nervous": Ibid.

10   Everyone was warmed up: George Gmelch, "Spring, and a Miss," *The New York Times,* April 29, 1998.

11   sue its way to greatness: Discussion with Daniel Popeo.

11 "standard[s] of right conduct": Benjamin Cardozo, *The Nature of the Judicial Process* (New Haven, Conn.: Yale University Press, 1921), p. 63.

11 When working properly: Paul E. Campos, *Jurismania* (New York: Oxford University Press, 1998), p. 58.

11 "conscious submission": Ibid., p. 128.

11 Several New York private schools: Anemona Hartocollis, "Nothing's Safe: Some Schools Ban Peanut Butter as Allergy Threat," *The New York Times,* September 23, 1998.

12 estimates range: Interview with Ann Munoz, Food Allergy Network.

12 Try getting peanuts: Scott McCartney, "U.S. Tells Airlines They Should Have Peanut-Free Seating," *The Wall Street Journal,* April 2, 1998.

13 allegorical figure of Justice: For discussion on the imagery of justice, see Dennis E. Curtis and Judith Resnick, "Images of Justice," 96 *Yale L. J.* 1727 (1987).

13 "the prophesies of": Justice Oliver Wendell Holmes, Jr., "The Path of the Law," 10 *Harv. L. Rev.* 457, 461 (1897).

14 The test of justice: Cardozo, *The Nature of the Judicial Process,* pp. 16, 104, 108, and passim. See also Oliver W. Holmes, Jr., *The Common Law* (Boston: Little, Brown, 1963), p. 36.

14 sandbox: Christopher B. Daly, "Stacey Versus Jonathan: Once in a Sandbox, Now in Court," *The Washington Post,* March 9, 1996; Leonard Pitts, "Tempest in a Sandbox," *The Atlanta Journal,* March 21, 1996; Zachary R. Dowdy, "Litigation Becoming a Pastime, Some Say," *The Boston Globe,* March 8, 1996.

14 "to keep each child": Daly, "Stacey Versus Jonathan: Once in a Sandbox, Now in Court."

15 "we need to": Ibid.

15 A bank robber: "Man Charged with Robbery Sues," *USA Today,* July 28, 1998.

15 Boston judge Hiller Zobel: Hiller B. Zobel, "In Love with Lawsuits," *American Heritage,* November 1, 1994.

16 Isaiah Berlin: Isaiah Berlin, *Four Essays on Liberty* (New York: Oxford University Press, 1969), pp. 118–31; see also pp. xxxvii–lxiii.

16 "A person's rights": Peter Weston, "The Empty Idea of Equality," 95 *Harv. L. Rev.* 537 (1982), quoting Paul Gewirtz, "The Basis and Content of Human Rights," 23 *Nomos: Human Rights* 119, 120 (1967).

17 "a framework of rights": Sandel, *Democracy's Discontent,* p. 290.

17 "a world of autonomous": Mark Tushnet, "Following the Rules Laid Down: A Critique of Interpretivism and Neutral Principles," 96 *Harv. L. Rev.* 781, 783 (1983).

17 A young couple: Discussions with witness and neighbors.

17 Seattle Police Department: Bill Richards, "Seattle Police Head Back to

Class for a Course in Chair-Sitting 101," *The Wall Street Journal,* March 24, 1999.

17 Miami had a rash: Lisa Getter, "Injury Benefits Helped Cripple City," *The Miami Herald,* December 15, 1996; Susan Crabtree, "Miami's Creative Compensation," *Insight* Magazine, January 27, 1997.

18 A depressive professor: Alice Dember, "Lawsuit by BU Professor," *The Boston Globe,* June 12, 1996. See also Ronald Smothers, "Rutgers Settles with Professor Accused of Sex Harassment," *The New York Times,* June 25, 1998.

18 are "not subject": John Rawls, quoted in Sandel, *Democracy's Discontent,* p. 290.

18 "as isolated islands": Tushnet, "Following the Rules Laid Down."

19 "It's driving me berserk": Patricia Wen, "Dealers Balk on Air-Bag Switches Fearing Possible Suits, Many Refuse to Install New Auto Safety Devices," *The Boston Globe,* February 16, 1998. See also "Dealers Balking at Installation of Air-Bag Switches," *The Florida Times-Union* (Jacksonville), June 2, 1998; Jody McPhillips, "Car Dealers Refuse to Install Air-Bag Switch," *Providence Journal-Bulletin,* May 20, 1998; Amy Argetsinger, "Who Will Remove Device?," *The Washington Post,* February 22, 1997.

20 "We're afraid": Wen, "Dealers Balk on Air-Bag Switches Fearing Possible Suits."

20 Harvard admitted an applicant: Alice Dember, "Out of Her Past," *The Economist,* April 15, 1995; Alice Dember, "Harvard Is Hit on Grant Case: Student Leader Calls for Rally on Behalf of Convicted Youth," *The Boston Globe,* April 12, 1995; "Harvard Turns Down Teen Killer," *The Times-Picayune* (New Orleans), April 8, 1995; Ben Gose, "Harvard's Decision to Withdraw Offer to Woman Who Killed her Mother Raises Tricky Questions," *The Chronicle of Higher Education,* April 21, 1995.

20 "afraid of telling": Ethan Bronner, "High Schools Fear Telling Colleges All About Johnny," *The New York Times,* March 11, 1998.

20 "They'll write that Johnny": Ibid.

20 "basic moral principle": Eugene Rostow, quoted in Ken Greenwalt, "The Enduring Significance of Neutral Principles," 78 *Colum. L. Rev.* 982, 1001, n.65 (1978).

21 $105.2 million: Warren Brown, "GM Negligent in Fuel Tank Case: Jury Awards $105 Million to Parents of Teen Who Died in Truck Crash," *The Washington Post,* February 5, 1993. See also David Margolick, "G.M. Verdict Intensifies Debate on Jury Awards," *The New York Times,* February 6, 1993.

21 $4.9 billion: Andrew Pollack, "$4.9 Billion Jury Verdict," *The New York Times,* July 10, 1999; Milo Geyelin, "How an Internal Memo

Written 26 Years Ago Is Costing GM Dearly," *The Wall Street Journal,*
September 29, 1999.

24   "corrosive effect": Robert Kagan, "Adversarial Legalism and American Government," 10 *Journal of Policy Analysis & Management* 369,
378 (1991).

25   "We know we": Marshall Kapp, *Our Hands Are Tied: Legal Tensions and Medical Ethics* (Westport, Conn.: Auburn House, 1998),
p. 16.

25   "to falsify records": Ibid., p. 18.

25   "turn over critical decisions": Dr. Christine Cassel, quoted in Kapp,
Our Hands Are Tied, p. 75. See also Marshall B. Kapp, "Treating
Medical Charts Near the End of Life: How Legal Anxieties Inhibit
Good Patient Deaths," 28 *U. Tol. L. Rev.* 521 (1997).

25   "has not moved": Kapp, *Our Hands Are Tied,* p. 83. See also Dr.
Muriel R. Gillick, "Rethinking the Role of Tube Feeding in Patients
with Advanced Dementia," *The New England Journal of Medicine,*
January 20, 2000.

26   "It is very difficult": Interviews in 1999 with physicians in Phoenix.
See also Lisa Belkin, "Sensing a Loss of Control, More Doctors Call It
Quits," *The New York Times,* March 9, 1993.

26   bad doctors: Chris Stern Hyman, "New York Protects Bad Doctors,"
The New York Times, July 29, 1995.

27   "conclusions masquerading as reasons": Cass Sunstein, "Propter
Honoris Respectum: Rights and Their Critics," 70 *Notre Dame L.
Rev.* 727, 742 (1995).

27   a homemaker brought: Interview with Professor John Jeffries.

29   McDonald's coffee spilled: Gerlin, "A Matter of Degree: How a Jury
Decided That a Coffee Spill Is Worth $2.9 Million."

31   A canoe rental company: Edward Felsenthal, "Modern Bathing Suits
Put a Damper on Summer Fun," *The Wall Street Journal,* June 24,
1993.

31   struck by lightning: Howard Pankratz, "Lightning Victim's Parents
Seek Damages from Denver," *The Denver Post,* March 18, 1998.

32   Nothing is sacred: Lisa Miller, "Surge in Malpractice Leads Pastors
to Offer Less Counseling to Parishioners," *The Wall Street Journal,*
February 5, 1998. See also Lisa Miller, "Federal Appeals Court Up-
holding Ruling Against Pastor Sued for Malpractice," *The Wall Street
Journal,* February 12, 1998; report on *CBS This Morning,* June 1,
1998.

33   "An act is illegal": Donald J. Black, "The Mobilization of Law," 2 *J.
Legal Studies* 125, 131, n.24 (1973).

33   1-800-Autopsy: Don Terry, "Autopsy Technician Turns Adversity and
an 800 Number into Success," *The New York Times,* April 20, 1998.

33 "an unattainable order": Vaclav Havel, *The Art of the Impossible* (New York: Alfred A. Knopf, 1997), p. 30.

34 Talk to principals: Thao Hua and Susan Deemer, "California and the West: District Policy Targets Rude Parents; Education: Capistrano Schools Try to Halt Threats and Other Such Behavior," *Los Angeles Times,* April 1, 1998.

34 "We're no longer educators": Interview with principal. See also George Barnes, "Athol School Chief Quits," *Telegram and Gazette* (Worcester, Mass.), September 22, 2000; UPI (Sacramento), "California schools fear lawsuits, study says," December 23, 1998; Vincent L. Ferrandino, "Remarks on Behalf of the National Association of Elementary School Principals," September 8, 1999, available at www.naesp.org.

34 "roam at large": Mary Ann Glendon, *Rights Talk* (New York: Free Press, 1991), p. 77.

34 "litigation neurosis": Chief Justice Warren E. Burger, "Isn't There a Better Way?," 68 *A.B.A. J.* 275 (1982).

35 "massive redefinition": Eric Foner, *The Story of American Freedom* (New York: W. W. Norton, 1998), p. 293.

36 America's awakening on racism: *Brown v. Board of Education,* 348 U.S. 886 (1954).

37 Herbert Wechsler: Herbert Wechsler, "Toward Neutral Principles of Constitutional Law," 73 *Harv. L. Rev.* 1, 34 (1959).

37 burgeoning regulatory state: Philip K. Howard, *The Death of Common Sense* (New York: Random House, 1995), pp. 12–15 and passim.

38 "principle of institutional settlement": Henry M. Hart and Albert M. Sacks, *The Legal Process: Basic Problems in the Making and Application of Law* (Westbury, N.Y.: The Foundation Press, 1994), pp. 4–5.

38 "The first recourse": Ibid., pp. lxxxiv, xci, xciv, 3–4.

38 "considerations of social": Holmes, "The Path of the Law," p. 467.

38 "The question is not": H.L.A. Hart, "Between Utility and Rights," 79 *Colum. L. Rev* 828 (1979).

38 "it appears beyond": *Conley v. Gibson,* 355 U.S. 41 (1957).

39 "the rules of the common law": U.S. Constitution, Amendment VII.

39 "I know it when I see it": *Jacobellis v. Ohio,* 378 U.S. 184, 197 (1964) (Stewart, J., concurring).

39 "respect people's freedom": Sandel, *Democracy's Discontent,* p. 8.

39 "Choosing among values": Charles E. Wyzanski, Jr., "Equal Justice Through Law," 47 *Tulane L. Rev.* 951, 959 (1973).

40 "Judicial power involves": Paul Gewirtz, "On 'I know it when I see it,' " 105 *Yale L. J.* 1023, 1025 (1996).

40 Americans do not distrust: Interview with Robert Samuelson; see

Samuelson's *The Good Life and Its Discontents: The American Dream in the Age of Entitlement* (New York: Times Books, 1995), pp. 141–54.

40 The new authority: George W. S. Trow, *Within the Context of No Context* (New York: Atlantic Monthly Press, 1997), pp. 51, 88, and passim.

40 "Legal principle rejected": P. S. Atiyah, "From Principles to Pragmatism: Change in the Function of the Judicial Process and the Law," 65 *Iowa L. Rev.* 1249, 1268 (1980).

41 Joey Fort: John Diaz, "4 Little League Coaches Sued over Boy's Injury," *The Record* (Hackensack, N.J.), May 8, 1995; AP, "Baseball Injuries Cause Stir in Court and Out," *Los Angeles Times,* July 11, 1985; AP, "Hurt Little Leaguer Wins Suit Settlement," *The Record,* August 11, 1985. See also Jack McCallum, "The Windup, the Pitch, the Suit," *Sports Illustrated,* January 15, 1996; Creighton Hale, "Litigation League," *The Wall Street Journal,* February 13, 1995; Lily Dizon, "Parents of Little Leaguer Injured by Wild Pitch Sue," *Los Angeles Times,* April 3, 1992.

41 Sister Gale Rawson: "Heard in Court," Center for the Community Interest, April 1996; interviews with participants and lawyers. See also James Pinkerton, "Softball Lawsuit Hits Home in Corpus," *Houston Chronicle,* October 26, 1996; John Leo, "The World's Most Litigious Nation," *U.S. News & World Report,* May 22, 1995.

43 "fairly safe course": Justice Louis Brandeis, Hearings before Sen. Comm. on Interstate Commerce, S. Res. No. 98, 62d Cong., 1st Sess. 1161 (1911).

43 Philosophy, to paraphrase Holmes: Richard A. Posner, *The Essential Holmes: Selections from the Letters, Speeches, Judicial Opinions, and Other Writings of Oliver Wendell Holmes, Jr.* (Chicago: University of Chicago Press, 1992), p. 105.

43 "extraordinary plasticity of legal rhetoric": Richard Posner, *Overcoming Law* (Cambridge, Mass.: Harvard University Press, 1995), p. 157.

44 "Rules travel in pairs": Jack Van Doren, "Is Jurisprudence Politics by Other Means?: The Case of Learned Hand," 33 *New Eng. L. Rev.* 1 (1998).

44 We conjure up: On judicial demographics, see generally Joan Biskupic, "Politics Snares Court Hopes of Minorities and Women: Federal Judges Are More Diverse, but Minority Nominees Still Twice as Likely to Be Rejected," *USA Today,* August 22, 2000.

45 "not what I believe": Cardozo, *The Nature of the Judicial Process,* p. 89.

46 "a knight errant": Ibid., p. 93.

46   "salutary disinfectant": James L. Oakes, "On the Craft and Philoso-
      phy of Judging," 80 *Mich. L. Rev.* 579, 588 (1982), quoting Judge
      Frank M. Coffin.

46   people start to go fishing: Daniel Kadlec, "Pitch In, Get Sued," *Time,*
      June 22, 1998.

46   major-league baseball: Rod Beaten, "Baseball: Stop Tossing Balls to
      Fans, Please," *USA Today,* May 21, 1999.

47   "oscillating verdicts": quoted in G. Edward White, *Tort Law in
      America* (New York: Oxford University Press, 1980), p. 185.

47   "the danger is": Ibid., pp. 190–91.

47   "Negligence": Oliver Wendell Holmes, Jr., "Law in Science and Sci-
      ence in Law," 12 *Harv. L. Rev.* 443, 458 (1899).

47   "larger orbit": David W. Peck, "The Complement of Court and Coun-
      sel," Thirteenth Annual Benjamin N. Cardozo Lecture, Association of
      the Bar of the City of New York, April 22, 1954, reprinted in *The
      Record,* June 1954, p. 272.

47   "interpreter for the community": Cardozo, *The Nature of the Judicial
      Process,* p. 16.

47   "replace the judgment": Hearn, "Social Regulation, The Rule of Law."

48   *Federalist 83:* Alexander Hamilton et al., *The Federalist Papers* (New
      York: Bantam Books, 1982), p. 421.

48   "a monument slowly raised": Learned Hand, quoted in Patricia M.
      Wald, "Some Thoughts on Judging as Gleaned from One Hundred
      Years of the Harvard Law Review," 100 *Harv. L. Rev.* 887, 897
      (1987).

49   "It was Marshall": Hon. Avern Cohn, "The Role of the Judge," 77
      Mich. B. J. 32, 35 (1998), quoting Walton Hale Hamilton, "The Legal
      Philosophy of Justices Holmes and Brandeis," 33 *Current History* 654
      (1931).

49   In an agrarian society: Arthur M. Schlesinger, Jr., *The Age of Jackson*
      (Boston: Little, Brown, 1953), p. 334.

49   A law of "contract": Kermit L. Hall, William M. Wiecek, Paul Finkel-
      man, *American Legal History* (New York: Oxford University Press,
      1991), pp. 171–86.

50   "loss from accident": Holmes, *The Common Law,* p. 76.

50   "takes upon himself": Chief Justice Lemuel Shaw, *Farwell v. Worces-
      ter Railroad Corporation,* 45 *Mass* (4 Metc.) 49 (1842). See generally
      Morton Horwitz, *The Transformation of American Law 1780–1860*
      (Cambridge, Mass.: Harvard University Press, 1977), pp. 208–10; L.
      Friedman and J. Ladinsky, "Social Change and the Law of Industrial
      Accidents," 60 *Colum. L. Rev.* 50, 53–58 (1967); Lawrence M. Fried-
      man, *A History of American Law* (New York: Simon & Schuster,
      1973), p. 301.

50   Shaw, "had a very real": Holmes, quoted in Schlesinger, *The Age of Jackson*, p. 340.

50   "infuse[d] . . . with the": Cardozo, *The Nature of the Judicial Process*, p. 93.

50   On formalism, Shaw, and Langdell: Grant Gilmore, *Ages of American Law* (New Haven, Conn.: Yale University Press, 1971), pp. 37–42.

51   "shift[s] responsibility": Richard A. Posner, "The Meaning of Judicial Self-Restraint" 59 *Ind. L. J.* 1, 6 (1984).

51   "The idea of a body of law": Gilmore, *Ages of American Law*, p. 64.

51   defective butter churn: Holmes, "The Path of the Law," pp. 474–75.

51   wiretap on a telephone: *Olmstead v. U.S.*, 277 U.S. 438 (1928).

52   "essentially stupid man": Gilmore, *Ages of American Law*, p. 42.

52   "[T]he life of the law": Holmes, *The Common Law*, p. 5.

52   The nadir of: *Lochner v. New York*, 198 U.S. 45 (1905). See also Gilmore, *Ages of American Law*, p. 63; Hall et al., *American Legal History*, pp. 388–92.

53   "The judge is": Cardozo, *The Nature of the Judicial Process*, pp. 133–35.

54   "must meet the needs": Archibald Cox, *The Role of the Supreme Court in American Government* (New York: Oxford University Press, 1976), p. 110.

54   "We don't expect": Jane Addams, quoted in Dominick Cavallo, *Muscles and Morals: Organized Playgrounds and Urban Reform, 1880–1920* (Philadelphia: University of Pennsylvania Press, 1981), p. 146.

55   "power goes to the most persuasive": Jeffrey Abramson, *We, the Jury* (New York: Basic Books, 1994), p. 246.

55   new federal courthouse: Linda Greenhouse, "Hear Ye! Hear Ye! See Ye! Too!," *The New York Times*, September 27, 1998.

55   "How do we judge": William J. Bennett, "Does Honor Have a Future?," *Imprimis*, December 1998, p. 2.

55   "empowered to keep watch": Derek Bok, "Law and Its Discontents: A Critical Look at Our Legal System," 37th Annual Benjamin N. Cardozo Lecture, November 9, 1982, reprinted in *The Record*, January/February 1983, p. 12.

56   "But how long": Atiyah, "From Principles to Pragmatism."

56   Dr. Ira Gore: *BMW of North America v. Gore*, 17 U.S. 559 (1996).

58   Morgan Stanley: Randall Smith, "Morgan Stanley Settles Its Legal Dispute with Former Analyst Christian Curry," *The Wall Street Journal*, September 15, 2000; Laurie P. Cohen, "Morgan Stanley Says Curry Had Over 150 Fake Expense Claims," *The Wall Street Journal*, June 8, 1999.

59   five-year-old Gregory: *Strothkamp v. Cheeseborough-Ponds, Inc.* 193 Mo. App. Lexis 417 (Mo. Ct. App. March 23, 1993).

60   "to assume the baffling task": Bok, "Law and Its Discontents,"
      p. 21.

60   "exercise of judicial power": Gewirtz, "On 'I know it when I see it.' "

61   Equals should be: Aristotle, *The Nicomachean Ethics,* H. Rackham, tr.
      (Cambridge, Mass.: Harvard University Press, 1990), p. 273.

61   "[T]o speak somewhat": Cardozo, *The Nature of the Judicial Process,*
      p. 109.

62   federal court in Kansas: Dirk Johnson, " 'F' for Kansas City Schools
      Adds to the District's Woes," *The New York Times,* May 3, 2000;
      Max Boot, "America's Worst Judges," *The Wall Street Journal,*
      May 28, 1998.

63   Playground Association of America: Henry S. Curtis, *The Play Move-
      ment and Its Significance* (New York: The Macmillan Company,
      1917), pp. 11–17.

63   "a new equilibrium": Cavallo, *Muscles and Morals,* p. 8.

63   "sense of balance": Ibid., p. 27.

63   "build up habits": Ibid., p. 138.

63   "One boy is": Ibid., p. 5.

64   John F. Kennedy's Council: C. W. Hackensmith, *History of Physical
      Education* (New York: Harper & Row, 1966), pp. 498–502; interview
      with Professor Lauri Macmillan Johnson.

64   "Children have always run": Curtis, *The Play Movement and Its Sig-
      nificance,* p. 226.

64   "It is reasonably": Ibid., p. 48.

65   "Better a broken arm": Lady Allen of Hurtwood, quoted in "Safety,
      Lawsuits Spur Changes in Playground Equipment," National Public
      Radio broadcast, Segment 04, Show Number 2236, June 6, 1996.

65   "Many of today's": The National Program for Playground Safety,
      "Working to Make America's Playgrounds Safe," n.d.

65   "Earth surfaces": Consumer Product Safety Commission, "Handbook
      for Public Playground Safety," November 28, 1999, p. 7.

65   broke his leg: Thomas Bevier, "Swings, Jungle Gyms Aren't Just
      Child's Play Anymore," *The Detroit News,* October 26, 1995; Lynne
      Van Dine, "Safety: Playgrounds Could Harbor Hidden Hazards," *The
      Detroit News,* August 14, 1996.

66   "all they had": Bevier, "Swings, Jungle Gyms Aren't Just Child's Play
      Anymore."

66   New York City cut the limbs: Interview with Professor Lauri Macmil-
      lan Johnson.

66   A school district: Celeste Fremont, "Are Schools Failing Our Boys?,"
      article posted at MSNBC website, November 25, 1999.

66   Philadelphia banned recess: Dirk Johnson, "Many Schools Putting an
      End to Child's Play," *The New York Times,* April 7, 1998. See also

Gerald S. Cohen, "Schools Cancel Field Trips—Fear of Suits," *San Francisco Chronicle,* August 30, 1989.

66   "that exceed the design": Interview with Hap Parker, playground equipment designer, Kompan, Inc.

67   bicycle helmet: The National Program for Playground Safety, "Wear Bike Helmets on Bicycles, Not on Playgrounds," *Playground Safety News,* Summer 1999.

67   "The spirit of distrust": Kagan, "Adversarial Legalism and American Government," p. 375f.

67   "eliminate altogether": Cardozo, *The Nature of the Judicial Process,* p. 173.

67   "You may say": Ibid., p. 135.

68   "a fair average": Ibid., p. 136.

68   "an objective way": Havel, *The Art of the Impossible,* p. 91.

68   "cannot be fair": Lon Fuller, "Forms and Limits of Adjudication," 92 *Harv. L. Rev.* 353, 373 (1978).

69   "they're letting lawyers": Robert Andrews, *The Columbia Dictionary of Quotes* (New York: Columbia University Press, 1993), p. 535.

69   "devastating critique": William Eskridge, Jr., and Philip Frickey, "Historical and Critical Introduction," *The Legal Process: Basic Problems in the Making and Application of Law* (Westbury, N.Y.: The Foundation Press, Inc. 1994) p. cxiii.

CHAPTER II.   THE COLLAPSE OF THE COMMON GOOD

71   George Reeves: *A Special Relationship: Our Teachers and How We Learned,* John C. Board, ed. (Wainscott, N.Y.: Pushcart Press, 1991), p. 150.

71   Bernard Baruch: Ibid., p. 92.

71   Floyd Patterson: Ibid., p. 313.

73   Professor William Sanders: Marilyn Marks, "The Teacher Factor," *The New York Times, Education Life,* January 9, 2000. See also William L. Sanders and Sandra Horn, "An Overview of the Tennessee Value-Added Assessment System (TVAAs)" (University of Tennessee, n.d.).

73   "What children learn": Christopher Jencks, "Is the Public School Obsolete?," *The Public Interest,* Winter 1966, p. 25.

73   kindergartners: Interview with Philippa Dunne, New York City, 2000.

74   "today's students know less": Laurence Steinberg, *Beyond the Classroom: Why School Reform Has Failed and What Parents Need to Do* (New York: Simon & Schuster, 1996), p. 65.

74   "We have vastly": Chester Finn, "The Greatest Reform of All," *Phi Delta Kappan,* April 1990, p. 588.

74 Several Philadelphia schools: Editorial, "When to Blame the Teachers," *The New York Times,* March 27, 1997.

75 Elementary schools become: Vivian S. Troy, "School Girds for New Regents Test Standards," *The New York Times,* September 4, 1996. See also Jodi Wilguren and Jacques Steinberg, "Under Pressure: A Special Report: Even for Sixth Graders, College Looms," *The New York Times,* July 3, 2000.

75 In Woodland, California: Lisa Richardson, "Test Prep Has Teachers in Trouble," *Los Angeles Times,* April 14, 2000.

75 In Reston, Virginia: "In Alarming Trend, Teachers Are the Cheaters," *USA Today,* July 13, 2000.

76 "telling them what": Carole Novak, "Interview with Linda Darling Hammond," *Technos Quarterly,* Summer 1994.

76 "little room for": Ralph P. Hummel, *The Bureaucratic Experience* (fourth ed.) (New York: St. Martin's Press, 1994), p. 40. See also John E. Chubb and Terry M. Moe, *Politics, Markets & America's Schools* (Washington, D.C.: The Brookings Institution, 1990), pp. 36–37 and passim.

76 In Gerald Grant's study: Michael Smith, quoted in Gerald Grant, *The World We Created at Hamilton High* (Cambridge, Mass.: Harvard University Press, 1988), p. 221.

76 "It's impossible": Interview with Jules Linden.

76 "Who's against": John McCormick, "Where Are the Parents?," *Newsweek,* September 1990 (Fall/Winter Special Edition), p. 54.

77 "Suffice it to say": Charles F. Wilson, *How to Develop and Apply Work Plans: A Federal Supervisor's Guide* (Washington, D.C.: U.S. Gov't Printing Office, 1974), p. 231.

77 "not burdensome": *Board of Regents of State Colleges v. Roth,* 408 U.S. 564, 591 (1972) (Marshall, J., dissenting).

77 Chester Barnard: Chester I. Barnard, *The Functions of the Executive* (Cambridge, Mass.: Harvard University Press, 1968), pp. 197–98.

78 "There was a trick": Studs Terkel, *Working* (New York: Pantheon, 1972), p. 174.

78 "The powers of": Friedrich Hayek, quoted in Lorenzo Infantino, *Individualism in Modern Thought from Adam Smith to Hayek* (London: Routledge, 1998), p. 6.

78 The ideal of: "Experience," in *Ralph Waldo Emerson: Essays and Lectures* (New York: The Library of America, 1983), p. 483.

79 "Just walk into": Interview with John Chubb.

79 " 'The trained instinct' ": Roscoe Pound, quoted in Benjamin Cardozo, *The Growth of the Law* (New Haven, Conn.: Yale University Press, 1924), p. 93.

79 In the 1980s: Interview with Nancy Udell.

80   "its central task": James Q. Wilson, "A Gap in the Curriculum," *The New York Times,* April 26, 1999.

80   "can either operate": Peter Drucker et al., in *Power and Democracy in America,* William W. D'Antonio and Howard J. Ehrlich, eds. (Notre Dame, Ind.: Notre Dame University Press, 1961), p. 13.

80   "Focus upon A": Robert K. Merton, "Bureaucratic Structure and Personality," 18 *Social Forces* 560, 562 (October 1939–May 1940).

80   "whisper to a child": Theodore and Nancy Sizer, "They Are Watching Us," *The New York Times,* April 1, 1999.

81   "cannot be apprehended": Aristotle, *The Nicomachean Ethics,* H. Rackham, tr. (Cambridge, Mass.: Harvard University Press, 1990), p. 351.

81   "Perception is not": "Self-Reliance," in *Ralph Waldo Emerson: Essays and Lectures,* p. 269.

81   Teachers "no longer believe": Grant, *The World We Created at Hamilton High,* p. 240. See also Sharon Rallis, "Room at the Top: Conditions for Effective School Leadership," *Phi Delta Kappan,* May 1988, pp. 945–46.

81   "You know what's": Grant, *The World We Created at Hamilton High,* p. 53.

81   "I'll go to": Jack Frymier, "Bureaucracy and the Neutering of Teachers," *Phi Delta Kappan,* September 1987, p. 12.

81   "Classrooms are filled": Steinberg, *Beyond the Classroom,* p. 13.

81   "Even the simplest": Ibid., p. 13.

81   The American teenagers: Ibid., p. 19.

82   Parents, the third: The National Commission on Civic Renewal, "A Nation of Spectators" (1998), p. 6.

82   PTA participation: Mary B. W. Tabor, "Comprehensive Study Finds Parents and Peers Are Most Crucial Influences on Students," *The New York Times,* August 7, 1996.

82   "Our subjective experience": Konrad Lorenz, *The Waning of Humanness* (Boston: Little, Brown, 1987), pp. 83, 197.

82   "Even the Tin Woodman": Daniel Dyer, "Help! The Teacher's a Robot!" *NEA Today,* April 1997, p. 41.

83   "In the past": Frederick Winslow Taylor, *The Principles of Scientific Management* (New York: W. W. Norton, 1967), p. 6.

83   "Industry" . . . is "warfare": Quoted in Andrea Gabor, *The Capitalist Philosophers: The Geniuses of Modern Business* (New York: Times Business, 2000), p. 6.

83   "science of shoveling": Taylor, *The Principles of Scientific Management,* pp. 64–68.

84   "The work of": Ibid., p. 39.

84   experiment at Bethlehem Steel: Ibid., pp. 40–46.

85   "mass production": Gabor, *The Capitalist Philosophers,* p. 43.
85   "find a principle": Ibid., p. 277.
85   scientific methods: Frederick C. Mosher, *Democracy and the Public Service* (New York: Oxford University Press, 1968), pp. 70–79.
86   New York State divides: Correspondence with state official.
86   South Dakota: Interview with state official.
86   "P.O.S.D.C.O.R.B.": Paul C. Light, *Thickening Government: Federal Bureaucracy and the Diffusion of Accountability* (Washington, D.C.: The Brookings Institution, 1995), p. 3.
86   In 1940: Gabor, *The Capitalist Philosophers,* p. 131.
86   This extraordinary success: Ibid., p. 136.
86   "Under McNamara": David Halberstam, *The Reckoning* (New York: William Morrow, 1986), p. 210.
87   "Bureaucracy develops the": Max Weber, *Economy and Society* (New York: Bedminster Press, 1968), p. 975.
87   "A great business": Henry Ford, quoted in Anthony Sampson, *Company Man: The Rise and Fall of Corporate Life* (London: HarperCollins, 1995), p. 44.
87   Alfred Sloan: Ibid., p. 70.
87   John D. Rockefeller: Ibid., p. 42.
87   "we are in the presence": Ibid., p. 37.
87   Larkin Building: Ibid., p. 54.
88   William H. Whyte: William H. Whyte, *The Organization Man* (London: Jonathan Cape, 1957).
88   "Most of us": John F. Kennedy, quoted in Christopher Lasch, *The Culture of Narcissism: American Life in an Age of Diminishing Expectations* (New York: W. W. Norton, 1991), p. 77.
89   "I prefer not to": Herman Melville, *Bartleby the Scrivener* (New York: Penguin Books, 1995).
89   "I'm not complaining": Franz Kafka, quoted in Sampson, *Company Man,* p. 63.
89   *Brave New World:* Aldous Huxley, *Brave New World* (New York: Harper Perennial, 1989).
89   "reject the evidence": George Orwell, *1984* (New York: Penguin Books, 1983), p. 69.
90   Chevrolet Chevette: *Car Talk* radio show, NPR, April 1, 2000.
90   "assigning points": Gabor, *The Capitalist Philosophers,* p. 140.
90   "rig the numbers": Ibid.
90   "dump[ed] thousands of parts": Ibid.
90   working overtime: Interview with Tim Bowling and Nye Stevens.
91   "As America's involvement": Gabor, *The Capitalist Philosophers,* p. 149.
91   "excessively mechanical system": Ibid., p. 147.

91 "we had to destroy": Hummel, *The Bureaucratic Experience,* p. 20.

91 "The parking lot": John Micklethwait and Adrian Wooldridge, *A Future Perfect* (New York: Crown Business, 2000), p. 64.

91 The Japanese: Sampson, *Company Man,* pp. 158–59.

92 Xerox discovered: Gabor, *The Capitalist Philosophers,* p. 151.

92 America's largest car companies: Ibid.

93 "management principles": Robert Hayes and William Abernathy, quoted in Sampson, *Company Man,* p. 205.

93 "the individual human": Thomas J. Peters and Robert H. Waterman, Jr., *In Search of Excellence* (New York: Warner Books, 1982), p. 8.

93 Jack Welch: Sampson, *Company Man,* pp. 216–18.

93 "360-degree evaluation": Eugene Kennedy and Sara C. Charles, M.D., *Authority* (New York: Free Press, 1997), p. 197.

93 Nordstrom's department store: Jennifer Steinhauer, "What Ever Happened to Service?," *The New York Times,* March 4, 1997.

94 young teacher: Interview with John Fager.

95 young principal: Interview with Paula Throckmorton.

96 mucus was dripping: Interview with Nancy Udell.

96 "I don't give a damn": Interview with John Fager.

96 banned visits to the parking lot: Grant, *The World We Created at Hamilton High,* p. 58. See also Dan McFeely, "Parking Loopholes' Days Are Numbered," *The Indianapolis Star,* July 16, 1999.

97 "You can't go": Interview with therapist in rural Pennsylvania.

97 "I'll call DYFS": Abigail Thernstrom, "Courting Disorder in the Schools," *The Public Interest,* Summer 1999, p. 21.

97 "I saw the kid cheating": Grant, *The World We Created at Hamilton High,* p. 53.

97 Schools make a point: Ibid.; Edward A. Wynne, "Courts, Schools, and Family Choice," *The Public Interest,* Spring 1982, p. 137.

98 "inclusion of cafeteria duties": Maria Newman, "Trading of Chalk for Whistles Is Out: A New Contract Would Bar Teachers from Policing Duties," *The New York Times,* November 28, 1995.

98 "disrespect students have": Public Agenda, "Given the Circumstances, Teachers Talk About Public Education Today" (1996), p. 15.

98 eighth-grader in Brooklyn: Thernstrom, "Courting Disorder in the Schools," p. 19.

98 two-thirds . . . cheated: Steinberg, *Beyond the Classroom,* p. 67; Harry Bruinius, "School Cheating Up as Stakes Rise," *The Christian Science Monitor,* December 14, 1999.

98 scared to use school bathrooms: Kennedy and Charles, *Authority,* p. 112.

99 teacher being threatened: Jackson Toby, "Getting Serious About School Discipline," *The Public Interest,* Fall 1998, pp. 76–78; Robert

Hardaway, "Too Many Rights Perpetuate Violence in Public Schools," *The Detroit News,* September 24, 1998.

99 Surveys of educators: Stephen Stolp, "Leadership for School Culture," *ERIC Digest 91,* ERIC Clearinghouse on Educational Management, June 1994.

99 Lord Moulton: Lord John Fletcher Moulton, "Law and Manners," *The Atlantic Monthly,* July 1924, p. 3.

101 "Ability is not something": Chester Barnard, quoted in Gabor, *The Capitalist Philosophers,* p. 81.

102 "education was a civil right": Richard Riley, "The Opportunity for a Quality Education: The Civil Right of the Twenty-first Century," speech, May 17, 1999; interview with Robert Kiley.

103 "look upon all authority": Alexis de Tocqueville, *Democracy in America* (New York: Vintage Books, 1990), vol. 2, p. 287.

103 "To the victor": William Marcy, quoted in Arthur M. Schlesinger, *The Age of Jackson* (Boston: Little, Brown, 1953), p. 178.

104 In 1878, 75 percent: Ronald N. Johnson and Gary D. Libecap, *The Federal Civil Service System and the Problem of Bureaucracy* (Chicago: University of Chicago Press, 1994), p. 15.

104 "The men who did": Michael Nelson, "A Short, Ironic History of American National Bureaucracy," *The Journal of Politics,* August 1982, p. 766.

104 The Secretary of War: Paul P. Van Riper, *History of the United States Civil Service* (Evanston, Ill.: Row Peterson and Company, 1958), p. 74.

104 The American minister: Ibid., p. 74.

104 General Winfield Scott's: Timothy D. Johnson, *The Quest for Military Glory* (Lawrence: University Press of Kansas, 1998).

105 forestry inspector: Leonard D. White, *The Republican Era* (New York: Macmillan, 1958), p. 172.

105 Artemis Ward: Van Riper, *History of the United States Civil Service,* p. 60.

105 "Tell all the office seekers": David Herbert Donald, *Lincoln* (New York: Simon & Schuster, 1995), p. 467. This quotation appears in slightly different form in numerous sources.

105 "Agitation over the spoils": Van Riper, *History of the United States Civil Service,* p. 88.

105 "Administration lies outside": Woodrow Wilson, "The Study of Administration," *Political Science Quarterly,* June 1887, p. 210.

105 "the demoralizing influence": Ibid., p. 83.

106 "A bureaucracy devoid": Nelson, "A Short, Ironic History of American National Bureaucracy," p. 764.

106 "if the front door": Van Riper, *History of the United States Civil Service*, p. 102.
106 "It is better": Ibid.
107 only 10 percent: Ibid., p. 105.
107 "blanketed in": Nelson, "A Short Ironic History of American National Bureaucracy," p. 766.
107 President McKinley: Van Riper, *History of the United States Civil Service*, p. 154.
107 "tried to increase": Nelson, "A Short, Ironic History of American National Bureaucracy," p. 766.
107 In 1913: Van Riper, *History of the United States Civil Service*, p. 222.
108 "The simple fact": Ibid., p. 287.
109 "straighten the paths": Wilson, "The Study of Administration."
110 "no constitutional right to be a policeman": *McAuliffe v. New Bedford*, 155 Mass. 216, 220, 29 N.E. 517 (1892). See generally Rodney Smolla, "The Reemergence of the Right-Privilege Distinction in Constitutional Law: The Price of Protesting Too Much," 35 *Stan. L. Rev.* 69 (1982).
110 "new property": Charles A. Reich, "The New Property," 73 *Yale L. J.* 733 (1964).
110 "No ideology, however noble": David Riesman, *Individualism Reconsidered* (New York: Doubleday Anchor, 1954), p. 27.
110 "witnessed a due process explosion": Henry J. Friendly, "Some Kind of Hearing," 123 *U. Pa. L. Rev.* 1263, 1268 (1975).
111 "free play of the spirit": *Keyishian v. Board of Regents of the State of New York*, 385 U.S. 589, 601 (1967).
111 "A teacher works": Ibid., p. 624 (Clark, J., dissenting).
112 "opportunity for the employee": *Cleveland Board of Education v. Loudermill*, 470 U.S. 532, 543 (1985).
112 black armbands: *Tinker v. Des Moines Independent Community School District*, 393 U.S. 503 (1969).
112 "enclaves of totalitarianism": Ibid., p. 511.
112 "schoolhouse gate": Ibid., p. 506.
112 four other students: *Goss v. Lopez*, 419 U.S. 565 (1975).
112 Powell, in dissent: Ibid., p. 593. See also Kay Hymowitz, "How the Courts Undermined School Discipline," *The Wall Street Journal*, May 4, 1999.
113 Justice Hugo Black: *Goldberg v. Kelly*, 397 U.S. 254, 271 (1970) (Black, J., dissenting).
113 " 'meaningful time and . . . manner,' ": *Goldberg v. Kelly*, 397 U.S. 254, 267 (1970), quoting *Armstrong v. Manzo*, 380 U.S. 545, 552 (1965).

113 "blur[red] any distinction": Harvard Law Review, Developments in the Law—Public Employment, "The Constitutional Rights of Public Employees," 97 *Harv. L. Rev.* 1738, 1744 (1984).

114 Even a reform leader: Diane Ravitch, "Let Our Schools Hire and Fire Teachers," *The New York Times,* July 1, 1995; "First, Save Our Schools," *The New York Times,* June 27, 1994.

114 Powerlessness Corrupts: I am unsure who first coined this variation on Lord Acton's famous observation, but I believe it may have been either Professor Rosabeth Moss Kanter or Michael Lerner.

114 New Jersey governor: Interview with Tom Kean.

116 *grève du zèle:* James C. Scott, *Seeing Like a State: How Certain Schemes to Improve the Human Condition Have Failed* (New Haven, Conn.: Yale University Press, 1998), p. 310.

117 "cheat to do your job": Interview with Gretchen Aylsworth.

117 "these people had to break": Editorial, "No Excuses," *The Wall Street Journal,* June 1, 1999. See also The Heritage Foundation, "No Excuses: Seven Principals of Low-Income Schools Who Set the Standard for High Achievement" (1999).

117 "I break every rule": Interview with Robert Kiley. See also Ruth Swinney, quoted in Clyde Haberman, "The Principal Wants Honor, Not Tenure," *The New York Times,* January 29, 1999.

117 "It took me ten months": Correspondence and interview with Linda Schrenko.

118 "the crazy acronyms": Hummel, *The Bureaucratic Experience,* p. 163.

118 "one-directional" language: Ibid., p. 163.

118 "silo system": Interview with Ann Nagle.

118 "hold a TQM meeting": Ibid.

118 "Meetings were held": Interview with teacher (anonymity requested).

118 "Meetings are a perk": Interview with Sam Schwartz.

118 Metropolitan Transit Authority barn: Interview with Robert Kiley.

119 rat poison: Report to Gov. Zell Miller, and interview and correspondence with Randy Cardoza.

119 selling real estate . . . hair care products: Interviews and personal observation. See Scott Shuger and Daniel Kaufman, "How to Cut the Bureaucracy in Half," *The Washington Monthly,* June 1990.

119 "Each job is a dead end": Interview with Thomas Dydyk.

119 "I can retire": Interview with Paul Beliotti.

119 usually an 80 percent pension: Interview and review of materials at Employee Benefit Research Institute in Washington, D.C.

119 "When you talk to anyone": Interview with Mary Tese (pseudonym).

120 "Only twenty-two more years": George Judson, "Where Teachers Share Trade's Tricks," *The New York Times,* August 5, 1996.

120 "We schedule meetings": Interview with town planner.

120 "I would type": Terkel, *Working*, pp. 350–51.
120 "At large meetings": Interview with Ross Sandler.
121 "I try not to help": Interview with Christie Beeman.
121 "had old carpet": Interview with Joe Tanner.
121 "temple of justice": Hiller B. Zobel, "Why Are So Many Temples of Justice Dilapidated?," *The Christian Science Monitor*, August 20, 1996.
122 bat droppings: Interview with Bill Richardson.
122 coal-fired furnaces: Jacques Steinberg, "Time Stands Still in Some School Boiler Rooms," *The New York Times*, November 15, 1995.
122 "When men do not choose": Barnard, *The Functions of the Executive*, p. 295.
122 statewide salary freeze: Memo by Max Cleland to Gov. Zell Miller.
122 "WordPerfect, not Word": Interview with Elizabeth Martin.
123 "The teachers started": Interview with teacher (anonymity requested).
123 Union newsletters trumpet: "Clerical's Out-of-Title Grievance Yields $8,000," *Public Employee Press*, May 9, 1997, p. 8.
123 took on responsibilities: Interview with Joe Quigley.
124 "So here this guy": Ibid.
124 new staff lawyer: Interview with Barry Goldsmith.
124 "Look around this office": Interview with Kathy Mone.
125 "If he was missing": Julian E. Barnes, "Man Charged with Receiving 7 Years of School Pay Illegally," *The New York Times*, April 29, 1999.
125 Joe Dear: Interview with Joe Dear.
125 "the first thing": John F. Kennedy School of Government, Harvard University, "The Washington State Workers' Compensation Administration: Reforming a Culture of Despair," C07-96-1317 (1996), p. 7.
125 Styrofoam cups: Stephen Barr, "For $117,000, Doctor Treats His Patience," *The Washington Post*, June 20, 1996.
125 "tendency to make animal sounds": *Dep't of Environmental Protection v. Golden*, City of New York Office of Administrative Trials and Hearings Index No. 1113/96, pp. 4–5 (1996).
126 scream at people: Interview with Elizabeth Martin.
126 "People forced to live": Bertrand Russell, *Authority and the Individual* (London: Routledge, 1996), p. 18.
126 food resale scam: Diane Ravitch and Joseph P. Viteritti, *New Schools for a New Century* (New Haven, Conn.: Yale University Press, 1997), p. 24.
126 "We just wanted to see": Interview with Pat Lancaster.
126 bottom level: Personal experience and observation. See Leonard Reed, "The Velvet Cage: The Life of a GS-15," *The Washington Monthly*, September 1979, pp. 34–36.
127 new Denver airport: Mike Causey, "The Design Police," *The Washington Post*, October 27, 1995.

128 "The school board": Christopher Jencks, "Is the Public School Obsolete?," pp. 22–23.

128 "a dysfunctional agency": Joe Sexton, "Child-Welfare Caseworkers Stage a City Hall Protest," *The New York Times,* May 15, 1996.

129 the system "tears": Hummel, *The Bureaucratic Experience* (third ed.), p. 129.

129 civil servants in Britain: Ron Winslow, "Lack of Control Over Job Is Seen As Heart Risk," *The Wall Street Journal,* July 25, 1997; M. G. Marmot et al., "Contribution of job control and other risk factors . . . in coronary heart disease incidence," *The Lancet,* July 26, 1997, p. 235.

129 tightly controlled cultures: James C. Scott, *Seeing Like a State,* p. 349.

129 morale among public employees: William T. Gormley, Jr., *Taming the Bureaucracy* (Princeton, N.J.: Princeton University Press, 1989), p. 131.

129 "At the core": William H. Swatos, Jr., Epilogue in *Bureaucracy Against Democracy and Socialism,* Ronald M. Glassman, William H. Swatos, Jr., and Paul L. Rosen, eds. (New York: Greenwood Press, 1987), p. 188.

130 "People didn't come here": Interview with OSHA official. See "Bureaucrats under Fire," *U.S. News & World Report,* June 11, 1979, pp. 52–56.

130 "I can't imagine": Interview with town planner.

130 "I feel very unimportant": Terkel, *Working,* p. 343.

130 "With each new employee": Interview with official (anonymity requested).

130 "Can't you see it?": Interviews with David Maloney.

131 Barry Goldwater: Dotson Rader, " 'This Country Has To Make a Decided Change,' " *Parade* Magazine, November 28, 1993, p. 4.

132 In 1960, over three-quarters: Peter W. Morgan and Glenn H. Reynolds, *The Appearance of Impropriety* (New York: Free Press, 1997), p. 40. See also "Deconstructing Distrust," The Pew Research Center (1997); "1996 Survey of American Political Culture," In Medias Res Educational Foundation (1996); "Public Confidence in Major Institutions," Gallup Poll Archives (1996).

132 Warren Rudman: Warren B. Rudman, "Take this Job. Please.," *The New York Times,* December 21, 1995; Adam Clymer, "Rudman, Irked by Senate, Is Retiring," *The New York Times,* March 25, 1992.

132 "How many times": Tim Wirth, "Diary of a Dropout," *The New York Times Magazine,* August 9, 1992, p. 36.

132 "Over the last twenty years": John Doble Research Associates, "Governing America: Our Choices, Our Challenge," National Issues Forums (1998), p. 10.

133 Many new teachers: Martin L. Gross, *The Conspiracy of Ignorance* (New York: HarperCollins, 1999); Jabari Asim, "Grading the Graders," *The Washington Post,* November 14, 1999; Walter Williams, "Educating Those Who Educate Others," *The Washington Times,* April 19, 1999; Heather MacDonald, "Why Johnny's Teacher Can't Teach," *City Journal,* Spring 1998, p. 14.

133 These teachers: Thomas Toch, "Why Teachers Don't Teach," *U.S. News & World Report,* February 26, 1996, p. 66.

133 In 1998, 60 percent: John Silber, "Those Who Can't Teach," *The New York Times,* July 6, 1998; Dina Nelson, "Teachers' Test Eased: Lower Score Now Passes," *The Patriot Ledger* (Quincy, Mass.), June 23, 1998.

133 even 2 percent: Lynette Holloway, "Weakened New York School Boards Lack for Candidates" and "Low Voter Turnout Cited by School Board Foes," *The New York Times,* May 12, 1999, and June 7, 1999. See also Fred Bayles, "Venerable Town Meeting Is Slowly Losing Its Voice," *USA Today,* April 14, 1998.

133 "Why go to the trouble?": John Doble Research Associates, "Governing America: Our Choices, Our Challenge," pp. 26–27.

134 A national survey: Ibid., p. 31.

134 Alan Wolfe found: Alan Wolfe, *One Nation, After All: What Americans Really Think About God, Country, Family, Racism, Welfare, Immigration, Homosexuality, Work, the Right, the Left and Each Other* (New York: Viking, 1998), p. 314.

135 "We are the ones": Stanley Hill, quoted in Mark Levinson, " 'Reinventing Government': Who Profits, Who Loses," *Public Employee Press,* December 24, 1993, p. 30.

135 "bowling alone": Robert D. Putnam, *Bowling Alone* (New York: Simon & Schuster, 2000).

135 Like them, instead: Robert N. Bellah et al., *Habits of the Heart* (Berkeley: University of California Press, 1996), pp. 23–25 and passim.

135 "perverse pleasure in powerlessness": Wolfe, *One Nation, After All,* p. 313.

136 "When every American": Kennedy and Charles, *Authority,* p. 17.

136 "If politicians have": Vaclav Havel, *The Art of the Impossible* (New York: Alfred A. Knopf, 1997), p. 198.

136 "The more systematically": Ibid., p. 107.

138 Nick's "intervenor": Pam Belluck, "Poor Teachers Get Coaching, Not Dismissal," *The New York Times,* December 8, 1996.

139 "Professional Development Center": Raymond Hernandez, "In Protecting Principals: A History of Problems," *The New York Times,* April 27, 1996.

139 PIPs: U.S. Merit Systems Protection Board, "Removing Poor Performers in the Federal System" (September 1995); interviews with Jim King.

140 teachers in Illinois: Andrew Goldstein, "Ever Try to Flunk a Bad Teacher?," Time.com, July 20, 1998.

140 In California: UPI (Sacramento), "California schools fear lawsuits, study says," December 23, 1998. See also Matthew Franck, "APS Eyes Cure For Lemon Teachers," *Albuquerque Journal,* February 21, 1999.

140 "In my twelve years": Interview with VA official (anonymity requested).

140 "impregnable position": Bruce Buchanan II, "Red Tape and the Service Ethic: Some Unexpected Differences Between Public and Private Managers," *Administration & Society,* February 1975, p. 437. See also Michael Chapman, "Why Bad Teachers Can't Be Fired," *Investor's Business Daily,* September 21, 1998.

141 Unless people can: Friedrich Hayek, *The Constitution of Liberty* (Chicago: University of Chicago Press, 1978), p. 76.

141 Principals are reluctant: Sol Stern, "How Teachers' Unions Handcuff Schools," *City Journal,* Spring 1997; Amita Sharma, "Tenure: A Two-Edged Sword for 80 Years," *The Press Enterprise* (Riverside, Calif.), April 7, 1999.

142 "Avoid giving an opinion": Albert C. Jurenas, "What You Say Can, and Will, Be Used Against You . . . ," *NASSP Bulletin,* October 1993, p. 76.

142 99 percent of teachers: Doug Cummings, "Grading Teachers in Center of Storm," *Atlanta Constitution,* February 8, 2000.

142 14 of 7,000 teachers: Ronda Steinke-McDonald, "Time for Watchdog on Teachers," *The Florida Times-Union* (Jacksonville), September 12, 1998.

142 In the federal government: Interview with Edward J. Lynch, senior research director, Civil Service Subcommittee, U.S. House of Representatives; U.S. Merit Systems Protection Board, "Federal Supervisors and Poor Performers," July 1999, p. 12.

142 "People we rated": Testimony of James B. King, Hearing before Subcommittee on Civil Service, Committee on Government Reform and Oversight, House of Representatives (October 12, 13, and 25, 1995), p. 57.

142 "certified": Frank J. Macchiarola, "Higher Standards, Worse Schools," *The New York Times,* March 8, 1999. See also "Rethinking Teacher Training," The Merrow Report, September 21, 1999, available at www.pbs.org/merrow; Betsy Streisand and Thomas Toch, "Many Millions of Kids, and Too Few Teachers," *U.S. News & World Report,* September 14, 1998, p. 24; editorial, "Who Should Teach?," *The Wall Street Journal,* July 15, 1999.

144 "The more we try": Philip Slater, *The Pursuit of Loneliness* (Boston: Beacon Press, 1990), p. 48.

144 P.S. 6: Interviews with Carmen Farina.

145 "You can do things here": Interview with Medea McEvoy.

145 "Writing Network": Interview with Barbara Rosenblum.

145 "Zero Period": Interview with Dr. Eileen Marzola.

145 "everything was mandated": Interview with Alice Hom.

145 "lunch with friends": Interview with Medea McEvoy.

145 garden club: Interview with Dr. Eileen Marzola.

146 Purple Pencil: Interviews with Carmen Farina.

146 "parents move to the neighborhood": Anemona Hartocollis, "A Principal with a Will of Steel Makes a Public School as Prestigious as a Private One," *The New York Times*, February 24, 1999.

146 new math program: Interviews with Carmen Farina.

147 understand the meaning of freedom: Hannah Arendt, "What Is Freedom?," in *The Portable Hannah Arendt* (New York: Penguin Books, 2000), pp. 438–48; Kennedy and Charles, *Authority*, p. 5.

147 The standard complaint: Interview with Tracy Harrell.

148 "prevent harm": John Stuart Mill, *On Liberty* (Cambridge: Cambridge University Press, 1989), p. 13.

148 student mural: Interviews with participants.

149 bell curve: Judith M. Bardwick, *Danger in the Comfort Zone* (New York: AMACOM, 1995), p. 83.

150 "Reducing anxiety absolutely": As summarized by Hummel, *The Bureaucratic Experience*, p. 151.

150 "High school students": Albert Shanker, "Where We Stand," *The New York Times* (advertisement), October 13, 1991.

150 "They don't let him": Jacques Steinberg, "Answers for City's Turnaround Schools," *The New York Times*, November 8, 1996.

151 Fear of our own incompetence: Havel, *The Art of the Impossible*, p. 53.

151 "preached for the whole period": Interviews with Carmen Farina.

151 twenty-three grievances: Ibid.

151 Other teachers got: Interviews with Carmen Farina and quoted in Hartocollis, "A Principal with a Will of Steel Makes a Public School as Prestigious as a Private One."

152 *authoritarianism*: "favoring complete obedience or subjection to authority as opposed to individual freedom . . . [1875–80]," *The Random House Dictionary of the English Language* (second ed., unabridged, 1987).

152 In ancient Rome: Arendt, "What Is Authority?," in *The Portable Hannah Arendt*, pp. 485–88; Leonard Krieger, "Authority," in *Dictionary*

of the History of Ideas, Philip P. Wiener, ed. (New York: Charles Scribner's Sons, 1973), vol. 1, pp. 141–46.

152　Confucius: Havel, *The Art of the Impossible,* p. 201.

152　"an obedience": Arendt, "What Is Authority?," in *The Portable Hannah Arendt,* p. 474.

152　"[A]uthority precludes": Ibid., p. 463.

153　" 'Moral authority' ": Gabor, *The Capitalist Philosophers,* p. 82; Barnard, *The Functions of the Executive,* pp. 282–83.

153　excellent fourth-grade teacher . . . science room: Interviews with Carmen Farina.

154　"the dreary standardization": Havel, *The Art of the Impossible,* p. 178.

154　1992 pilot program: Interview with Bill Roper.

154　Georgia governor Zell Miller: "State of the State Address," January 10, 1996.

154　"I can't remember": Interview with Paul Burkhalter.

154　*Federalist 10:* Alexander Hamilton et al., *The Federalist Papers* (New York: Bantam Books, 1982), p. 42.

155　"out of here": Interviews with Carmen Farina.

155　"We need due process": Sharma, "Tenure: A Two-Edged Sword for 80 Years."

156　Maria Tuma: *Dade County School Board, Florida v. Tuma,* DOAH Case No. 96-0820 (1986).

158　"One might think": Robert Wright, *The Moral Animal* (New York: Vintage Books, 1994), p. 281.

158　1999 study: Justin Kruger and David Dunning, "Unskilled and Unaware of It: How Difficulties in Recognizing One's Own Incompetence Lead to Inflated Self-Assessments," 77 *Journal of Personality and Social Psychology* 1121 (1999). See also Erica Goode, "Incompetent People Really Have No Clue, Studies Find," *San Francisco Chronicle,* January 18, 2000.

158　"The only one who doesn't know": Andrea R. Waintroob, "Don't Fool With Incompetent Teachers," *Education Digest,* October 1995, p. 36.

158　Disciplinary hearings turn into: Testimony of G. Jerry Shaw, Hearing before the Subcommittee on Civil Service, Committee on Gov't Reform and Oversight, House of Representatives, October 26, 1995, pp. 111–17; Sharma, "Tenure: A Two-Edged Sword for 80 Years."

159　literally years: See Jolayne Houtz, "Bad Teachers—One of Education's Toughest Problems Has No Easy Solutions," *The Seattle Times,* May 23, 1999; Joseph Berger, "$600,000 Settlement Said to Be Awarded to Ousted Principal", *The New York Times,* June 24, 1999; "Silber Decries Efforts Needed to Fire Teachers," *The Patriot Ledger* (Quincy,

Mass.), November 23, 1999; Alison Gendar, "Schools Chief: Dump Lemons," *Daily News* (New York), March 1, 2000. See also Walter Olson, *The Excuse Factory* (New York: Free Press, 1997), pp. 172–73.

159 "it is simply": U.S. Merit Systems Protection Board, "Removing Poor Performers in the Federal Service," September 1995, p. 2, and "Federal Supervisors and Poor Performers," July 1999.

159 "Imagine yourself": Charlie Peters, "A Kind Word for the Spoils System: Special Anniversary Section: Who We Are, What We Believe, Why We Believe It," *The Washington Monthly*, February 1989.

159 "Dismissing a tenured teacher": Sharma, "Tenure: A Two-Edged Sword for 80 Years."

160 "cries on Mondays": Houtz, "Bad Teachers—One of Education's Toughest Problems Has No Easy Solutions."

160 Failure of a few: See Testimony of G. Jerry Shaw, Hearing before the Subcommittee on Civil Service, October 26, 1995, p. 114; statement of Allan Heuerman, ibid., p. 154.

160 Surveys of school administrators: Houtz, "Bad Teachers—One of Education's Toughest Problems Has No Easy Solutions"; Sharma, "Tenure: A Two-Edged Sword for 80 Years."

160 A student stringer: Jassmine Marwaha, "Bad, Badder, Baddest," *The Seattle Times,* May 23, 1999.

161 New Jersey Transit: Richard Perez-Pena, "Few Engineers Commit Most of Rail Errors," *The New York Times,* July 22, 1996.

161 thirty sick days: Brian Thevenot and Anand Vaishnav, "Sick and Tired," *The Times-Picayune* (New Orleans), March 28, 1999.

161 In Framingham: Matt Carroll, "Municipal Records Show Sick-Day Abuses," *The Boston Globe,* May 2, 1997.

161 "I guess some people": Thevenot and Vaishnav, "Sick and Tired."

161 Willie Woods: Stephanie Simon and Paul Feldman, "Search Goes on for Answers to Violence in the Workplace," *Los Angeles Times,* July 30, 1995.

161 Jay Dubner: Sam Dillon, "Teachers and Tenure: Rights vs. Discipline," *The New York Times,* June 28, 1994.

162 In Hamden: "Hamden School Superintendent Sentenced for Drunken Driving," *The Hartford Courant,* April 9, 1994; editorial, "David Shaw's Golden Parachute," *The Hartford Courant,* June 22, 1994. See also Olson, *The Excuse Factory,* pp. 127–28.

162 None of the people just described: Same sources as cited above.

164 Due process: U.S. Constitution, Amendment V.

164 "we have been re-defining deviancy": Daniel Patrick Moynihan, "Defining Deviancy Down," *The American Scholar,* Winter 1993, p. 19.

164 " 'society that loses its sense of outrage' ": Daniel Patrick Moynihan, quoting Judge Edwin Torres of the New York State Supreme Court,

Twelfth Judicial District, in "Defining Deviancy Down," p. 26. See
also David L. Kirp and Donald N. Jensen, "What Does Due Process
Do?," *The Public Interest,* Fall 1983, p. 75.

164 The ones "just doing": Kennedy and Charles, *Authority,* p. 110. See
also John C. Jeffries, Jr., "In praise of the Eleventh amendment and
Section 1983," 84 *Va. L. Rev.* 47, 75 (1998) ("the incentives of government officers are skewed . . . toward inaction, passivity, and defensive behavior").

165 Natural selection: Wright, *The Moral Animal,* p. 186.

165 "merit is loudly celebrated": Edward Gibbon, *The Decline and Fall
of the Roman Empire* (New York: Everyman's Library, 1993), vol. 2,
p. 397.

165 Shakespeare: William Shakespeare, *Two Gentlemen of Verona,* Act I,
Scene 2.

165 Camus: Albert Camus, *The Fall* (New York: Vintage Books, 1991),
pp. 132–33.

166 pointing their fingers: Editorial, "Mark Common Sense Absent,"
Chicago Tribune, April 16, 2000.

166 bottle of Advil: Albert Shanker, "No Laughing Matter," *The
New York Times,* November 10, 1996; Dennis Cauchon, "Schools
Struggling to Balance 'Zero Tolerance,' Common Sense," *USA Today,*
April 13, 1999.

166 metal-spiked ball: Kay S. Hymowitz, "Who Killed School Discipline?,"
City Journal, Spring 2000, p. 39.

166 "If it can be measured": Interview with Bill Coats.

167 "vagueness of . . . morals": Janet Bingham and Beth DeFalco, "Jeffco
Board to Review School Discipline Code," *The Denver Post,* June 15,
1999.

168 basic ACLU principle: Grant, *The World We Created at Hamilton
High,* p. 51.

168 "wholesome sense": Julius Menacker, "The Courts Are Not Killing
Our Children," *The Public Interest,* Spring 1982, p. 135.

168 Life is a game: See Grant, *The World We Created at Hamilton High,*
pp. 63–65; William Raspberry, "Zero-Tolerance Laws Breed Youth
Contempt," *The Detroit News,* June 21, 2000.

169 "no real faith in democracy": Henry Steele Commager, *The American
Mind* (New Haven, Conn.: Yale University Press, 1950), p. 319.

169 "But it is also a myth": Alan Brinkley, "What's Wrong with American
Leadership?" *Washington Quarterly,* Spring 1994.

169 "The confusion": Lippmann, quoted in Commager, *The American
Mind,* p. 320.

169 "seeds of . . . destruction": Paul P. Van Riper, *History of the United*

States Civil Service (Evanston, Ill.: Row Peterson and Company, 1958), p. 530.

169 Almost twenty million: U.S. Census Bureau, *Statistical Abstract of the United States* (119th ed., 1999), table 689.

169 Executive Order 10988: Ronald L. Johnson and Gary D. Libecap, *The Federal Civil Service System and the Problem of Bureaucracy* (Chicago: University of Chicago Press, 1994), p. 100.

169 One out of ten: Myron Lieberman, *The Teacher Unions* (New York: Free Press, 1997), p. 2; Sol Stern, "How Teachers' Unions Handcuff Schools," *City Journal,* Spring 1997.

169 "an education bill"; Diane Ravitch and Joseph P. Viteritti, *New Schools for a New Century* (New Haven, Conn.: Yale University Press, 1997), p. 33.

170 "only 13 teachers": Lawrence C. Hall, "School Chiefs Want to Oust Bad Teachers," *The Morning Call* (Allentown), March 13, 1998.

170 boycott of Pepsi products: "Bullies Block Scholarships," *The Wall Street Journal,* December 5, 1995.

171 "the rule of nobody": Arendt, *Eichmann in Jerusalem: A Report on the Banality of Evil,* in *The Portable Hannah Arendt,* p. 381.

171 "I believe in face-to-face": Havel, *The Art of the Impossible,* p. 126.

171 "We got better and better": Interview with Carmen Farina.

CHAPTER III.   THE LEGAL WEDGE IN THE RACIAL DIVIDE

173 "They hit the track": Interview with Darnell Williams.

173 "would be telling": Ibid.

173 "My manager would": Ibid.

174 "The subtle part": Stephan and Abigail Thernstrom, *America in Black and White: One Nation, Indivisible* (New York: Simon & Schuster, 1997), p. 520.

174 "often . . . people will": Joe R. Feagin and Melvin P. Sikes, *Living with Racism* (New York: Beacon Press, 1994), p. 141.

175 "worked to their disadvantage": Ellis Cose, *The Rage of a Privileged Class* (New York: HarperCollins, 1993), p. 44.

175 Racism "is worse": Thernstrom, *America in Black and White,* p. 494.

175 "African Americans increasingly believe": Alan Wolfe, *One Nation, After All: What Americans Really Think About God, Country, Family, Racism, Welfare, Immigration, Homosexuality, Work, the Right, the Left and Each Other* (New York: Viking, 1998), p. 210.

175 "so angry": Ibid., p. 211.

175 "racism has not": Thernstrom, *America in Black and White,* p. 494.

176 one-quarter of all black males: Dinesh D'Souza, "The Forum," *USA*

Today, June 2, 1999. See also Vincent Schiraldi and Jason Ziedenberg, "The Punishing Decade," The Justice Policy Institute, December 1999, p. 4.

176   "They give them": Sharon Davis, "Minority Execs Want an Even Break," *Workforce,* April 2000.

177   "racism plays a part": Ibid.

177   "would have to think": Cose, *The Rage of the Privileged Class,* p. 63.

177   John Dovidio: Samuel L. Gaertner and John F. Dovidio, "The Aversive Form of Racism," in *Prejudice, Discrimination and Racism* (Orlando, Fla.: Academic Press, 1986), p. 63.

177   "We do not converse": David K. Shipler, *A Country of Strangers: Blacks and Whites in America* (New York: Vintage Books, 1998), p. 562.

178   "The wall between": Thernstrom, *America in Black and White,* p. 519.

178   Black distrust of whites: Brenda Major and Jennifer Crocker, "Social Stigma: The Consequences of Attributional Ambiguity," in *Affect, Cognition and Stereotyping,* Diane M. Mackie and David L. Hamilton, eds. (San Diego: Academic Press, 1993), pp. 345–70.

179   For the last two decades: John J. Donohue III, *Foundations of Employment Discrimination Law* (New York: Oxford University Press, 1997), pp. 234–39; "Civil Rights Complaints in U.S. Circuit Courts, 1990–98," Bureau of Justice Statistics Special Report, January 2000.

179   "necessary to encourage": Legislative History: H.R. Rep. No. 102-40 (1991); Civil Rights Act of 1991 P.L. 102–66.

179   "Monetary damages": Ibid.

179   "manna from heaven": Robert J. Grossman, "Law in the Slow Lane," *HR Magazine,* July 2000.

179   Discrimination-type employment: Ibid.

180   "There are some people": "In Federal Work Force, Some See a Culture of Complaint," *The Boston Globe,* January 19, 1999.

181   "effect is to neutralize": H. B. Karp and Nancy Sutton, "Where Diversity Training Goes Wrong," *Training,* July 1993.

181   "white males encouraged": Ibid.

181   "removed one more racist": "Workforce Diversity: PC's Final Frontier?," *National Review,* February 21, 1994.

181   "everyone walks": Davis, "Minority Execs Want an Even Break."

181   "It's one thing": Ibid.

182   "You can make": Interview with Darnell Williams.

182   "Sometimes people": Davis, "Minority Execs Want an Even Break."

182   "No Euro-American person": Orlando Patterson, *The Ordeal of Integration: Progress and Resentment in America's "Racial" Crisis* (New York: Basic Civitas, 1997), p. 2.

183 "whites have to prove": Shelby Steele, *A Dream Deferred* (New York: HarperCollins, 1998), p. 156.

183 "are becoming flooded": Maureen Mineham, "Employment Litigation an Ongoing Concern," *HR Magazine,* August 1997.

183 "almost anyone not selected": Ibid.

184 "You could've done": Wolfe, *One Nation, After All,* p. 213.

184 "Career-enders": Conversation with Tony Carnevale.

184 "lack of performance": Jon Brock, "Equal Employment Opportunity in the U.S. Department of Health, Labor and Commerce," Kennedy School of Government study (1980).

184 "It was one thing": Ibid.

184 "simply cannot understand": Wolfe, *One Nation, After All,* p. 211.

185 "twiddle their thumbs": Davis, "Minority Execs Want an Even Break."

186 "not by the color": Coretta Scott King, *The Words of Martin Luther King* (New York: Newmarket Press, 1984), p. 95.

186 Chester C. Davenport: Seth Schiesel, "How One Man Used Corporate Affirmative Action in Ameritech Deal," *The New York Times,* April 12, 1999.

188 "The human brain": Robert Wright, *The Moral Animal* (New York: Vintage Books, 1994), p. 280.

188 "Men being partial": John Locke, *Second Treatise on Government: An Essay Concerning the True Original Extent and End of Civil Government,* C. B. Macpherson, ed. (Indianapolis: Hackett Publishing Co., 1980), p. 66.

188 "It is through": Elliott Jaques, *A General Theory of Bureaucracy* (London: Heinemann, 1976), p. 15.

188 James Harris: Donn Esmonde, "Branding Five on Board Racists Cloaks Accusers in Shame," *The Buffalo News,* April 25, 1999.

189 Bosnian refugees: Paul Zielbauer, "Looking to Prosper as a Melting Pot," *The New York Times,* May 7, 1999; Paul Lipkowitz, "Bosnians Start Anew in Utica: The SUNY City Attracts the State's Largest Population of the Ethnic Group," *The Post Standard* (Utica), November 20, 1998.

190 "niggardly with this": Melinda Hennenbarger, "Race Mix-Up Raises Havoc for Capital," *The New York Times,* January 29, 1999.

191 "nice to meet you": Shipler, *A Country of Strangers,* p. 450.

191 somebody flipping her hair: Lena Williams, *It's the Little Things* (New York: Harcourt, 2000), p. 14.

192 FAA's air traffic: G. Pascal Zachary, "Pursuit of Diversity Stirs Racial Tension at an FAA Center," *The Wall Street Journal,* December 3, 1998; interviews with Ed Drury.

195 "Each meticulous gesture": Everett C. Hughes, "Institution Office and

the Person," *The American Journal of Sociology*, July 1937–May 1938, p. 406.

195   "face-to-face interactions": Patterson, *The Ordeal of Integration*, p. 115.

196   "Conflict in organizations": Linda L. Putnam, "Productive Conflict: Negotiation as Implicit Coordination," *Using Conflict in Organizations* (London: Sage Publications, 1997), p. 147.

196   an "intriguing symmetry": Shipler, *A Country of Strangers*, p. 544.

197   "judge an institution": Harold J. Laski, *Authority in the Modern State* (North Haven, Conn.: Archon Press, 1968), p. 68.

197   "Black Americans cannot": Glenn C. Loury, "Beyond Civil Rights," address before the National Urban League, in *The State of Black America 1986* (National Urban League, January 23, 1986), p. 450.

197   "Freedom does not": Arthur M. Schlesinger, Jr., *The Age of Jackson* (Boston: Little, Brown, 1953), p. 523.

198   "It's really hard": Interview with Darnell Williams.

198   "If each side": Shipler, *A Country of Strangers*, p. 563.

Chapter IV.   The Secret to Freedom

199   "[I]f an American": Alexis de Tocqueville, *Democracy in America* (New York: Vintage Books, 1990), vol. 1, p. 250.

199   "mother of . . . progress": Ibid., vol. 2, p. 110.

200   "I've had almost": NIF Reports on Issues, "Governing America, Our Choices, Our Challenges" (John Doble Research Associates, 1998).

200   "self-interest": Tocqueville, *Democracy in America*, vol. 2, p. 123.

201   "For my own part": Tocqueville, *Democracy in America*, vol. 2, pp. 320–21.

201   "No one has a greater asset": Andrea Gabor, *The Capitalist Philosophers: The Geniuses of Modern Business* (New York: Times Business, 2000), p. 57.

202   "lack confidence in": The National Commission on Civic Renewal, "A Nation of Spectators" (1998), p. 6.

202   "Spontaneity and instinct": "Self-Reliance," in *Ralph Waldo Emerson: Essays and Lectures* (New York: The Library of America, 1983), p. 269.

202   "Our freedom depends": Larry M. Preston, *Freedom and the Organizational Republic* (New York: Walter de Gruyer, 1991), p. 138.

203   "salvag[e] the individual": Henry Steele Commager, *The American Mind* (New Haven, Conn.: Yale University Press, 1950), p. 49.

203   "each citizen will voluntarily": Donald Black, "The Mobilization of Law," 2 *Journal of Legal Studies* 125 (1973), p. 138.

204   a "perfect whole": Isaiah Berlin, "The Pursuit of the Ideal," in *The*

Crooked Timber of Humanity (New York: Alfred A. Knopf, 1991), p. 13.

204 Professor Carl Bogus: Carl T. Bogus, "Liability Lawsuits Help Consumers," *America's Victims, Opposing Viewpoints* (San Diego: Greenhaven Press, 1996), p. 165.

204 "a crossword puzzle": Vaclav Havel, *The Art of the Impossible* (New York: Alfred A. Knopf, 1997), p. 105.

205 Professor Lani Guinier: Lani Guinier, "Bias in Higher Education," *The New York Times*, June 24, 1997.

206 "The gulf separating": Alan Brinkley, "What's Wrong with American Leadership?," *Washington Quarterly*, Spring 1994.

207 "There is no private life": George Eliot, *Felix Holt, The Radical* (London: Penguin Books, 1866).

208 "We are only": Dominick Cavallo, *Muscles and Morals: Organized Playgrounds and Urban Reform, 1880–1920* (Philadelphia: University of Pennsylvania Press, 1981), pp. 93–94.

209 "It covers the": Toqueville, *Democracy in America*, vol. 2, p. 319.

210 Frank Mickens: Maria Newman, "Trading of Chalk for Whistles Is Out," *The New York Times*, November 28, 1995.

212 Americans "feel they have lost": Alan Wolfe, *One Nation, After All: What Americans Really Think About God, Country, Family, Racism, Welfare, Immigration, Homosexuality, Work, the Right, the Left and Each Other* (New York: Viking, 1998), p. 300.

213 "Bigness, loss of community": Robert F. Kennedy, quoted in Sandel, *Democracy's Discontent*, p. 301.

213 "an end to giantism": Ronald Reagan, quoted in ibid., p. 311.

213 "purely passive or bovine": Chester I. Barnard, *The Functions of the Executive* (Cambridge, Mass.: Harvard University Press, 1968), p. 117.

213 "The belief that adherence": Hayek, *The Constitution of Liberty*, p. 219.

214 "Men are misled": "The Conservative," in *Ralph Waldo Emerson: Essays and Lectures*, p. 187.

214 *Eichmann in Jerusalem*: Hannah Arendt, "Eichmann in Jerusalem: A Report on the Banality of Evil," in *The Portable Hannah Arendt*, pp. 344, 385.

214 Bradshaw on Arendt: Leah Bradshaw, *Acting and Thinking: The Political Thought of Hannah Arendt* (Toronto: University of Toronto Press, 1989).

214 "We seek to find": Cardozo, quoting John Dewey, in *The Growth of the Law*, p. 67.

214 "personality of the judge": Eugen Ehrlich, quoted in Cardozo, *The Nature of the Judicial Process* (New Haven, Conn.: Yale University Press, 1921), p. 17.

214 "What keeps the law": "The Conservative," in *Ralph Waldo Emerson: Essays and Lectures,* p. 188.

214 "Find men esteemed": Matthew Crenson, *The Federal Machine: Beginnings of Bureaucracy in Jacksonian America* (Baltimore: The Johns Hopkins University Press, 1975), p. 171.

215 "No man is a warmer": George Washington, quoted in Abner J. Mikva, "From Politics to Paranoia," *The Washington Post,* November 26, 1995; letter to Bushrod Washington, November 9, 1787, at www.virginia.edu/gwpapers/constitution/1787/bwshton.html.

215 "what can one humble:" Bertrand Russell, *Authority and the Individual* (London: Routledge, 1996), p. 30.

216 "There is an amazing": Tocqueville, *Democracy in America,* vol. 1, p. 247.

217 "not to believe in anything": Havel, *The Art of the Impossible,* p. 4.

217 homemaker in Atlanta: Wolfe, *One Nation, After All,* p. 3.

ACKNOWLEDGMENTS

This book was made possible through the help and generosity of many friends, colleagues, and government officials. Initial research was supported by the William and Mary Greve Foundation, and Tony Kiser has been an adviser throughout the five years of this project. Funding for research into civil service issues was provided by The Manhattan Institute and the J. M. Kaplan Fund. The Arthur Ross Foundation also supported initial phases of the project. My agent, Andrew Wylie, is as wise as he is astute; his support has been invaluable.

My editor, Robert Loomis, is as remarkable as everyone says—patient, encouraging, with the gift of understanding. The rest of the team at Random House was thoughtful and attentive, including production editor Sybil Pincus, art director Andy Carpenter, and Ivan Held. Allison Dickens at Ballantine was wonderfully flexible.

Henry Reath lent his expertise and judgment at every stage. Senator Zell Miller, when governor of Georgia, organized the support of his cabinet to catalogue the frustrations of bureaucratic organization; Joe Tanner was particularly helpful. Bob Stone and Greg Woods at the National Performance Review opened many doors. Richard Bartlett was an astute reader. Neal Dolan at Harvard kept the spirit of Emerson alive. Professors John C. Jeffries and Richard Merrill of the University of Virginia Law

School gave critiques on certain sections. My colleagues at Howard, Smith & Levin, later Covington & Burling, were patient and encouraging: Len Chazen, Barbara Carley, Adam Siegel, and Barbara Hoffman were thoughtful sounding boards; librarians Karen Schubart and Greta Boeringer were resourceful; and the staff, particularly Sarah Sears, were devoted beyond reason. Scores of other friends and strangers volunteered their time and resources. Thank you all.

Research was vital to this project, and Tom Kollar devoted almost three years, with patience, excellent organization, and a clear head. Ken Weine worked a year and a half to help get the project off the ground. Andrew Tannenbaum culled electronic libraries with Olympic skill. Richard Boulware was helpful in several phases, and his judgment critical in one area. Holly Ketron organized a troop of interviewers around the country, and their enthusiasm helped put a human face on the bureaucratic dilemma. Others who helped with research included Heather Wright, Alan Effron, Paul Halajian, Daniel Scardino, Keith Halverstam, Jonathan Holub, Lori Price Abrams, and Charles Euchner. Philippa Dunne was indispensable in the last year.

Getting the message out is a critical aspect of these projects, and Bob Dilenschneider has volunteered his wisdom and connections generously, and to great effect. John Scardino has been loyal and resourceful, helping me negotiate the shoals of government with help from Bob Neuman. Donna Thompson of the Manhattan Institute is a natural crusader. Ron Sachs and Cathy Wilson spread the word in Florida. Charles Nesbit, Ken Godat, and Anthony

McCall helped sharpen the message. Dick Rogers, astute and caring in his last moments, led me to improve the conclusions.

My family has been more generous than anyone. My brothers, John Allen and Bobby, picked up the slack on the southern front. My father, Rev. John R. Howard, ninety, never let me forget core values. My children, Olivia, Charlotte, Lily, and Alexander, figured out how to keep me involved as a dad even when my time with them was stolen for the book. My wife, Alexandra, did the job of two parents with love and great success.

© Charles Nesbit

ABOUT THE AUTHOR

Philip K. Howard, a lawyer, is the author of *The Death of Common Sense*. He has advised leaders of both parties on legal and regulatory reform. Howard grew up in small towns in the South and is the son of a Presbyterian minister. He is a managing partner of an international law firm and lives in Manhattan with his wife and four children.